UNFINISHED JOURNEY

"Two People, Two Worlds . . .
From Tyranny to Freedom"

Nancy Rosenfeld

Foreword by Alan M. Dershowitz

UNIVERSITY
PRESS OF
AMERICA

Lanham • New York • London

Copyright © 1993 by
Nancy Rosenfeld

University Press of America®, Inc.
4720 Boston Way
Lanham, Maryland 20706

3 Henrietta Street
London WC2E 8LU England

Library of Congress Cataloging-in-Publication Data
Rosenfeld, Nancy.
Unfinished journey : two people, two worlds : from tyranny to
freedom / Nancy Rosenfeld.
p.   cm.
Includes index.
1. Tarnopolsky, Yuri, 1936–   .   2. Refuseniks—Biography.
3. Political prisoners—Soviet Union—Biography.   4. Jews—Soviet
Union—Biography.   5. Rosenfeld, Nancy—Journeys—Soviet Union.
6. Union of Councils for Soviet Jews.   I. Title.
        DS135.R95T296   1993
947'.004924'092—dc20   93–17961 CIP
[B]

ISBN 0–8191–9195–7 (cloth : alk. paper)
ISBN 0–8191–9196–5 (pbk. : alk. paper)

 The paper used in this publication meets the minimum requirements of
American National Standard for Information Sciences—Permanence
of Paper for Printed Library Materials, ANSI Z39.48–1984.

To Marty, without whose love and patience this book
could never have been written

CONTENTS

ACKNOWLEDGMENTS

The writing of this book could not have been accomplished without the help, encouragement, devotion, and expertise of many extraordinary people.

With love and gratitude I wish to thank my wonderful family, who supported me with their loving patience first throughout the years I spent as an activist for Soviet Jewry and then for two more years while I wrote and then searched for a publishing house. My husband, Marty, my most ardent supporter, read and critiqued many chapters, as did our children, Steve, Rob, and daughter-in-law, Sherri. My parents, Ruth and Milton Glassenberg, read the entire manuscript while it was still in its infancy, supplying details of our family roots.

Yuri Tarnopolsky, friend and fellow author, was the one who initially encouraged me to write this book. He had just completed the first draft of *Memoirs of 1984*, and he felt it would be interesting if the story was portrayed from the American side. Over the past two years Yuri has read and reread every page of my text, and he remains my sharpest critic. The two of us have detailed a single experience from our two distinct perspectives, and now it seems only fitting that our books are being published together at the same house.

A special tribute goes to all my friends and fellow workers with whom I worked side-by-side at Chicago Action for Soviet Jewry. To name a few: Pamela Cohen, co-chairman of CASJ and president of the Union of Councils for Soviet Jews, who never wavered in her support for the work I was doing on behalf of the organization. Marillyn Tallman, co-chairman with Pam and teacher of Jewish history, was my mentor, adviser, and the first person to read and critique the manuscript. Hetty De Leeuwe, financial chairman, backed me unquestionably. I shall always remember the late Betty Kahn, beloved by the entire organization and a master of creativity. When Pam Cohen phoned from Israel on Sunday, March 15, 1983, to inform me that Yuri had just been arrested in Kharkov, it was Betty who rushed into the office to help get out press releases.

Jeannette Zupan, my dear friend and counterpart in France, offered invaluable help and continuous support through her painstaking effort and work, which she supplied on a weekly basis.

I also wish to extend my appreciation to Rabbi Herbert Bronstein and Rabbi Stephen Hart from North Shore Congregation Israel. Professor Jonathan Sarna, Brandeis University; Paul J.J. Payack; Fanchon and Manuel Silberstein; Michael Steinberg, literary agent; and Christine Benton, my editor.

Finally, I wish to thank Professor Alan M. Dershowitz from Harvard University, who wrote the beautiful foreword to my book. Professor Dershowitz was one of two international attorneys representing the Tarnopolsky case.

FOREWORD

The partial, and as yet incomplete, rescue of Soviet (now former Soviet) Jewry, first from the anti-Semitism of the communist regime and now from the anti-Semitism of extreme nationalists, is one of the great success stories of international human rights. Although governmental actions by the United States, Israel, and other Western nations contributed significantly to the rescue, the primary impetus for governmental intervention came from private groups and individuals.

We know a great deal about the "wholesale" aspects of the rescue: successful efforts to increase the gross *numbers* of Jews allowed to leave. But we know very little about the "retail" aspects of the rescue: efforts, some successful, some not yet successful, to bring out *individual* refuseniks or refusenik families. This is a book about the rescue of an individual named Yuri Tarnopolsky.

The drama of individual cases is always more intense than the story of statistics. Just as the world came to understand the tragedy of the Holocaust more perceptively through the diary of one young girl, Anne Frank, than through the abstract statistics of the Nuremburg and Eichmann trials, so too we can empathize with the plight of Soviet Jewry through the story of Dr. Tarnopolsky.

But this is really two stories. It is also a story of grass-roots efforts by a small but devoted group of people in America. These are people who took seriously the Talmudic precept that those who save a single person are as if they saved the entire world. Just as the world is composed of individuals, so too was Soviet Jewry composed of individuals like Yuri Tarnopolsky.

In my professional life as a lawyer, I have had many gratifying moments. But none has been as gratifying as those occasions on which I have greeted Soviet Jews whom I have helped, in some small way, to emigrate. Whether at the airport in New York or Tel Aviv, the hugs, the tears, the optimistic looks toward the future, these are what one remembers.

As I write these words, both Mikhail Gorbachev and Boris Yeltsin have finally, and belatedly, acknowledged the continuing impact of anti-Semitism in Soviet life and have condemned it, though not as forcefully as one would have hoped.

The future of the undetermined number of Jews who still live within the former Soviet Union is not certain at this time. The need for continued vigilance in relation to Soviet, and Eastern European, Jewry has not abated. With changed circumstances comes the need for different tactics. But this is surely not the time for lethargy.

Jews and non-Jews alike who care about human liberty can learn a great deal from the stories of courage, persistence and the intelligent use of democracy presented in this book. It is a book about courage, determination, and success.

ALAN M. DERSHOWITZ
Cambridge, Massachusetts
January, 1993

INTRODUCTION

Article 124 of the Soviet Constitution "ensured to citizens freedom of conscience . . . freedom of religious worship and freedom of anti-religious propaganda. . . ." Article 125 stated that "the citizens of the USSR were guaranteed by law:

    a)   freedom of speech;
    b)   freedom of the press;
    c)   freedom of assembly, including the holding of mass meetings;
    d)   freedom of street processions and demonstrations;

Article 128 said, "The inviolability of the homes of citizens and privacy of correspondence are protected by law."

These rights were honored only in the frequency with which they were ignored by Soviet authorities. In keeping with the propaganda motives of the Soviet government, throughout the late 1970s, a large wave of Jewish emigration was allowed. After the invasion of Afghanistan in 1979, the door to the free world closed and the Great Refusal began.

As thousands of refuseniks[1] clamored to leave, a few spoke out openly in defiance of their forced confinement. These brave activists were systematically arrested and imprisoned for insisting upon inalienable rights granted every Soviet citizen within the written Constitution of the USSR. The personal sacrifices of these prisoners of conscience[2] helped ultimately to reopen the door to freedom for others waiting to be delivered.

Unlike the United States, where a person is innocent until proven guilty, in the Soviet Union there was a presumption of guilt. Trials were Kafkaesque showcases where the defendant stood alone at the whim of the state bereft of family, friends, and even selected legal counsel.

Yuri Tarnopolsky knew these risks, yet his conscience spoke louder than his palpable fear when he arranged to smuggle out the following article and have it published.

---

[1]Soviet Jews who had been refused the right to emigrate.

[2]People who had been imprisoned for seeking to emigrate.

SOVIET JEW DESCRIBES
STATE OF REFUSAL

"Otkaz is the most comfortable concentration camp that ever existed."

In a paper received by Chicago Action for Soviet Jewry, Soviet Jewish scientist Yuri Tarnopolsky describes the prolonged agony of tens of thousands of refuseniks who were forced to suffer while waiting for exit permits to leave the Soviet Union. The following is a condensed version of the original:

DESCRIPTION OF A DISEASE[1]

In 1954, a Japanese schooner was caught in the sea by the radio-active fallout after a nuclear test. The very moment of contamination passed quite unnoticed by the fisherman, but soon they discovered that they had gotten the radiation sickness.

In summer and autumn 1979, many thousands of Soviet Jews were informed of a six-month delay in getting permission to leave the USSR for Israel. Happy and lighthearted people swarming to the OVIR office in Kharkov were a little bit confused, but nevertheless full of optimism. Had they been told then that they had become victims of a deliberate, inhuman experiment, and that they had been infected with a new, yet unknown disease, they would not have believed it. However, in time they discovered in themselves numerous symptoms of a painful and exhausting ailment, the so-called "otkaz" (refusal). This disease is so endemic that the Russian word "otkaz" has been inserted into foreign languages, like another notorious Russian word: Pogrom.

A year later, in the autumn of 1980, in the Kharkov OVIR one could observe depressed, worried and harassed people who avoided looking at each other. Now, in 1982, there is no crowd at the OVIR doors. The refuseniks have stopped complaining, arguing, and asking OVIR officials to let them leave for Israel. Twice a year they send by mail or hand over their re-applications. In 1982, the standard answer from OVIR is: "You are refused. The refusal is final. Your case will not be reconsidered. You will never leave."

---

[1]This is the edited version of the excerpted "Description of a Disease," published in *News Bulletin* by the Israeli Public Council for Soviet Jewry on December 31, 1982.

You will immediately recognize the symptoms of the "otkaz" sickness: Permanently depressed mood, changing into irritation; languor; insomnia; lack of interest in life; headache; exacerbation of the heart and other chronic diseases; fixed ideas and phobias; deep anxiety for the family; distress; powerless hatred for the tormentors. You will see that a refusenik turns to the "otkaz" no matter what topic you discuss with him. He speaks about the "otkaz" for long hours, with the same expression, repeating the same ideas, asking the same questions.

What are the results of the first three years of the "otkaz"? It is not the same in different cities. I know only the situation of educated people, engineers, and scientists. The refuseniks of our city are deprived of everything which is the essence of a normal life of an average man in time of peace. The refuseniks do not sew yellow six-pointed stars on their clothes. The yellow stars are replaced by work-books (service records) where all the jobs of a man during his life are recorded.

It is difficult to keep from becoming angry while thinking about the tragedy of the young generation. Young people, in their best years, are doomed to slowly wasting away. The "otkaz" has built an insurmountable wall between them and the rest of youth. The "otkaz" separates young lovers more than the walls of a medieval castle. Young men of "otkaz" families often work or study in other cities where nobody knows they are refuseniks. Our youth is deprived of the right to family life, happiness, joy, and a future.

Elderly people are losing hope of returning to professional work as they near the retirement age. Old people are dying in the "otkaz" without seeing their relatives abroad, without seeing the deliverance of their relatives here. Children are being born in the "otkaz." Like radiation damage to the still unborn generation, the "otkaz" damages children still in their mothers' wombs, because they will grow and develop in an atmosphere of fear, alarm, and stress, and will live with the consciousness of inferiority. "Otkaz" is the content of the children's games.

The "otkaz"--with what can it be compared? It is very much like compulsive treatment in a psychiatric hospital. Of course, "otkaz" is better than prison. However, there is no difference as to their results. These years are wasted and crossed out of life. "Otkaz" is the most comfortable concentration camp that ever existed. It is a giant, invisible ghetto where an oppressed minority vegetates. People are unable to fight omnipotent evil. They can only challenge it by sacrificing themselves. The "otkaz" is also a kind of war, a bloodless, absurd, and nevertheless, cruel war of nerves, a war with an invisible and heartless enemy, a war for moral destruction, a war for happiness of the family, a war for the dignity of the Jewish people and the human race.

Why, then don't the refuseniks give up? Why do they stubbornly bring their re-applications to OVIR together with a heart medication in their pocket? Because whatever reasons for emigration they had three years ago, now all the reasons are over-shadowed by a new reason: One should not stay in a country where the "otkaz" is possible.

I don't think that the Great Otkaz will influence the fate of nations. But, I am sure it is no longer a set of family disasters, due to its duration and the multiplicity of its victims. It is, at the very least, a development in history. This page is written with the tears of Jewish women. What will we see on the next page? If they have bereaved us of three years, they will bereave us of four. If four, then five is easier to take away. If today we have no job, tomorrow we will have no foreign mail and telephone calls. The day after tomorrow, there will be no higher education for our children, and no free access to other places in the country. They will start putting us into prison for the slightest protest. The noose around our neck will tighten notch by notch, and the world will be inured to that process.

Listen to our voices. They are still heard, but they could stop in the nearest future. Listen to our voices. It is probable that we will pay for that with our freedom. Don't wait until the Biblical forty years are up. You may be too late. Afterwards, possibly, our names will be honored, too, regardless of who intended to go to Israel and who intended to go to the USA. Because nobody will have arrived anywhere, except at the common grave of the "otkaz." Forget temporarily all your discussions and unite in order to save living persons.

Our ship has been caught by the radioactive fallout of our alarming times. We are Jews. We are deadly sick with the "otkaz". Save our souls!

YURI TARNOPOLSKY
Dr. of Chemistry
May, 1982

PART ONE: JOURNEY BEGINS

"If I am not for myself, who will be for me? And if I am only for myself, what am I. . . . And if not now--when?"

Hillel

Chapter 1

ARREST[1]

There was a knock at the door; a voice called out, "Telegram." A man shrank from behind the door as four uniformed men filled the hallway. Outside were the investigator, Shenger, a second official, and two witnesses. Behind the door was Yuri Tarnopolsky.

Tarnopolsky was a distinguished forty-seven-year-old doctor of organic chemistry, author of several scientific articles published in the Soviet Union, the recipient of nine patents in his field of science, a poet, a writer, and a linguist versed in eight languages.

He had just come in from walking his dog, Nika, and now Investigator Shenger was showing him a search warrant. His mother, wife, and daughter were seated in the room. They watched in hushed silence. Tarnopolsky gritted his teeth and stared angrily at the "Gestapo" agents who pushed their way into his home. He had concealed nothing slanderous or anti-Soviet in the apartment. Searches such as this were merely commonplace. In fact the search came as no surprise; he had more or less expected it to happen. Many of his refusenik friends had been subjected to such harassment.

The usual routine began. All confiscated items were tossed into a bag, later to be used against him as "evidence of the crime." The bag contained nothing more incriminating than a few color photographs sent from abroad, all of Tarnopolsky's foreign correspondence, and letters and petitions to Soviet officials demanding exit visas. In spite of previous searches, neither he nor his close friends had received anything more than an official KGB warning . . . except for one. Alexander Paritsky had been arrested two years earlier.

This, as became immediately apparent, was *no* warning. Tarnopolsky was manacled, escorted out of the apartment building and into a waiting black Volga, the official car of the Soviet police. Aware that he would be treated like an

---

[1]Some material in this chapter, as well as wording, has been documented from a letter written by Yuri Tarnopolsky on June 1, 1986, from Kharkov and sent out of the country via the Diplomatic Pouch for obvious security reasons. Other information was obtained through conversations and letters from him.

animal, not like a man, his body stiffened. He would, he knew, be granted no rights, permitted no contact with anyone from the outside. The injustice and the inhumanity of the procedure were undeniable.

The date was March 15, 1983, and Yuri Tarnopolsky was charged with "Slandering the Soviet State."

Tarnopolsky was driven directly to KGB headquarters, where his glasses were seized by a man conducting the interrogation. He immediately refused to answer questions or participate in the interrogation because of the absurdity of the charges. Afterward he was sent to Kharkov City Prison to await trial.

He remained in Kharkov in a small prison cell with five other inmates, isolated from the outside world.

He declared a hunger strike to denounce the senseless confiscation of his eyeglasses. When officials promised to return them on the sixth day of the strike, he ended the fast. His head was shaven completely bald, and he was taken for psychiatric evaluation. He refused to participate in the interrogation and refused to sign his name to any official papers. "You don't want to speak to me?" questioned the alleged psychiatrist. "Very well, it will make my situation even easier." Tarnopolsky's position was clear. He had committed no crime; rather he was the victim of a crime. His "crime": he was a Jew and had spoken out in public about his intention to emigrate.

* * *

Yuri Tarnopolsky lived with his wife, Olga, their eleven-year-old daughter, Irina, and the beloved family dog, Nika. He had resided in Siberia for seventeen years, in the city of Krasnoyarsk, where he engaged in scientific research and taught as an assistant professor at the Siberian Institute of Technology. It was there that he had met his wife and his daughter had been born. Then, in 1977, he returned with his family to Kharkov, in the Ukraine, to the same apartment in which he had spent most of his life since early childhood. At this time, he was working as a patent consultant and Olga was self-employed as an English instructor.

After the Tarnopolsky family first applied for emigration in December 1979, they waited three years before learning their applications had been denied.

Yuri Tarnopolsky was an active member of the Kharkov refusenik group, one of the founders and teachers of a special university set up for children of the refusenik families, most of whom had been denied admission to regular universities. The "university" met in the group's homes.

In November 1980, he was among the group of Kharkov refuseniks who undertook a hunger strike to coincide with the Madrid Conference on Security and Cooperation in Europe (CSCE). Later his telephone was disconnected as punishment. In August 1981 Tarnopolsky's apartment, along with the apartments of his friends Eugene Chudnovsky and David Soloveichik, was raided by KGB. Many books and papers were confiscated at that time. He lived "on the razor's edge."

On October 1, 1982, five months before his arrest, Tarnopolsky began a forty-day hunger strike, protesting the repeated refusals of authorities to allow him to emigrate. A chilling statement, sent to the West on a postcard, fully declared his intentions:

> We hope that in the New Jewish Year, people, especially Jews all over the world, will understand that our authorities are successfully exterminating us, without gas chambers, incinerators, and other offensive things. They are burning alive our hopes, human dignity, future, past, happiness, capabilities and sense of logic. The result is the same. They are hiding their crime as their predecessors did, and many of our powerful brothers abroad are watching impassively. The refusal is by no means a waiting for visas. It is a slow dying, an agonizing tragedy. Perhaps, a new batch of jail-birds is cooking by MR. CAGEY BEE out of those who dare to expose the crime. Nevertheless, we shall overcome!

We in the West heard that desolate cry for help, and we responded. It took forty years for Moses to lead the Jews out of Egypt and into the land of Canaan. Would Tarnopolsky's forty-day hunger strike be loud enough to draw world attention to the plight of thousands of Soviet Jews hoping to leave the USSR for freedom? He maintained his strike until November 9, when the Conference on Security and Cooperation in Europe, formed to monitor the Helsinki Accords, reconvened.

As he described later in a letter sent overseas, "Throughout the hunger strike, I felt humiliated and thought I would go mad. I slept away the days and lost all taste for food. There was a constant foul taste in my mouth, accompanied by continuous stomach cramps. I vomited daily." Yet he persevered, his only goal a visa for himself and his family so they could be free to live their lives as civilized human beings.

"I wish to live as a man, not as a domesticated animal."

Tarnopolsky sent a message to the West that he could no longer continue to exist in an uncivilized and primitive country. He felt that he had so much to offer the world, yet his knowledge was being wasted, imprisoned behind the walls of this barbaric country.

A mounting and incessant feeling of hopelessness and despair had intensified his sense of confinement even before his formal arrest and incarceration. Rapidly approaching the age of fifty, he felt his time to leave his mark on society was running out.

One day, in the middle of his hunger strike, a man and a woman appeared at the door. The woman was an officer at the OVIR (visa department) office, and the man was purportedly a "concerned physician." Suspecting a probable KGB setup, Tarnopolsky refused to allow them entry into the apartment.

"You are anti-Semites," he said, "You are fascists. We have nothing to talk about."

Tarnopolsky released a second statement to the West during a telephone conversation with Chicago Action for Soviet Jewry (CASJ). The hunger strike had already taken a heavy toll:

> I feel myself not deadly [sic], there is no reason to worry about my health except my sight. Two blind spots have appeared in both eyes, but they don't affect the central sight yet. I don't expect a quick release. I want to tell people abroad that the refusal is a humiliation and organized and moral torture, and I want to protest it. I don't want to be a silent victim of a crime. The hunger strike is the only possible way to strike my protest in a convincing form. If you have both of my statements made about the hunger strike, please publish it without any hesitation. Though I have received an indirect threat from the authorities, I intend to continue the hunger strike.

A civilized man could have nothing in common with the Russian provocateurs: no common language, no common goals. To participate in the ridiculous interrogation would only have dignified and justified the behavior of the accusers. The only acceptable response was nonparticipation.

Tarnopolsky expressed his desire and determination to emigrate in his third appeal to the world:

SAVE OUR SOULS

> The authorities tell us repeatedly: "Renounce your desire to emigrate, we will return your job, and you will live as before." Why, then, don't the refuseniks give up? Why do they stubbornly bring their reapplications to the exit visa office, together with a heart drug in the pocket? Because whatever reasons for emigration they had three years ago, now all the reasons are overshadowed by a new reason: One should not stay in a country where the "otkaz" is possible. How is one to describe the gnawing despair, the stagnant anxiety, the tantalizing uncertainty, the unbearable frustration of our ordeal? . . . Every wound of the heart heals, every wound but that of the "otkaz."

> . . . There are other aspects of the problem. If they have bereaved us of three years, they will bereave us of four. If four, then five is still easier to take away. If today we have no job, tomorrow we will have no foreign mail and telephone calls. If tomorrow we have no mail, the day after tomorrow there will be no higher education for our children and no free access to other places in the country. They will start putting us into prison for the slightest protest. The noose around our neck will tighten step by

step, and the world will be adapted to that process.

We address the Jewish people concerned with our plight.
We are Jews. We are deadly sick with the "otkaz." SAVE OUR SOULS!

Ten days before being arrested, he sent a fourth statement in a letter to CASJ:

Dear Friends,

If the reason for my hunger strike was obscure to you, I am going to explain myself one more time. . . . I see the history of the Jews, and I see its last tragic chapter, "The Holocaust." This chapter is not history for me because I am living it. I see, and I am convinced that my eyes do not deceive me: It's an extermination, well-camouflaged and slow. That's why neither public opinion nor the victims themselves can see its real nature because they are sensitized to the physical extermination only. And even if they see it, they substitute action to hope or hope to humility. The Jews of the world are separated. Where are the guards of morality, conscience, and honor of our ancient people? I am neither a judge nor a prophet, but I cry like our ancient prophets cried. We, the refuseniks, myself and my family, are we to be sacrificed to give again a lesson to the world? Wasn't the preceding lesson sufficient? My strike and my statement had been only so that this question can be shouted as loudly as I could. But, not all people like it when someone yells in their ears. . . . If I am arrested, I will not take any part in the inquest and at the trial. I will not answer the questions, and I won't sign anything so that I will not take part knowingly in the illegality of the proceedings. Therefore, I will not give it an air of legality.

Thank you, my friends, for your warm hearts.
Yours truly, Yuri

We immediately made the letter public in a press release, and four days after receiving it I spoke with Tarnopolsky. He warned me that he might need to reach us very quickly. He was never afforded the opportunity; he was arrested before he could contact us.

A few days prior to the trial, he was asking his interrogator, Shenger, how he could go along with the absurdity of this prevaricated "crime" filed against him. Shenger replied, "I am a soldier, and I should follow orders."

On June 29, 1983, Yuri Tarnopolsky was officially tried and convicted of the charge "Anti-Soviet Agitation and Propaganda with the Intent to Defame the

Soviet State." This charge, under Article 187/1 of the Ukrainian Criminal Code, carried a maximum sentence of three years' imprisonment at hard labor.

At the opening of his trial, he spotted his wife and daughter seated in the half-empty courtroom. He had not seen them for three and a half months. All meetings with family and friends, as well as all correspondence, had been disallowed prior to the hearing. He had been totally isolated from the world outside the prison walls, and the only people attending the trial were other refuseniks, friends and relatives of the accused. Others--who were usually invited to attend the hearings--interested Russians but those not closely connected, such as law school students and people from work, were not present. Yuri refused representation by an attorney, aware that all Russian lawyers were appointed by the state and did not actually represent their clients. He would represent himself.

What was the evidence used against Tarnopolsky?

1. His request to the Soviet authorities that his family be granted the right to emigrate

2. Four postcards in English and French to friends abroad

3. Postcards written in Russian to relatives in America comparing the refusal with historic incidents of anti-Semitism

4. Humorous poems he had composed for a Purim celebration

5. The statement from official OVIR authorities that he had informed a woman, during his forty-day hunger strike, that he was conducting this strike as a kind of treatment for his health; also that she had been called a "fascist"

The prosecutor opened the trial with a statement that all those people wanting to leave the Soviet Union had already received permission and departed. He went on to state that only 1.5 percent of those wanting to leave had been denied because they possessed "state secrets."

Among the witnesses for the state was a female mail clerk who happened "by chance" to find one of Tarnopolsky's "slanderous postcards," written in French to friends in Paris. Though the mail clerk could not read French, she "knew" it was "slanderous" and turned it over to KGB.

Another incident occurred in Moscow, when one of Tarnopolsky's other postcards was "coincidentally discovered" by some "stranger" who "happened to be passing through town." She picked it up and took it to KGB headquarters.

Photographs were shown to him, and besides the familiar faces on some of them, there were others he was unable to recognize. In one of the photos sent from France, there was a picture of a dog named Capi. There were no people in the photograph, but the dog was "registered" as a familiar "person," and this nonperson was entered into the case against Yuri.

There was harmful testimony from his mother, who stated that they had no relatives abroad, a prerequisite for applying to emigrate. She later retracted the statement.

The trial concluded. Tarnopolsky stared into the cavernous space of the half-empty room. Rising, he stood to face the tribunal. The "executioner" pronounced the sentence. It came as no surprise.

Before departing for the labor camp, Yuri was granted two meetings with relatives, which were conducted through a prisoner's window. He was allowed to speak to his visitors by telephone.

On August 17, five months after his arrest, the condemned man began the long, arduous journey to eastern Siberia by train, confined to a prison car. Traveling in a direction unknown to either him or the rest of the world for nearly three months, he arrived at Chita prison camp on November 7. There he would be incarcerated for three long and painful years.

Another refusenik had been banished. Another Jewish voice would be silenced.[2]

I am the person who led the international rescue attempt for Dr. Tarnopolsky on behalf of Chicago Action for Soviet Jewry. My name is Nancy Rosenfeld.

---

[2]At the time of his arrest Tarnopolsky was one of sixteen political prisoners who were incarcerated for long years in the harsh Siberian wilderness, far removed from family and friends. Most of these politicals were leaders in the Jewish emigration movement.

Chapter II

A JEW IN AMERICA

$\mathbf{M}$y role as an activist for Soviet Jewry is not difficult to explain. It is, in fact, a by-product of my heritage and my life. Like many Jewish Americans growing up in the postwar years, I was immersed in the social "progress" of those prosperous fifties and sixties, but as I matured I became increasingly aware of what seemed to be missing from my world. It was a sense of connection to the past, to great-grandparents and their great-grandparents, and the rich history that linked us all. Eventually I went in search of that bond. My journey took me through a study of Jewish history and exploration of my family's roots. It led me to the present plight of Jews in the former Soviet Union. Denied on a broad and blatant scale the right to be and to take pride in who they are, these people are being persecuted just as their forebears were.

During the great emigration period, which began in the late 1800s, Jews were fleeing Eastern Europe because of massive waves of persecution. Czar Alexander III ascended to the throne in 1881 and unleashed a campaign of Jewish hatred and Russification. Jews were cited as "infidels" and blamed for the assassination plot of Alexander II. Pogroms exploded throughout southern Russia and the Ukraine. Jewish homes were destroyed, their shops plundered, the people massacred. Police only looked away, pretending not to notice.

The May Laws were established in 1882, making it illegal for Jews to settle in rural areas. All exits from congested cities to villages were sealed off. Jews were expelled from trades and deprived of their professions. Many were driven to starvation.

In 1891 the Jewish community was evicted from Moscow and the synagogue was boarded up. This mass expulsion of Jews from an urban community was systematically repeated in other cities as well.

Parents were fearful that their sons would be conscripted into the army of the czar. Memories of atrocities of the reign of Nicholas I evoked feelings of terror. Jewish boys had been snatched from their families, driven off on carts, starved, tortured, and forced to submit to baptism in the presence of the czar. Most of these children were never seen or heard from again. It was this fear of conscription that drove my father's maternal family out of Minsk in the late

1800s. They came to America and succeeded in the grocery business.

By 1920 nearly three million Jews had fled to the shores of America. Most came by steerage on crowded ships, anxiously awaiting their first glimpse of the United States. The vast majority of immigrants entered the New World through Ellis Island. They were detained for days and weeks as the seemingly endless process of interrogation and examination took place. Those failing to pass inspection were sent back.[1]

My paternal grandfather left Minsk with three of his siblings in the early 1900s. After resettling in New York, they sent for the rest of the family. Their eldest brother remained in Russia and was never heard from again. My grandfather struggled in search of "the American Dream," and after several years he achieved a modest success as a retailer.

Mother's father was born in Lithuania to orthodox parents. Fearful that they would be confronted with anti-Semitism even in America, they anglicized their name before leaving the old country in 1901. As a young man of nineteen, my grandfather found work as a watchmaker in Chicago. When he and Grandma were married, he forsook the orthodox customs since she was not religious. They even wholeheartedly embraced the American traditions of Christmas.

My maternal grandmother was born in Budapest in 1891. After her birth, her father set out alone for America without waiting for the new infant to be old enough to travel. He resettled on the West Side of Chicago, where he earned a living as a peddler. Seven months later my great-grandmother packed her belongings and with the children left Budapest to rejoin her husband. By that time he had managed to save enough money to buy a small store in the Maxwell Street area, where they lived behind the shop.

My own family--mother, father, my younger sister, Linda, and I lived on the first floor of a six-flat building in Chicago's East Rogers Park. It was a neighborhood that had attracted many upwardly mobile Jewish families who had left the deteriorating West Side. Its lakefront location, convenient transportation, and comfortable mix of Gentiles and Jews made it an attractive stopping point on what was for some an ultimate flight to the suburbs.

Our large extended family in Rogers Park spanned four generations. We enjoyed a warm feeling of community that was bolstered by the strong Jewish tradition of family support that shaped my formative years. Even now, the image of Grandpa seated at the head of the Passover table leading the seder evokes tender feelings.

One of my most vivid memories of those days was the metal bars on my bedroom window. Although I knew Dad had installed them for my protection after a local child had been abducted and her body dismembered, they made me

---

[1]Historical data from this chapter are documented in *The Course of Modern Jewish History*, by Howard Morley Sachar (New York: Dell, 1977).

feel imprisoned. The vision of these bars was to flash before me after Yuri Tarnopolsky was arrested in the Ukraine and sent to prison in Siberia.

When I was six, we moved to the affluent North Shore suburb of Winnetka. It was a primarily white, Anglo-Saxon, Protestant community, which my parents chose because of its excellent schools. We had a nice home on a quiet street. There was also a new baby, my sister Jane. Our move to suburbia symbolized the American dream; the congested ghettos of the old Pale of Settlement were only a distant legend.

Yet life in the suburbs was unsatisfying in some ways. Little crime existed, but even as a child I noticed how alike everyone seemed to be. As I grew older I yearned for the ethnic diversity of the city and the easy trips to museums and theaters that those who lived downtown take for granted.

I also missed the sense of connectedness I'd felt in Rogers Park. Though we were only about ten miles north of our former home, the tight link among generations seemed broken. And as Jews we did not fit the profile most of our neighbors shared.

Flagrant anti-Semitism did not exist in the 1950s, but it did manifest itself in subtle ways. Instead of swastikas painted on walls, deed restrictions were placed on property by individual home owners in Winnetka. This made it impossible for Jews to purchase houses in certain parts of town. An organized and institutionalized effort on the part of real estate agents further augmented this discriminatory practice. Cooperative real estate listings were labeled ORRT (owners right to reject any and all offers). By the end of the decade, enforcement of deed restrictions was deemed unlawful after being overturned by the U.S. Supreme Court.

"Gentlemen's agreements" were harder to crack, however. These barred Jews from membership in private clubs, giving rise to Jewish clubs throughout the Chicago area. Discrimination in employment was also rampant in both suburbs and city. One-third of all job listings at employment agencies noted, "No Jews."[2]

Ironically, involvement at the synagogue, where I should have felt at home, only underscored my sense of being uncomfortably different. I was sent to North Shore Congregation Israel to study Judaism and Jewish culture. It was a Reform temple--more so than Reform Judaism today--where little Hebrew was used in the service, and most children were confirmed instead of bar or bat mitzvahed. I learned about a place called Israel as some faraway land, never imagining that one day my two sons would be bar mitzvahed in Jerusalem. Most other children who attended this religious school lived in villages with a high percentage of Jewish households. Being isolated in a Gentile community, I did not know them and felt like a pariah.

On the High Holy Days, I was also one of the few students absent from

---

[2]All references to discrimination were obtained from the Anti-Defamation League.

public school. Throughout these formative years it seemed to accentuate the difference between Jews and non-Jews, when most kids equated acceptance with conformity. Insinuated resentment of our extra days off was always felt.

It was not until after the Six Day War in Israel, when the pendulum began swinging closer to conservative Judaism, that most Jews started looking upon their heritage with renewed respect.

After a few years of living in a predominately non-Jewish environment and trying to fit in with "the crowd," my parents succumbed to our pressure and permitted us to put up a Christmas tree along with our Chanukah decorations. Winnetka was a world away from the shtetls. Nevertheless, the overwhelming pressure of trying to assimilate in a Gentile world sent conflicting signals, which further sublimated my identity.

Winnetka is the home of New Trier High School, which remains one of the most highly rated schools in the country. Although I cultivated new friendships, stereotyped attitudes prevailed among students, reflecting the feelings of their parents. New Trier was a microcosm of "movers and shakers." A hierarchical stratification of cliques ruled. These tightly formed clans were referred to as "our crowd" and "their crowd," and little crossover existed between Jewish and non-Jewish circles. Acceptance rested on one's group affiliation. Interaction between Jews and Gentiles was confined to membership on athletic teams, school-affiliated academic clubs, and extracurricular activities. There was little social carryover.

As a teenager, I was self-conscious about my appearance because I was tall for my age and had a bad complexion. Since I did not like my own image, I couldn't imagine how anyone else could like me either. Being unsure of myself caused me to retreat into the background. In school I was satisfied to receive average marks and had no real aspirations. It was a lonely adolescence, compelling me to learn to shield my most personal feelings.

When I graduated from New Trier, I attended the University of Iowa. Like most other coeds from the North Shore, I was programmed to further my education, become socially adept, and receive my "Mrs." degree. This is the life I had been prepared to meet, the life for which I had been intended. My "profession": homemaker.

A turning point in my development was my introduction to a young woman whose family had fled Nazi Germany in 1938 and immigrated to Israel. Ruthie would become a close friend. Born in Israel (a Sabra), she later moved with her family to Canada before they finally settled in Chicago. When we met, I had transferred to Roosevelt University and Ruthie, fluent in seven languages and a graduate of Northwestern University, was working at the Canadian Embassy as a translator. I loved to listen to her relate stories about Israel, and I admired her strength, intelligence, and outgoing personality. She exhibited a certain toughness, characteristic of native Israelis, that I envied. As a child of survivors, she also kept a positive outlook on life and was unafraid of challenge.

"My parents fled Hitler to build a new life in a strange land," she told me one day as we were eating lunch. "After a few years, my father saved enough money to buy a small store, which later become one of Tel Aviv's leading department stores. The decision to move to Canada was a political one."

Ruthie was so different from my other friends; all of us had led such sheltered lives. "I'm a Sabra," she would say. "We worked with our hands in Israel, and our feet are tough from going barefoot." Her life in Israel was almost beyond my imagining, but I saw how her uniqueness attracted others. When she entered a room people noticed. It was Ruthie who opened my eyes and made me comprehend not only that it could be good to be different but also that I could take tremendous pride in my heritage.

I met my husband, Marty, at a New Year's Eve party while I was still in college, and we were married a year after my graduation from Roosevelt. It was a whirlwind romance. He was handsome, dashing, fun to be with, bright, genuinely warm, and sensitive. Marty would stand me in good stead throughout the years to come as I went through the trials and tribulations of a Soviet Jewry activist. He was there when I most needed him, to support me emotionally during the trauma of my breakdown. He sympathized with my compulsion and was a rock when I fell.

Chapter III

A LOOK BEYOND

In the spring of 1971 Marty and I moved, with two small children, from our city apartment to the suburb of Deerfield. Despite having scorned suburbia as a child, I followed the course my parents had traveled: seeking the best life for our offspring. We chose Deerfield, twenty-five miles north of downtown Chicago and just west of the lake, with care. The small, quiet community, with nice homes and good schools, seemed to be just right for us. It was more affordable than the long-established, well-to-do towns along the shores of Lake Michigan. Just as important, though, it had a mixture of Gentiles and Jews. There the boys--Steve was two and a half years old and Rob was a baby--would not grow up bearing the stigma of "token Jews" or experience the humiliation of being called "kikes."

We quickly settled into a lifestyle typical of young, upper-middle-class suburban American families. Marty, a CPA, had started his own accounting firm the prior year, and his office was conveniently located close to home. I had retired from working in the field of social service to stay home and raise the children. Life was simple then, and we were happy.

By the time Steve and Rob were old enough to enter the public school system, they were involved with Little League Baseball, Indian Guides, and Cub Scouts. There were tennis lessons and ice skating lessons; violin, saxophone, and guitar. The boys went to summer camp, we attended family camp, and there were nice family vacations. Besides typical auto excursions, we became involved with the children on long-distance biking tours, canoe trips, and tent camping. It was an active life for all of us.

Although Marty had been born and raised in a Conservative Jewish family from Chicago's East Rogers Park neighborhood, we decided to join North Shore Congregation Israel, which was a Reform synagogue. We eventually sent the boys to religious and Hebrew school at the synagogue and found our choice of communities affirmed when we could see that they never felt like outcasts as I had felt a generation earlier. Many of their classmates from public school attended with them.

Each morning after Marty left for work and the children went to school, I busied myself with household chores. Laundry, marketing, car-pooling, cooking, and typing financial statements for Marty's new business took up most of my day. During free time I enjoyed home decorating activities, and I was always working on an art project. My friends and I, most of our time spent at home with children, had time for gourmet cooking. So dinner parties on weekends were a big part of our social life.

Still, missing from our life was the community feeling that in years past was fostered by generations of family living in close proximity, the feeling I remembered from East Rogers Park. Fragmentation of the family structure began manifesting itself as society became more mobile. As segments of family moved away from the city, they began restructuring their own lives. The feeling of unity and support, once cherished, had disappeared. The telephone, as for most modern-day Americans, became the lifeline with relatives and friends who were geographically scattered. Grandchildren of immigrants never seem to lose that longing for a sense of community.

Perhaps that's what led me to become involved in community affairs when the woods behind our home was threatened by developers. Although never political, I suddenly found myself helping to circulate petitions and attending public meetings. We saved our trees.

In a relatively affluent town like ours, it wasn't difficult to get things done. Two doors down from our house was a park where the boys played football and baseball after school. When a group of us complained that we shouldn't have to car-pool our kids to the other side of town to skate when we had a neighborhood park, an ice skating rink was agreed on by the village.

I had also done volunteer work since as far back as high school, working with both terminally ill and severely handicapped children. Later, my involvement extended to schizophrenics, teenage drug addicts, and youngsters who had attempted suicide. They were scared and lonely, but their faces lit up when I entered the room. Often, I, too, felt lonely. When a child wrapped his tender arms around my neck, however, it made me feel needed.

Staying busy is not always enough. Suburban living can be dull, and that trek into the big city is worth the required time and planning. Suburbs like ours are placid with little crime, but they can also be sterile, lacking in culture. To break the monotony of this cultural wasteland, a trip to the city for a visit to the Art Institute of Chicago, the Museum of Science and Industry or the Chicago Symphony Orchestra offered our family more stimulation than "going to the mall." We hoped the boys would begin to see beyond their backyard.

Marty and I began to expand our horizons further in 1979, with our first trip overseas. Before a planned return to Europe the following year, we decided to reach out and accept an exchange student from France into our home for the summer. Our involvement with NACEL, the North Atlantic Cultural Exchange League, opened a new door to the world, giving us a broader perspective and awareness by allowing us to experience everything through the eyes of a foreigner.

Becoming more cosmopolitan, we reapplied for an exchange student the following summer. A longstanding relationship developed with the family of the second boy, and we visited them at every opportunity. Their two younger children arrived from France a year later, and subsequently the eldest son returned for a second visit. Both our boys were invited to spend a summer in France, and each went abroad at the age of thirteen.

Neither Marty nor I wanted to shelter the boys by allowing them to think our very sterile and stereotyped way of life was the norm. We lived in a place of fresh air, an abundance of luxury, and the possibility to attain great heights through the finest educational system. Nevertheless, there was more to the world.

Although rarely cognizant of how good life was because things didn't always go perfectly, we hoped to teach the children to look beyond themselves, to be thankful for their own lives, and extend a hand to others. Only a small percentage of the world lived this way, and we were determined to show the boys there was life outside "Suburbia, USA."

Chapter IV

ISRAEL

As Steve approached his thirteenth birthday, we began to consider plans for his bar mitzvah. Marty had always regretted not being bar mitzvahed, but at the age of thirteen he had dropped out of the program following the death of his grandfather. Perhaps that contributed to our decision to celebrate Steve's bar mitzvah in Israel. To prepare for the event, Marty and I enrolled in classes of Jewish history taught by Marillyn Tallman. Later Marillyn, co-chairman of Chicago Action for Soviet Jewry, also would become my mentor as my dedication to that cause increased in intensity. We began observing traditional Jewish customs in our home, lighting candles on Shabbat and holding special Friday night dinners. We made sure to set aside time for discussions with the boys, sharing knowledge as we looked forward to the trip.

The memory of my friendship with Ruthie flashed back often as I vividly remembered the influence she had had on my life. Unfortunately neither her positive attitude nor her strength of character, both as an Israeli and as a child of survivors, could protect her from the multiple sclerosis that had taken her life a few years earlier. She would always be missed.

Steve would be symbolically sharing his bar mitzvah with Roman Rozental, a boy from Kishinev, a city in Moldavia on the border of Romania. A "twinning" bar mitzvah ceremony is a symbolic b'nai mitzvah between an American boy or girl and a Soviet child from a refusenik family. The uniting of two families has served as a lifeline to hundreds of Soviet Jewish families denied a visa to emigrate and forbidden by law to practice their religion.

On June 13, 1981, Marty and I, Steve, Rob, my parents and sister, Jane, departed for Israel despite my father's recent heart attack. Marty was saddened that his parents would not be in attendance on this joyous occasion. His father had died when Marty was sixteen and his mother's death came two weeks before our departure. Since it is Jewish custom to continue with life following the death of a loved one, we were encouraged by our rabbi to proceed with plans for the trip. Three generations would be experiencing together the wonders and meaning of the Jewish state.

"Welcome home!" cried the hotel doorman as he opened our car door when we arrived in Israel. We shall never forget that reception. Nor will I forget the overwhelming joy that filled me as I gazed proudly on our loving family. The seven of us had made it to Israel, in spite of illness and death. Little has had as much meaning as the blessings of three generations of a family united in Israel for a child's bar mitzvah.

After checking into the hotel, we received another wonderful surprise. It was a letter from Roman Rozental's grandparents: they were coming to the hotel the next day.

When we met, Blima and Misha Rozental reached out to us as if we were truly a lifeline to their family in Kishinev. Though they had to speak through a sister-in-law who had come along as interpreter, with Dad conversing in Yiddish, their feelings could not have been plainer. Their eyes told all--their worry about family members left behind, their difficult adjustment to Israel. They were heartbroken over being separated from their children and grandson, still captive in the Soviet Union. Though they had achieved the miracle of arriving safely in Israel, they did not speak Hebrew, and housing was poor. They clung to the hope that one day soon their family would be granted visas and all would be reunited in Israel.

For the Rozentals it was a desperate hope born of the urgent need to escape persecution. We, on the other hand, had come to Israel from the perspective of freedom, so it was with unalloyed joy that we were able to take in the profoundly affecting sights and sounds around us.

The most striking observation to an American Jew was being aware that this was a country where Jews were a majority. People on the street, shopkeepers, cab drivers, hotel employees, police, soldiers, government officials . . . all were Jewish. Some had fled from persecution and had arrived as refugees; others had emigrated from other nations because they believed in Zionism (establishment and preservation of the Jewish state). *This* was what Ruthie had spoken of, this pride and passion that I never found in Winnetka when I was growing up.

In Israel, a Jew can hold up his head with dignity and pride, without fear of hostility and revenge or the humiliation of being called a "kike." Freedom to live a Jewish life with respect and honor is unattainable in the former Soviet Union, and even in America this freedom can be elusive.

To walk through the Jewish state and witness the Jewish spirit untrammeled by bigotry--from out-and-out persecution to the "little" prejudices-- was a transforming experience. Here was Ruthie's homeland and the home of my ancestors. Our home. The more deeply we probed the land of our heritage, the more deeply we felt that bond.

We began at the Diaspora Museum in Tel Aviv, where Marty and I searched eagerly for information regarding our family's heritage. There one could trace family roots back to Eastern Europe, which was a great gift to Jews of the Diaspora visiting Israel. Though we were unable to find anything new about our specific family, the records were rich in historical value.

Next we visited Meggido, where three thousand years ago, during the time of King Solomon, the need to survive forced Jews to construct a water tunnel to maintain their civilization. As we walked 183 steps down into a shaft that led to the tunnel, I realized with profound shock that this staircase, recorded in the Bible, had been climbed centuries ago by my ancestors. And their ingenuity! This extraordinary engineering accomplishment, dramatically documented in James Michener's book *The Source* (though he called it Tell Hazor, which is the site of another ancient water tunnel, now in ruins), left me breathless.

On another day we drove to Masada, the location of one of the most dramatic episodes in history, which occurred three years after the destruction of the Temple of Jerusalem by Titus in 70 A.D. As told by Josephus, one of the commanders in the revolt against Rome, 960 Zealot defenders committed suicide on Masada (including women and children who were put to death by heads of families) rather than surrender to the invading Romans. As I stood there with my family, overlooking the Dead Sea, I felt the strength of our ancestors fill me.

On the road to Jerusalem, we watched eagerly for the first glimpse of the Old City. As we spotted it from a distance, it seemed to beckon us. The pinkish-golden stones of the ramparts were glowing, and the city seemed to possess celestial magic. Gleaming majestically amid the towers and turrets within the ancient walls was the golden Dome of the Rock. Following the War of Liberation in 1948, the Old City was barricaded by the Arabs and Jews were forbidden to enter. It remained closed to Jews until 1967, when Israel defeated its Arab neighbors in the Six Day War. From the beginning of time our people had been forced to fight for survival. From Meggido to Masada to Nazi Germany, and now to oppression in the Soviet Union. When will it end?!

Inside the ramparts we gazed at the Western Wall, the symbolic link for Jews throughout the world. Since the destruction of the Second Temple, Jews have come from all over the Diaspora to pray here. We did so as well, on the eve of Shabbat. We prayed for peace.

Har El Synagogue in Jerusalem was the setting of the bar mitzvah. Rabbi Ben Chorin spoke about the beauty of this experience--the uniting of the Diaspora in Israel, extended to Russia by symbolically bringing together Steve and Roman. As Steve stood on the podium next to the rabbi, we noticed he was pale and unsteady. The evening before, he had become ill, burning with fever and dysentery. We had been awake all night. But then Steve smiled. After chanting his portion of the Torah and Haftorah, Steve spoke about Roman: "This is an especially happy time for me, because not only do I have the pleasure of having my bar mitzvah in Jerusalem, but I am also sharing it with a refusenik, whose name is Roman Rozental. . . . Since Roman and his family live in the Soviet Union, he has been denied the right to practice Judaism. His grandparents, who were fortunate to leave Russia and immigrate to Israel, had been invited to my bar mitzvah. They were unable to attend because Roman's grandfather was too ill to travel from Tel Aviv. . . . This morning, as I recite the blessings in Jerusalem,

Roman will be doing the same thing privately in Kishinev with his parents. . . .
This morning, we are taping the service and sending it to the Soviet Union, so
Roman can hear our twinning ceremony. . . ."

Steve remained weak, but he kept up with us for the rest of the trip. A
memorable but disturbing highlight was a visit to Yad Vashem. "Even unto them
will I give in mine house and within my walls a place and a name . . . ": Isaiah
56:5. From this verse came the name Yad Vashem, the memorial to the six
million Jews who perished in the Holocaust. A tree-lined path, the Allees des
Justes, leads to the monument, each tree honoring one of the righteous Christians
who risked their lives to save Jews. Had it not been for their courage, many more
would have perished. The entrance to the monument is beyond the eternal flame,
and inside are photos of victims, some life-sized. Both Steve and Rob stood
speechless before pictures of children in the death camps.

Though overcome myself, I stood back for a moment and watched my two
sons. Here was Steve, sensitive and shy, vulnerable to peer rejection and easily
hurt as I had been. He was, however, more inquisitive than I, excelling in math
and science.

There was Rob, the effervescent one in the family: very outgoing, always
surrounded by other boys and girls, a natural athlete who constantly had us on the
floor laughing.

Two boys, so different, yet so alike at this moment. As they stared at the
hollow eyes and emaciated bodies of those children of fifty years ago, they both
seemed to ask, "Why?" The walls echoed silence. The message from those
sacrificed cried out, "Never forget!"

When we left Jerusalem, we headed toward a kibbutz in the Upper Galilee,
where we were reminded that Israel's struggle is never ending. Constantly on our
minds was the smallness of the country, its borders dangerously close to enemy
Arab countries. It took no time to travel from one frontier to the other. Israeli
soldiers were posted everywhere on twenty-four-hour patrol, but citizens carried
on with their everyday lives. When we arrived at the kibbutz, we thought we
heard a sonic boom but soon discovered a border skirmish had taken place. The
kibbutz was located close to the Syrian border, and the series of cross-border
missile attacks had reached its peak.

Our experiences in Israel left me with a dizzying array of new thoughts
and emotions. These were simultaneously disturbing and exhilarating. While the
boys were going through early adolescence, I had been happily involved with
suburban living, focused on children, home, and family. But recently, as the boys
began to need me less, I had become engulfed by a growing feeling of emptiness.
The realization had hit home that there must be more to life than raising children
and being a housewife. Now I had an idea of what might fill up that emptiness.
I did not know where my actions might ultimately lead me, but I knew that what
was important right now was extricating the Rozentals from the USSR. I also
knew where to turn. Through Marillyn Tallman I had become interested in

Chicago Action for Soviet Jewry. CASJ had shown me that efforts of individuals and groups of individuals can make a difference, that battles had been fought and won, and that all was not hopeless for Soviet refuseniks.

When I returned to Chicago, I immersed myself in work with CASJ, concentrating on the Rozental case.

As a result of support solicited by public officials and political heat generated by the Soviet Jewry movement, the Rozentals received permission to emigrate within thirteen months.

Chapter V

CHICAGO ACTION FOR SOVIET JEWRY AND THE UNION OF COUNCILS FOR SOVIET JEWS

"Once you become involved with this organization you cannot stop. It becomes part of your life, and the members are like family."

When you entered the door of Chicago Action for Soviet Jewry in the early 1980s, you were immediately aware of the constant tension in the office. Phones rang with calls from abroad. "Hello, dear, your party is on the line," said the saccharine-sweet Moscow operator. Calls to and from Washington were taking place hourly as news was monitored minute by minute.

Moments after an arrest was made anywhere in the USSR, Chicago Action, located on Chicago's North Shore, received information and began transmitting news throughout the world. Telegrams and press releases were issued, and frequently the news media moved in with massive pieces of equipment, preparing for live television coverage of some major event that had just taken place. Concurrently, tourists were being briefed for missions to the USSR.

Lining the office walls were photos of prisoners of conscience, and a large map of the former Soviet Union hung ominously over the conference table. Shelves were lined with articles of material support that were carried into the USSR with tourists to be distributed among prisoners and refusenik families. A full inventory of food (dried fruit and juice, powdered milk, coffee, and chocolate), clothing (mostly winter), medicine, Jewish books and news magazines, electronics, and other supplies was checked regularly. A scarcity of these foods prevailed, and the other items were usually unattainable. Boxes of postcards to prisoners and Soviet officials were stacked on the floor, waiting to be distributed to groups and organizations throughout the United States for mass mailing into the

Soviet Union.

Ten years later, in the early 1990s, a daily core group of ten to fifteen people continues to work in this very busy, unpretentious office. It is a grass-roots operation, not a bureaucracy, with 99 percent of the staff volunteers. Most of them are women who reside in this affluent area, and they dedicate huge amounts of their time to the cause of rescuing Russian Jews. In doing so, they have earned the understanding and respect of their families. Leisure time seldom exists for this small group of people.

The movement remains in a constant state of flux. There is and always has been a steady flow of visiting activists, educators, politicians, and religious leaders. Weekly staff meetings are held to ensure that members are aware of all developments taking place. New programs are discussed, ideas are exchanged--a revolving "think tank" is always in progress. No set routine exists. Everyone is busy doing his or her job, and all work is carried out with the greatest efficiency and accuracy.

In the Soviet Jewry movement there is no room for error. One mistake can cost a person's life.

One important aspect of the organization has been to educate the community to establish public awareness. To accomplish this task a monthly refusenik newsletter is published, edited during the 1980s by Linda Opper and now by Laura Bramlet. In addition, a Speaker's Bureau sends out lecturers to address groups throughout the area. Anti-Semitism in the Soviet Union was and is so widespread and threatening that it is beyond the imagination of most Americans. Russian Jews fear for their safety and the safety of their children.

Without strong support from the American Jewish population, it would be impossible to generate the political action necessary to fight this persecution. Both workers and financial backers are needed to underwrite rescue efforts. Hetty De Leeuwe, financial chair of CASJ, volunteers five days a week, keeping a watchful eye on the monetary situation. A Holocaust survivor from the Netherlands, Hetty was hidden by a Gentile family for two years during WWII. Her parents were hidden separately from her. In 1944 Hetty's mother was arrested by the Gestapo and shipped from one concentration camp to another. She was liberated from Mauthausen, a camp in Austria. Hetty's father, who worked in the underground, was caught listening to an English radio station just two months before the war ended. Since his Jewish identity was unknown, he was jailed instead of being executed. The family was reunited in early 1945.

Hetty came to the United States as a new bride in 1962. She had met her Dutch-born American husband in the Netherlands. In 1976, she learned about a Jewish prisoner of conscience from the Soviet Union, Mark Nashpitz, who was being held captive in the Gulag. "You can't go to bed at night knowing people need your help," reflected Hetty one day. Immediately she began writing regular letters to Mark. His mother contacted Hetty from Israel to ask her to send him a coat so he could survive the harsh Siberian winter. Hetty followed her instructions and sent the coat into the USSR with Lorel Pollack, who was chairman of CASJ at the time. Lorel dropped it off in Moscow at Ida Nudel's apartment. For years Ida served as "Guardian Angel" for all prisoners of conscience, until she herself was arrested.

The following year Lorel recruited Hetty for CASJ, and she was instantly hooked. "Once you become involved with this organization," she remarked, "you cannot stop. It becomes part of your life, and the members are like family."

CASJ could never have achieved the many successes it has without its heart and soul, current co-chairmen Pamela Cohen and Marillyn Tallman. Pamela and Marillyn have dedicated their lives to the cause of liberating Soviet Jews. A demanding schedule involving complete attention and constant supervision is carried out with love and devotion. These two outstanding women serve as an inspiration to other activists, while giving hope to Russian Jews through their unwavering support and friendship.

Marillyn's devotion to human rights and the Jewish people began in 1942, when she was a student at the University of Illinois and active with the Hillel Foundation. Upon graduation from Illinois with a degree in education, she directed the Hillel Foreign Student Service, a project organized to rescue college-age people from Displaced Persons Camps after the war. Thousands of applications from all over Europe began pouring in from young men and women who were unable to enter the United States under the quota system. One hundred twenty-five candidates were selected, among whom was Tom Lantos. Tom was later to become a California congressman.

In 1968, four years before the advent of the Soviet Jewry movement, Marillyn traveled to the Soviet Union with her husband, Sefton. She returned ten years later on a mission to meet refuseniks, after having been formally briefed by Lorel at CASJ. Her involvement with Chicago Action began when she came home. "I recognized the terrible need for Soviet Jews to get out, and CASJ was the only organization working for this *single goal*. My whole life has been directed towards rescuing Jews," said Marillyn. "But as a Jew this is not a remarkable thing. Being involved in history, in rescue . . . this is part of my Jewish identity." Marillyn has also been teaching Jewish history to adult education classes for over twenty years and has lectured throughout the United States and Canada. "I learn from my students, and they are *my* teachers." Marillyn has many followers, and it has often been said that she has the talent to make the *ordinary* (people) *extraordinary*.

Looking at her co-workers around the conference table in 1992, Marillyn said, "At CASJ we are like family. We are personally involved in each other's lives and remain fine-tuned to emergencies. Despite the tension which fills the office, we still find time to relax and enjoy one another's company. We laugh and cry together. As Jews, we have something important in common. We are taught in the Bible that it is our responsibility to 'rescue the captives.'"

It is difficult for many Americans to understand the urgency of that mission--that life in the Soviet police state was a humiliation for many. But being treated as an animal rather than as a human being is and was intolerable. A person who was content to live within the "accepted" Soviet structure, adhering to all restrictions, had fewer problems. Being told what to do, how to think, how to behave, what to say and not to say was simply unnatural. There was *only* one "right" approach, the Soviet approach, and any deviation from the accepted way of thinking was punishable by the authorities. "Big Brother" was always watching.

Since the former USSR was an atheist society, and people were forbidden to practice religion, Jews held underground meetings at each other's apartments. At times scholars were present to teach, but usually Jews were self-taught from rare books shared among friends. Samizdat, literature unpublishable in the USSR that was self-published and circulated underground, contained good information but was risky if discovered by KGB. *Exodus*, by Leon Uris, was one of the most sought after books translated into samizdat.

Lack of telephone communication exacerbated the information vacuum. Although a majority of Russians are nonpolitical, intellectuals craving news found it futile trying to obtain information through normal channels. The two state-operated newspapers, *Pravda* and *Izvestia,* remained silent on major news events: natural disasters within the country, airplane and train wrecks, fires, etc. Even the death of Khrushchev received only a one-sentence obituary. A thirty-minute nightly television news program offered little except collective farm reports, sports announcements, and propaganda. It was possible to obtain information (when broadcasts were not jammed) through Voice of America, Radio Liberty, BBC Radio and Kol Israel. Clandestine meetings with foreigners were arranged, and on occasion a few Soviet Jews organized meetings with Western journalists.

Jews were disqualified from most careers, except in the fields of science and the arts. Promotions were difficult to achieve without party membership, and employers were fearful of Jewish employees, knowing they might try to emigrate.

At best, life was drab and unexciting. Nobody smiled, and the clothing was as drab as the colorless lives. Most things taken for granted by Westerners as "essential" were forbidden to Soviet citizens. They had no control over their lives, very few ever saw life beyond the USSR, and for years they remained in constant fear of harassment and arrest, justified by their failure to accept the "norm" as defined by Soviet law.

Internal passports, mandatory for all Soviet citizens, were to be carried at all times. These identification cards were clearly stamped with each person's nationality: Russian, Georgian, Latvian, or Jew. At age sixteen, children from mixed marriages were compelled to declare their nationality, Jew or that of the other parent.

In 1948, before the Soviet Jewry movement began, Golda Meir, the Russian-born minister to Moscow for the new state of Israel, went to the USSR, and fifty thousand cheering Jews from all over the Soviet Union arrived in the capital city to see her as she addressed them before attending Moscow Synagogue for the High Holy Days.

Following the 1967 War in Israel, Soviet Jewry awakened and became alive. After years of oppression under Stalin, many became inspired to learn Hebrew and practice Judaism. With the newly kindled desire to go to Israel, thousands of visa applications began flooding offices of the Soviet government.

In 1970, when Silva Zalmanson and her "co-conspirators" attracted world attention to their plight by attempting to "hijack" a plane to Israel via Sweden, the Soviet Jewry movement was born. Although their mission was foiled by KGB infiltration, the Jews of the USSR were silent no longer. They knew their attempt was doomed to fail, but they were willing to make the sacrifice to open the doors to thousands of other Jews held hostage in the USSR. The group was arrested, tried, and sentenced during the infamous Leningrad trials. Two of the offenders were sentenced to death, and the rest were given severe labor camp sentences. However, due to world pressure, the Soviet Union commuted the two death penalties to fifteen years' imprisonment.

Pamela had been listening to Marillyn express her convictions. She nodded in agreement. "'Never again' has a deep, relevant meaning. Soviet Jews represent the third largest Diaspora community, and we will not permit our people to be lost a second time."

As a teenager, Pamela was a voracious reader and avidly concentrated upon the Jewish historical cycle from Abraham to modern times. In high school she studied Russian literature and began to "feel a connection."

It was the heroism of Silva Zalmanson and her friends that first spurred Pamela Cohen to action. As an American Jew, she viewed the incident as an opportunity to create awareness so that others would not commit the "sin of silence."

Pamela mobilized her resources and embarked on a plan to collect information. She became active in a branch of the Council of Jewish Women, attended committee meetings on Soviet Jewry, and involved herself on the Social Action Committee at Congregation Solel. In addition, she attended Jewish history classes taught by Marillyn. Soon afterward she met Lorel.

When CASJ first opened in 1972, the office was located at Spertus College of Judaica in Chicago. Lorel, who had been one of the founders of the organization, resigned from her position just two weeks before Marillyn's second trip to the Soviet Union in 1978. Pamela then became the new co-chairman along with Carole Boron, and the office of CASJ was relocated to Highland Park. When Marillyn was asked to join them, she became the third co-chairman. Hetty, already involved for some time, was office manager. Eventually Carole gave up her position to work for the American Israel Public Affairs Committee (AIPAC).

That winter Pamela and her husband, Leonard, made their first trip to the

USSR. Their second trip would not take place until 1988. In the intervening ten years Pamela attended annual meetings in Israel, sponsored by the Union of Councils for Soviet Jews (UCSJ), to establish links with members of separated families whose loved ones were unable to leave the USSR. Since 1989, Pamela has increased her visits to Israel to twice a year.

As the Soviet Jewry movement grew more intense after the door to the free world closed in 1979, the work at CASJ became more involved. Night after night, Pam took her work home. She gave meaning to the words "The walls dividing the Jewish community are nonexistent." Visiting activists often stayed at her house. "The Jewish world lives in our kitchen," she commented. "It's like a Moscow kitchen, and when I'm there [in Moscow] I feel at home. There's no difference."

One former prisoner of conscience, Ari Volvovsky, whose case she embraced wholeheartedly, had a deep, personal impact on her life. So much so that in 1984, when Pam learned about Ari's attempt at keeping a kosher home in Gorky, she felt compelled to make her kitchen in Deerfield kosher. Since shoiket (ritual slaughter) did not exist in Gorky, the observance of dietary laws was far more difficult than in the West, where easy access to kosher food exists.

"Our real responsibility is to *people*," said Pamela. "Reaching out to individuals on a case-by-case approach is what makes the movement work."

Leonard Cohen takes pride in Pam's career and is proud of her performance. "It would be impossible for me to commit so much time to this cause if it were not for the support of my husband," she said. "We're a team, and we help each other."

Living with a mother who was passionately involved as a human rights advocate was not as easy for the Cohens' three children. The constant traffic of visitors in and out of the house created a lack of privacy. Nevertheless, in retrospect they understand how this all-consuming experience helped mold their lives. As young adults, they know what it means to be a Jew.

CASJ, which has been the active voice of Soviet Jews since 1972, works nationally and internationally as part of the Union of Councils for Soviet Jews. Located in Washington, D.C., UCSJ is operated by the national director, Micah Naftalin. Pamela, in addition to her duties as co-chairman for CASJ, is also the national president of UCSJ. At the time of this writing in early 1993, Pamela had held this position for six years. UCSJ has over thirty grass-roots councils located within the United States and is closely involved with independent Soviet Jewish groups in Canada, England, France, and Israel. In 1993 it was also sponsoring three human rights bureaus, which were located in Moscow, Kiev, and St. Petersburg. Another bureau, scheduled to open later in Central Asia, was targeted for Bishkek, Kyrghyzstan. The sole purpose of the organization now is to help Jews who continue to live in the former USSR and to sustain and protect them. The majority of Russian Jews in the former Soviet Union (FSU) will remain there because they are unable to enter the United States, don't want to go to Israel, or see existing possibilities for themselves in the FSU. Therefore, the role of UCSJ is to guard their safety, dignity, and right to democracy.

The most traditional activity of UCSJ is the monitoring of rescue and exit issues. UCSJ keeps a watchful eye on emigration legislation in the FSU including the Baltic States and Georgia. The Baltics (Latvia, Lithuania, and Estonia) did not join the new Commonwealth of Independent States because they denied ever being part of the USSR. Georgia also remained outside the commonwealth because it was in the middle of a civil war.

Jewish survival and empowerment in the former Soviet Union are confronted daily by UCSJ. In safeguarding Jewish lives, UCSJ supports groups and projects that serve this goal. Its grass-roots efforts have been responsible for initiating programs such as the twinning bar mitzvah ceremonies. Since a new generation of activists has come forward following the departure of former refuseniks, new leadership within the communities must be enforced. UCSJ is in tune with the suggestions and wishes of Jews who are living there.

To help monitor news of interest about Jewish communities across the new independent states, a weekly digest is published in Moscow. It has a network of correspondents throughout the FSU who collect data on anti-Semitism, Jewish culture, and other issues of concern. *The Monitor* is produced jointly by the Union of Councils for Soviet Jews, the Center for Jewish Renewal (a joint project of UCSJ and the Bay Area Council for Soviet Jews), and the International Bureau on Human Rights (IBHR) and Rule of Law. *The Monitor* includes weekly reports from IBHR's political monitoring publication, *Russia Inside,* and from IBHR's *Jewish News Weekly.* David Waksberg, director of the Bay Area Council for Soviet Jews, coordinates this effort.

During the 1980s, when I joined CASJ, thousands of Soviet Jews had begun to fight for their freedom. A massive emigration movement had culminated in the late 1970s, when (within a one-year period) fifty thousand Soviet Jews received permission to leave "Mother Russia." In 1979, after the invasion of Afghanistan, the Soviets knew they could no longer expect favors from the United States, and the door to the free world was again closed.

The Soviet Union never had an emigration policy, and the opportunity to leave came solely from worldwide Jewish pressure. Under Stalin's terrorist reign, Jewish emigration could never have existed, but his successors adhered to detente, releasing some Jews to appease the West. The Soviets disposed of "troublemakers," hoping to cripple the emigration movement by deporting its leaders, but new leadership quickly formed to fill the voids.

Those who emigrated during the 1980s were considered "Betrayers of their Motherland." Emigres were limited as to what they could take, and most came out to begin their lives with only one suitcase apiece and under $100 cash.

In 1982, Marty and I were to travel to the Soviet Union on a mission under the auspices of CASJ. At that time, there were nearly 550,000 known refuseniks out of a population of approximately three to five million Jews. This was to be a journey that changed our lives forever.

PART TWO: INSIDE THE SOVIET UNION

"I went to Russia drawn by the silence of its Jews. I brought back their cry."

Elie Wiesel

Chapter I

PREPARING FOR THE SOVIET UNION

"Neither oceans nor miles nor oppressive governments will keep us away from our people."

One day, toward the end of 1981, I approached Marillyn and told her Marty and I were hoping to travel to the Soviet Union in the spring. At this time, we had not entertained the idea of going on a real "mission" because our main goal was to meet the Rozentals in Kishinev.

At the onset of my involvement with the organization, I had felt completely inadequate about embarking on a serious mission. In the early 1980s the only Americans traveling to the Soviet Union on missions to meet with refuseniks were dedicated individuals, many of whom were scholars of Judaica, doctors, lawyers, or political figures. I was a suburban wife and mother, not a great scholar, and neither Marty nor I could foresee how we could be of service on a wide-scale basis.

Marillyn emphasized how critical the situation was for Jews behind the Iron Curtain, saying the need for tourists was great and we *would* be qualified to do the job. She stressed the fact that to go to the Soviet Union without seeing the truth and hearing the real story, as told by many families rather than one "special" family, would be regrettable. When Marillyn equated the situation to the late 1930s in Nazi Germany, we realized how wrong it would be to go to the Soviet Union without attempting to reach out to as many refuseniks as possible. She said that during the genocide years of World War II, American Jews did *not* act to help victims of the Holocaust. "We know," said Marillyn, "what is taking place today behind the Iron Curtain, and the situation must be monitored to prevent another crime. *Neither oceans nor miles nor oppressive governments will keep us away from our people.*" The purpose of our trip to the USSR had become much bigger than just our own special family, the Rozentals.

Before our mission, we were briefed thoroughly by Marillyn and Pamela. Both of them filled our heads with facts about everything we needed to know concerning the Russian people, the culture, and the refuseniks.

Marillyn began. "Never make any phone calls from your hotel room. Remember that all calls are monitored. Always use telephone booths on the street to phone refuseniks."

"But we do want them to make one call from their room as soon as they check into the hotel in Moscow," interjected Pamela. "Be sure to phone the American Embassy to let them know you are there. In case of emergency, they'll know who and where you are."

"That's very important," agreed Marillyn before continuing. "Also be aware that the maids are all KGB, as well as the key ladies on every floor."

"And don't talk in taxicabs," warned Pamela. "When you get to an apartment, ring the doorbell; *never* knock. The KGB knocks."

It sounded like something out of a good spy novel. Marty and I looked at each other, and at that moment we both wondered what we were getting ourselves into.

Noticing our concern, Marillyn quickly proceeded. "There are two books that are mandatory reading. *The Russians*, by Hedrick Smith, and *The Last Exodus*, by Leonard Schroeter. These are read by all of our tourists and will give you historical background as well as up-to-date facts."

Pamela handed us a folder that she and Marillyn had carefully prepared for our trip. It contained case histories of every refusenik with whom we were to meet and key people to contact in each city. Lists of instructions were included. "Contact Lev in Moscow, but wait until after 5:00 p.m.," cautioned Pamela. "When you meet, ask him who the prisoner contact is in Kiev--or should aid be left in Moscow with Natasha? Also, does Natasha want articles in the newspapers about herself?"

"It's important to find out who does *not* want publicity," added Marillyn. "We also need to know what's happening with the Sverdlovsk trial."

"Find out if it's true that Gorodetsky's fiance has been arrested," continued Pamela. "Ask if it's safe to visit Polina Paritsky. Inform them of Kazachkov's sentence . . . fifteen years' strict regime labor. . . ."

The briefing continued for hours. I felt overwhelmed by the vast amount of information conveyed to us. So much would have to be memorized. We could only take brief notes with us into the country, and they would need to be coded. I glanced over at Marty, and he smiled reassuringly.

Suddenly Hetty came rushing into the conference room. "Joseph Begun has just been rearrested!" The briefing ended abruptly. Pam and Marillyn activated the emergency system for disseminating news. Within moments Pam was on the phone to Washington, and Marillyn directed a staff member to send out a press release.

"NBC is on the line," shouted Linda.

Marillyn took the call from the TV reporter. After hanging up, she announced there would be a live broadcast from the CASJ office in one hour.

Cameramen from NBC were on the way over to interview Pam regarding Begun's arrest.

Marty and I left quietly. We felt deeply affected by what had just occurred. This was not a cloak-and-dagger operation. It was real life, happening to real people, and it was frightening. We wanted to help.

Before long I became completely immersed in studying the material. The deep absorption of new data was all-consuming. Stacks of notes were piled high on my desk along with newspapers, journals, and books. I kept myself awake with large doses of caffeine.

One morning I called Dad to ask him to join me for coffee--and would he stop to pick up some chocolate donuts? Knowing my craving for chocolate, he didn't even hesitate. I frequently pig out on it when nervous. When he arrived with dozens of donuts, he found me studying in the kitchen. Papers were all over the table, floor, and countertops. We both laughed, which relieved the tension and allowed me to relax.

If Marty and I were to be able to move independently, we would need to become familiar with the Cyrillic alphabet and learn to speak some simple phrases. In addition, Marty and I each had our own responsibilities as well as strengths. His job was official photographer, handler of all foreign currency, and guide for Soviet cities, which was aided by his keen sense of direction. I was responsible for imparting official business to the refusenik community and recording all information in our notebook. This meticulously documented material would be taken back to the United States and evaluated during debriefing.

After months of planning and preparation, the time for departure had finally arrived. Like most Westerners embarking on a mission to the USSR, we were nervous, due mostly to ignorance and fear of the unknown. When the day arrived, we had come a long way toward mastering our fear after being instilled with confidence that we would be prepared to meet the challenges ahead.

Friday, May 8, 1982, at O'Hare Airport, Marty and I boarded the plane that would take us to Moscow.

Chapter II

MOSCOW

$\mathbf{W}$e approached customs with some trepidation as we carried several pieces of luggage bursting with material support for refusenik friends. Moments earlier we had landed at Moscow's Sheremetyevo Airport. It was Sunday night.

By standing in two different lines, we hoped to draw less attention to ourselves since we were bringing many things into the country. Several hours earlier we had been in Copenhagen, where we had sat in the airport in between flights for four and a half hours, reading and consuming last-minute notes, anxiously awaiting the next leg of our journey. Marty's line appeared to be moving more quickly than mine, and from across the crowded room I watched as his luggage was opened and methodically searched. Unfortunately, Marty had grabbed a suitcase containing a fur-trimmed sweater destined for a refusenik family, and the customs agent knew at once that he was either homosexual or traveling with a woman. Immediately, I was summoned and asked to join him in line. We suspected they were thinking, "Zionist conspirators." At first it appeared they would confiscate our Hebrew items and magazines, because these things were temporarily removed. Eventually, however, everything was returned. In our anxiety to leave the premises, we quickly tossed everything back inside the cases. Our small notebook of carefully coded names and messages had gone undetected inside Marty's breast pocket. Besides a Berlitz phrase book, we also carried a magic slate to write down sensitive things we felt could not be discussed freely in carefully bugged rooms.

After a tiring and somewhat unsettling introduction to "Mother Russia," we checked at the Intourist desk to obtain the name of our hotel. Foreign tourists to the USSR were never permitted a choice. We exchanged dollars for rubles and waited for the airport "limousine" that would take us to the National Hotel. While waiting for the van to arrive, we met a Pennsylvania businessman who stared in utter amazement at the number of bags we were carrying. With one small hanging case in tow, he remarked condescendingly, "Experienced travelers always travel light." We agreed and nodded politely.

Arriving at the National, conveniently located across the street from the Kremlin, we registered and went directly to our room. The dingy hotel room proved to be furnished in spartan fashion with two twin beds, one dresser, and a lamp. As we unpacked, we were careful to remove all sensitive items, which we did not want to leave for the surreptitious inspection of the hotel maid. Little conversation of any substance took place in the room. Anything important was discussed outdoors, where we felt comfortable to speak freely. If something significant needed to be communicated, we would write messages to each other on our magic slate. Any notes on paper were shredded and flushed down the toilet a few pieces at a time.

The task of unpacking completed, we followed our instructions and phoned the American Embassy. Then we eagerly left the room for a quick jaunt around Moscow to orient ourselves. It was a holiday, Victory Day, and thousands of people had gathered in Red Square to view the fireworks display. It looked like the Fourth of July.

We found a telephone booth around the corner from the hotel and made a call to our first refusenik, to set an appointment for the next day.

"Lev, it's Nancy and Marty from Chicago, and Marillyn and Pamela send their fondest regards." The mention of Marillyn and Pam immediately told him who we were.

"We're in town for a couple of days and would like to see you. When would it be convenient?" Lev quickly gave us instructions on when and where to meet him; refuseniks were not permitted to enter hotels designated for foreign tourists.

We returned to the National Hotel late that night and collapsed into bed.

Rising early, we met our group for breakfast in the hotel dining room, anxious to know what types of people signed up for a tour of the Soviet Union. Traveling with Intourist, on a tour approved by the Russian government, we discovered that our group consisted of twenty-three people, mostly elderly, seasoned tourists from all over the United States. Marina was our Intourist guide. There was one young couple in the group, whom we befriended, knowing they might be helpful to us at the end of the trip, when we needed to get through customs. The majority of the group had come to the Soviet Union as tourists; as Jewish activists we had little in common with our traveling companions. We felt isolated.

We joined the group for an organized city tour of Moscow that first morning, trying to appear to be ordinary sightseers. Walking through Red Square, we were struck by the powerful presence of the Kremlin. We visited St. Basil's Cathedral and saw Lenin's Tomb. The daily line waiting to view the body at this central shrine appeared endless, wrapping around several blocks. The passive faces, mostly peasants, stared directly ahead in silence as they stood two abreast.

After lunch at the hotel with our tour group, Marty and I felt free to go out on our own. We had plenty of time before our rendezvous with Lev. Briefly we visited GUM, the largest department store in the USSR, located directly across the street from the Kremlin at 3 Red Square. This two-story building housed many departments, but merchandise was shabby and shelves were sparsely filled. I remembered reading in *The Russians*, by Hedrick Smith, that only goods which nobody wanted remained on the shelves, and even Russian housewives refused to purchase them. Imported products, when available, were the only items worth buying. Racks of clothing, mostly suits and coats, seemed plentiful, but when we examined them closely we found them to be poorly made and out of style. Certainly we could find no resemblance between GUM and Chicago's Marshall Field's!

As we made our way down Kalinina Prospekt, walking toward the Kremlin on the way to the Metro, Marty and I nearly collided with a group of militia. They were standing on the sidewalk in front of a government building. When we realized we would have to either walk right through them or make an obvious detour to cross the street, we decided to proceed through the "blockade" rather than call attention to ourselves. It was slightly unnerving because of the contents of our tote bags, but we received nothing more than menacing stares. The bags were so heavy that both Marty and I had deep indentation marks on our shoulders for weeks.

We found the streets in downtown Moscow thronged with people, their faces blank, their clothing colorless. Walking through the downtown section, we noticed attractive storefronts, but we soon realized they were only facades. The shop interiors were run-down, barren, and stocked with poor-quality merchandise. Storefront displays were usually filled with imported products, most of which were unavailable inside. Russians, mostly women, waited for hours in long lines, queuing up to purchase goods as they stood with shopping bags brought from home. Since separate lines existed for each item (bread, fish, meat, eggs), shopping for groceries was an all-day process. The only well-stocked stores were bookstores, filled to capacity with propaganda.

We admired the beautiful facades of churches and palaces, now museums, which had been built at the time of the czars. The large synagogue in Moscow was open, but the rabbi was appointed by the state and reported daily to KGB. We later discovered the same situation existed at the Leningrad Synagogue, and the majority of synagogues in the Ukraine had been converted into gymnasiums.

Housing in the USSR was terrible, built with shoddy construction and poorly maintained. Buildings were erected practically overnight, and edifices began to deteriorate almost as quickly. Paneled prefab structures were monotonously produced with leaking roofs and crumbling stone walls. In a country where private property did not exist and everything was owned by the state, the result was apathy; no one cared about workmanship. Most apartments were stark, small, and substandard.

We made good use of underground passageways on our way to meet Lev since the weather was inclement--the Moscow climate matched the drab of the buildings and the expressionless faces of the Russians. Entering the Metro on Karl Marx Boulevard (Prospekt Marxa), we lingered on the platform as had been

arranged. Would we recognize each other? we wondered. Then along came a
man, smiling broadly, who gave us a wink. It was Lev. With our Western
clothing and bursting bags, we were not difficult to spot. He too was easy to
identify; we recognized the familiar wool hat pulled down low over his eyebrows
from several photographs we had seen. Since Marty and I were each carrying two
bags apiece, Lev took mine, and silently we all walked to catch the train for his
apartment.

The first thing we noticed when Lev opened the door to his flat was that
it was heavily padded to help muffle sounds from within. Once inside, we felt
warmth and comfort despite our run-down surroundings. There was an old sofa,
a cocktail table, a wooden chair, and a lamp. The gray walls echoed the sounds
of family long since departed, and photographs of a woman and two children hung
crookedly on the living room wall. There was a small kitchen, where Lev busied
himself in preparation for guests. There was a water closet, but the toilet didn't
flush. We communicated through our magic slate.

Lev Blitshtein had been chief administrator in the Ministry of Meat and
Dairy Production before applying for a visa in 1974. One year later he was forced
to divorce his wife, Bluma, so she could obtain a visa. That was a common
practice that had been inflicted on Soviet Jews, and officials seemed to delight in
breaking up families. Husbands and wives separated voluntarily to save at least
one spouse and the couple's children. The alternative was unthinkable: to remain
in Russia was like being buried alive. Bluma was able to leave the country with
their two children, Boris and Galina, but Lev was denied permission on the
grounds that "his work was secret and he knew too much about the time for
storage of canned meats." Although Lev had been a national authority on
breeding and meat processing in the ministry, he had *no* access to secret
documents. As was common practice, Lev had been reapplying every six months
and had been denied repeatedly. His "unofficial *refusenik* occupation" was "chief
Moscow contact" to foreign activists, helping to coordinate meetings with other
Jewish dissidents.

While we were visiting with Lev, Abe Stolar, the well-known "Chicago
hostage" and long-term refusenik, entered the apartment. He was wearing an
American-made plaid shirt, which we had seen on him in almost every
photograph. Abe was born in Chicago in 1910, but his Russian-born parents had
chosen to return to the Soviet Union during the Depression. They believed in the
pure form of communism, the ideal as defined by Marx and Engel in the
Communist Manifesto. They had believed life would be better for them in their
motherland, but they were soon disillusioned. Unfortunately for the Stolar family,
by the time they realized their mistake it was too late to leave the USSR. They
were trapped. Abe's father disappeared shortly after their arrival in Moscow and
was never seen again. During World War II, Abe fought for the Red Army and
lost an eye. After all these years he still spoke English with a Chicago accent and
thought of himself as an American. Proudly, he showed us his American passport.

Before retiring in 1974, Abe had been a Russian-English translator serving as an official interpreter for some well-known personalities, among them Henry Kissinger. Abe was a frequent and welcome visitor at the American Embassy.

In 1975, Abe told us, the Stolar family was granted permission to leave the country for Israel, but they were literally pulled off their plane shortly before takeoff because of what the Soviets described as a "technicality in Gita's passport." Gita, said Abe, was very depressed about the refusals, and he himself felt he would never again set foot outside the USSR.

Despite their plight, Abe told story after story that allowed us to laugh together, such as the one about a parcel sent to him by a class of American schoolchildren. Soviets were required to pay duty on all parcels before being permitted to examine the contents, so after being summoned to the post office to pick up this package Abe was compelled to pay a duty of fifty rubles--about $50, the equivalent of one-third to one-half of a typical monthly salary. Inside he discovered one pair of "slightly used" blue jeans. Shortly thereafter he was summoned to the post office for a second parcel. This time the duty on the package cost him one hundred rubles. Upon opening the box, he found two pairs of "very small" blue jeans, totally unusable. Obviously Abe's sense of humor had helped him survive fifty-two years as a hostage inside the Soviet Union.

In the middle of Abe's story, a familiar face appeared in the doorway. I immediately recognized Ida Nudel, one of the most well-known former prisoners of conscience. Ida had just been released from four years in Siberia, and we were the first Westerners to meet her since her arrest. Called the "Guardian Angel," because of her selfless and tireless campaign on behalf of Soviet prisoners of conscience, Ida wrote regular letters to prisoners, sending both emotional and material support necessary for their survival. One day, after hanging a banner outside the balcony of her apartment stating her desire to go to Israel, she was arrested for "malicious hooliganism" and sentenced to four years' internal exile.

Ida appeared pale and had lost a lot of weight during her long captivity. She was an amazing woman, still strong as steel after all she had endured, the personification of a modern Jewish hero. Unfortunately, she had just lost her *propiska*, an official residence permit authorizing a person to reside in a particular city. As a result she was to be resettled outside of Kishinev, but she emphasized that the West should not be distracted by this information since her only goal remained a visa for Israel. She would continue to maintain a low profile and said any help on her behalf was to be given only quietly at the highest level.

Ida inquired about our itinerary after departing Moscow. She wondered if we would visit Polina Paritsky in Kharkov, whose husband, Alexander, was then a prisoner of conscience. We promised to try to meet with her. Ida told us that if we went to Polina's we should take extreme caution since her apartment was under constant surveillance and visitors had been "roughed up" by militia. She nearly had not made it to Lev's apartment that day because her faithful dog, who had accompanied her to Siberia, had been poisoned by a piece of tainted meat, which she felt had been maliciously thrown up to the balcony.

During the course of our conversation, Natasha Khassina walked into the apartment. Throughout Ida's long years of isolation and confinement, Natasha had taken her place in working for the prisoners of conscience. She reiterated the need for "quiet diplomacy." A strong, intelligent, and vocal woman, Natasha was most helpful to Marty and me in arranging for a meeting with our Kishinev family, the Rozentals. They would be summoned to meet us in Odessa, at the home of activist refusenik friends of Natasha's.

We had dinner at Lev's, which he prepared in our honor. There was beef tenderloin, sausage, delicious bread, ice cream, and plenty of vodka, scotch, and orange water. I thought about the many hours that Lev had had to stand in long lines to purchase that food. Although we were expensive to entertain, the appearance of Western tourists was a celebrated event shared by the entire refusenik community. Since Lev's birthday was May 17, Marty had brought a fine bottle of scotch as a gift. Lev insisted upon opening it immediately, and we clicked our glasses and toasted his birthday.

Following the meal we got down to business and emptied the bags of clothing we had brought. Certain items had been earmarked for specific refuseniks in Moscow, and news magazines would be shared by all. There was dried food and coffee for prisoners, items that complied with regulations established by prison guards, and Hebrew books and cassettes for the general refusenik community. Underneath turtleneck sweaters we were each wearing dozens of chais (the Hebrew character symbolizing *life*) and Mogen Davids (six-pointed stars) to be distributed amongst refuseniks. Marty peeled one off and handed it to Lev. We showed him photographs of his granddaughter, Masha, whom he had never met. Excitedly, he reached for the pictures, kissing them one by one. We shared some photos of our own family and friends, and he gave us two nested Russian dolls as souvenirs. All exchanges were written on our magic slate.

At breakfast the following morning, our tour group quizzed us as to our whereabouts the previous day. They had been to the Bolshoi to see a beautiful ballet. How could we have missed such a grand event? We responded that I had become ill and had been resting quietly in our hotel room with a headache. There was talk among the group about how beautiful Moscow appeared--what type of "propaganda" were *we* being fed at home about the "poor Russians"? We bit our tongues, seething inwardly, and said nothing. They, of course, were not privy to our information. They would never see what we saw or hear the harrowing and tragic stories that we had been told. We did not blame them for their naivete.

On an excursion to the Pushkin Museum, I was ordered to check my purse since it was oversized. My stomach churned at the thought, but I acquiesced so as not to attract unnecessary attention by leaving the museum. The Pushkin is a stately museum, housing a beautiful collection of art by some of the most famous masters.

We returned to Lev's that evening, and more guests arrived. There was Alexander Yoffe, a doctor of mathematics, who had been "demoted" following his application to emigrate in 1976. Marty discussed with Yoffe the possibility of photographing his scientific papers so we could take them to France and deliver them to Professor Paul Kessler in time for the scientific conference, set for later that month in Paris. We would be going there to visit our exchange family in Normandy after we left the Soviet Union. He responded that it "sounded very good," and we arranged to go to his apartment.

Soon we found ourselves adopting the demeanor and behavior of longtime refuseniks. As we huddled together for hours, we noticed each other slouching, and our faces were as grim as those of our refusenik friends. We took turns speaking and listening, our voices subdued, while constantly writing all important messages in our notebook.

Natasha returned to Lev's that evening, and we also met Mike Lumar. Mike was the one who had gone to Siberia to escort Ida Nudel back to Moscow. He, accompanied by two other refuseniks, spent one week in Siberia before flying back with Ida and her dog.

Another refusenik, Joseph Pekar, arrived at Lev's. Joe was an unemployed physicist. He was anxious for us to meet his family and offered to escort us to his place. The most difficult part of each day was spent searching for taxis, which is something we never would have thought twice about in Chicago. Here, however, they were few and far between. When they did stop, drivers frequently drove off in a hurry, leaving us behind after determining our destination, unwilling to drive into the sections of town where we were headed. At last Joseph hailed a van, and the driver accepted. Marty and I felt uncomfortable for Joe because he had tried unsuccessfully for over half an hour to flag down a cab.

The Pekars' apartment was located in a dilapidated section of the city, the building in a state of decay, but inside we discovered a tastefully decorated flat. Joe's lovely wife and three beautiful young children greeted us. They were a musically talented family, and the children were anxious to perform. Their older son rendered several classical numbers on the piano. The younger son gave us a piano and then violin recital, and their small daughter displayed her ability on the violin. As we relaxed with the Pekars, Joseph opened a drawer and proudly pulled out a bar mitzvah invitation. Their oldest child, Alexander, had recently been twinned with a boy from Chicago.

Day number four began with a typical Russian-style breakfast of black bread, cheese, a thimble full of undrinkable coffee, and a hard-boiled egg. There was no such thing as orange juice, for which I had a craving throughout the entire trip. It is a strange comparison, missing this little pleasure in the midst of the subsistence living we were viewing firsthand.

On a tour of the Moscow Metro system, we were acutely aware of its overwhelming cleanliness and elaborate displays. Floor sweepers, mostly peasant women, were positioned throughout the underground. No graffiti existed anywhere in the USSR. People had been shipped to Siberia for lesser offenses! Inside the Metro we saw bronze statues, beautiful paintings, crystal chandeliers, and stained-glass windows. As part of the great Moscow facade, it makes an indelible impression on touring Westerners.

As soon as possible, Marty and I slipped away from the group and returned to Lev's. This was our last full day in Moscow, and there would be another group for us to meet at his apartment. Before they arrived, I asked Lev if there was some way we could contact the Rozentals since it was Roman's fourteenth birthday. Immediately Lev went to the telephone and called Kishinev. Roman's mother, Era, had been frantically waiting by the phone for word from us after learning of our visit through the network of Jewish activists. She and her family had originally wanted to meet us in Moscow, but she did not know where to find us since the person who had phoned with news had fearfully hung up before she had an opportunity to question him. Era said she had purchased airline tickets to Moscow, but she would sell them and meet us in Odessa.

Two of the first to arrive at Lev's were long-term refuseniks, Judith and Leonid Byaly. Leonid had recently recovered from a massive heart attack. Judith walked with great difficulty because one of her legs was shorter than the other. Her condition was the result of a serious automobile "accident," which she suspected had been deliberately staged by KGB. When the accident occurred, Judith had been driving her aunt, who had received a visa to emigrate to Israel, to the airport. Her aunt was killed in the accident, and Judith was hospitalized for nearly a year, casted from neck to toe. She remains in constant pain.

Other refuseniks who arrived included Mark Nashpitz, the former prisoner of conscience to whom Hetty had been writing since 1976. Before his arrest Mark had been a dentist in Moscow. Hetty sent a warm-up suit with us to give to him along with a photograph of her family.

When it was time for Marty and me to go to Alexander Yoffe's, the Byalys offered to drive. They were one of the few refusenik families to own a car, and they always helped by chauffeuring their refusenik friends and foreign visitors.

Alex's entire family was waiting to meet us, as were Abe and Gita Stolar. We sat around the living room dining table, a Russian custom reserved for entertaining friends, while Marty photographed documents. Before departing, Alexander's wife, Rosa, handed us a Russian-made doll. "Please accept this souvenir as a gift from our family. Remember us!"

The Byalys drove us to a Beriozka shop. Beriozkas, which are found throughout the Soviet Union, are stores catering only to Westerners and accept only foreign currency. Russians are forbidden to shop there, and rubles are not accepted. Goods found in Beriozka shops were of better quality, more abundant in supply, and even some Western items could be purchased. There was a plentiful stock of Russian fur hats, amber jewelry, lacquered boxes and nests of wooden dolls. We bought nothing for ourselves. The Russian-made souvenirs we took home were all gifts presented by refusenik friends. Our only reason for going to the Beriozka was to shop for Anatoly Sharansky, then a long-term prisoner in an Eastern Siberian labor camp. We purchased some instant coffee and dried sausage, which were picked up later in the day by Ida Milgrom, Sharansky's mother. Ida Milgrom lived in Moscow and shared an apartment with Lev Blitshtein's mother.

Our final hours in Moscow were spent alone "window shopping." We walked into a large bookstore teeming with propaganda displays and soon settled on one small item, a calendar. Taking our place in line, we were soon spotted as foreigners by the cashier and motioned to move to the front. Western customers were considered more desirable than Russians.

There was time for one brief stop at Lev's before returning to the hotel to meet our group for the flight to the Ukraine. As we embraced before our departure, we conveyed to Lev the closeness we had come to feel in such a short period of time. At that moment I recalled Marillyn's words uttered shortly before our departure. "It won't take long before you feel closer to your new refusenik friends than to some people whom you have known for many years." It was difficult to imagine, when she made the comment, but her message now rang loud and clear. The intensity of our meetings, held under difficult circumstances on alien soil, created a special bond that few relationships could transcend.

Lev was a warm and gentle man who went out of his way to help others. He had become a real friend. As we parted, he cautioned us about seeing the Rozental family more than once, since repeated visits were thought unsafe in'the Ukraine due to a higher ratio of KGB to foreign visitors. Ukrainians were isolated behind an invisible wall. But it was in Kharkov that we would have our fateful meeting with a person who would play a significant role in my life.

Chapter III

KHARKOV

Kharkov, our first stop in the dreaded Ukraine, is an industrial city and regional capital with almost one and a half million people. Arriving in time for dinner, our group was staying in town at the Intourist Hotel.

The following morning we decided there was time to join the group for a tour of the Children's Health Center. Those we wished to visit were more likely to be at home in the late afternoon than earlier in the day. Aboard the bus, on the way to the health center, our Intourist guide gave us the latest news of the day: a Soviet spaceship had been launched, the U.S. Embassy in Buenos Aires was being evacuated, and there had been an attempt on the pope's life in Portugal.

As we sat in the large assembly room of the health center, we were addressed by a heavy-set female professor clad in a white lab coat. The room was stark white, and a large picture of Lenin, placed prominently in front of us on the wall directly behind the professor, seemed to be watching. We were ushered on a tour of the facility, which was sterile and modern with up-to-date equipment, a real showplace for western tourists.

That afternoon, we slipped quietly away from the group and walked a few blocks away before boarding the number 8 bus for downtown Kharkov. Trying to look as if we belonged there, we hailed a taxi and went to our first meeting.

We arrived at Krasnoznammeny Pereulok 2, the apartment building of Yuri Tarnopolsky. In the big cities of Moscow and Leningrad, it was possible for Western tourists to phone ahead and warn refuseniks of a visit. In the Ukraine it was ill advised because there were fewer tourists and the likelihood of being shadowed by KGB was much greater. Even had we been able to phone ahead, the Tarnopolskys had no telephone.

I will never forget how I entered Yuri's name in our code book so I would remember "Tarnopolsky." The code for Tarnopolsky was "Don't forget to polish the tarnished silver."

As we walked into the building, we had to avoid garbage strewn all over the floor of the entry hall. We climbed to the fourth floor and rang the doorbell. In a moment, Yuri appeared at the door. I softly whispered, "Tarnopolsky, shalom!" He stood there, stunned, his eyes filling with tears. Yuri showed us into the apartment, and we made our introductions. He hastily asked to be excused for a minute to freshen up, feeling slightly embarrassed at having been caught off-guard, unshaven and wearing an unpressed shirt. He returned within moments with a clean shirt, but hadn't taken time to shave. A tall, ruggedly handsome man with slightly tousled brown hair, rounded shoulders, and blue eyes, Yuri offered us coffee, which he ground fresh, and sat down with us at his desk.

Seated in the rather worn-looking living room, it was apparent that he was a highly learned and cultured man. Yuri possessed a fine collection of some very rare books and recordings: Plato, Spinoza, Einstein, and Francis Crick lined the shelves, and there were albums of Mozart, Beethoven, Bartok, and Stravinsky.

In a soft-spoken, articulate manner, he apologized for his stunned behavior. He said he could not believe our presence, since nobody from the West had visited Kharkov in over three years.

Suddenly, he arose and rushed to look out the window. "Were you shadowed on your way to the apartment?" he asked us with obvious concern. We responded that we had been on the alert but had not seen anything out of the ordinary. Relieved, he sat back down.

I related to him the intricacies of the Soviet Jewry movement and what was happening politically. He had been worried about worldwide apathy toward the refuseniks, but we reassured him we were all united by a common goal. The citizens of Kharkov had been told that Prime Minister Begin had said immigration had stopped and nobody was coming to Israel anymore. We told him it was pure propaganda.

I began to relate the story of our own family's Russian roots and our feeling of kinship. Had our ancestors not fled the Eastern European countries when they did, we, too, might have been refuseniks. I shall never forget his look of intensity and how his eyes glazed as we spoke. I never forgot his face.

Yuri told us the refusenik community in Kharkov was completely cut off, and without periodic visits to Moscow they would be isolated from the rest of the world. He appeared gravely troubled, paralleling the situation in Kharkov to Nazi Germany in the 1930s.

He mentioned the keen interest Kharkov Jews had in the American hostage situation in Iran and how they had followed the developments as closely as possible. They felt that the difference between American hostages in Iran and their own dilemma was that the United States had come to the immediate aid of the Iranian hostages, but with Soviet Jews their government was holding its *own* citizens hostage. Current Soviet actions notwithstanding, he expected a transition period in the government to follow soon since Brezhnev was ill and nobody in the hierarchy of Soviet government could be held responsible for anything.

As we opened our bags, Yuri promised to distribute the items among the refusenik group. He told us, that without such help from abroad, Kharkov refuseniks would be unable to survive since many were unemployed, and those working had meager incomes. Occasional parcels of clothing were still being received from Denmark (once or twice a year) in spite of the city's being cut off from Western tourism.

At the time of this meeting Yuri had just returned from a visit to Moscow, where he had met with Robert Gillette, a correspondent from *The Los Angeles Times*. It was fate that brought us to Kharkov at this time . . . one day earlier and we never would have met.

Yuri reached into his desk and pulled out a manuscript he had written shortly before our arrival. Entitled "Description of a Disease" and dated May 1982, it speaks of the prolonged agony of the refusal or "otkaz." We would be taking the paper out of the country, and it was to have great significance in the future. For now, though, its author would have to remain anonymous.

Yuri then began to relate his personal story.

There must have been some misunderstanding, Yuri felt, when one year of waiting passed without an answer to his family's application for an exit visa. After the second year, the situation became "questionable." After three years, it was a "*crime*." Yuri had an aunt in New York and a cousin in Israel, but his own family had applied too late and had been trapped when the door to freedom closed. His relatives left in June of 1979. Two months later emigration had come to a halt. The "Great Refusal" had begun.

When he found out that we had no plans other than spending time with him and his family, Yuri invited us to accompany him to a scientific seminar for Kharkov refuseniks at the apartment of David Soloveichik. On our way out we met Yuri's daughter, Irina, who had just returned home from school. On impulse I opened my purse and handed Irina a package of chewing gum. Her face lit up at the tiny gesture; the fact that it was American made it special.

As we descended the stairs to the ground floor, we encountered another man coming up. Without a word or other acknowledgment he turned and continued walking down with us. When we were safely outside the building, Yuri introduced us to his good friend Eugene Chudnovsky.

Eugene, Yuri, Marty, and I took a bus to the Soloveichiks' apartment. Escorted into the living room, we were introduced to the gathered scientists and members of their families. Some of them had been unemployed for years, while others were working as firemen, nightwatchmen, and in other nonscience jobs; one was employed as a landscaper.

These weekly seminars had just been reconvened after having been broken up by KGB during the 1981 raids. We sat around in a horseshoe, with Marty and me at the head. Instead of their usual scientific discussion, we began to inform them about the strength of the Soviet Jewry movement. We brought them up to date on the political situation in the United States and related stories about Israel.

David Soloveichik began to respond. He described how thoroughly Kharkov refuseniks were cut off: mail was frequently undelivered, radios were jammed, and no visitors were allowed. Kharkov was described as a ghetto without walls, where local authorities were giving refuseniks final verbal refusals.

Feelings of helplessness were rampant. Only the strongest were able to survive, the group members said. They aged quickly after being subjected to constant pressure, harassment, and increasing threat of arrest and imprisonment. I glanced quickly at Liliya Zatuchnaya, who resided with her mentally handicapped son, Vladimir, aged 20, and her elderly mother. My heart was rent by the sadness I saw in her eyes.

Many of these scientists' families and friends had left the USSR before June 1979. In 1979, eighteen hundred Jews received visas in Kharkov; in 1980, the figure had dropped to 300 Jews who received exit visas; and in 1981 only 70 Jews from Kharkov received permission to emigrate. No one knew of a single family from Kharkov who had been granted permission to emigrate since 1981.

When a Soviet Jewish family applied for a visa to emigrate to Israel, their lives were further threatened. Parents lost jobs, children had difficulties in school, family possessions were forsaken as refuseniks were forced to surrender apartments and move into more cramped accommodations. For scientists it was worse, because they were overqualified for most positions, and if caught not working, they could be arrested for "parasitism." It was a veritable Catch-22. These refuseniks had been relegated to the position of "nonpersons"; they were unable to work in their fields, their knowledge was wasted, and they were forbidden all rights since they had lost their credentials.

They stressed the urgency of getting their scientific papers out of the country, and we were asked to take some documents out with us. We agreed.

Following the exchange of information, Marty and I joined the group for dinner. David's wife, Lina, had prepared a meal typical of Soviet "Jewish" hospitality. She served us trays of cheese and herring with bread and wine. A Hebrew toast, which would be repeated many times in apartments throughout the Soviet Union, was made: "L'Shana Haba 'ah Bi-y'rushalayim" (Next year in Jerusalem). We shared a Russian toast, "Zah vahsheh zdahrov'yeh" (To your health) as glasses clicked in unison. In the background, Israeli music played on a phonograph. This could have been a setting with good friends anywhere in the world, but it was a ghetto deep within the walls of the dreaded Ukraine.

When we finished eating, Yuri felt it was time to depart. Earlier in the evening he had asked us if we wanted to visit Polina Paritsky. We agreed. The warning from Ida Nudel had flashed in our minds, but it would not deter us from visiting her. We felt safe in the company of our refusenik friends.

We left the Soloveichiks, flanked by Yuri and Eugene. Both of them had been quite frank concerning the situation surrounding the Paritskys' building. They reiterated the incident involving a British couple who had been beaten outside the apartment complex. Nevertheless, under the protection of both men, acting like two bodyguards, we remained unafraid.

The first thing we saw when Polina opened the door was her packed suitcases in the middle of the living room. She was preparing to leave for Siberia to visit her imprisoned husband, Alexander. Her two daughters, Dorina and Anna, looked forlorn as they sat shyly in the room. Polina's mood reflected despair. The apartment was gloomy and depressing. Later Yuri told me that the Paritskys' apartment was an exact replica of his apartment in Krasnoyarsk (a "professor's dwelling"). Though obviously fatigued, Polina insisted we sit down and join her for tea and homemade matzoh, which she apologetically told us was the only food remaining in the apartment.

Slowly she began to talk about her husband. As the story unfolded, she sat with bowed head and her brow furrowed as if in deep pain. They had first applied for emigration in 1976, only to be refused a year later because of the catchall "security risk." Alex, an acoustic physicist, had been employed for eleven years at the Kharkov Institute of Meteorology. He was designing highly precise ultrasonic devices for measuring distances, which also were used in research of sea waves. Nevertheless, all the devices were openly produced, and neither principle nor construction constituted any secret.

In 1977 Alex was stripped of his scientific degrees as a result of his request to emigrate. One year later a file was opened against him after a vicious article appeared in the Kharkov evening newspaper *Vecherny Kharkov*, entitled "Contrabanda." The article accused Alex of black marketeering, racism, incitement against the Soviet Union, making propaganda for aliyah (immigration to Israel) and provocation disseminated in the West (through "anti-Soviet" letters and phone calls abroad).

In August 1981, Alexander Paritsky was arrested under Article 191/1, "Defamation of the Soviet State." Three months later he was sentenced to three years in a Siberian labor camp. After the trial, Alex informed Polina he had been threatened with being tried for "treason" during the entire time he was held incommunicado. He was told that factories throughout Kharkov had held meetings, and employers were warned of an "anti-Soviet, Zionist conspiracy" led by Paritsky.

Polina felt Alexander's release would come only as the result of a "high official request," not loud protests. She also feared that nothing further could be done from the West if she was unable to help him herself.

She described the labor camp as a "concentration camp," with the average age of inmates being from twenty to twenty-two years. Alex, at forty-four, was much older, and it was harder on him physically. The other prisoners had been soldiers and criminals, arrested for violation of military laws. Alex's crime: he was a Jew.

She depicted his condition in camp as "grave" since he had not been allowed to receive medication and was suffering from very low blood pressure. Alex had lost a lot of weight, and when she last visited him at the prison camp he had been "unrecognizable." Polina hoped to spend the summer months in Siberia to be closer to him.

While Polina would be living in Siberia for the summer, her girls were planning on spending those months with Ida Nudel at her summer dacha (country house). Neither Dorina nor Anna had seen their father since the previous January. Even then they were able to visit only through the prisoner window, speaking through a telephone. The girls appeared quite nervous. They sat fidgeting in their seats, with drawn faces and tears in their eyes. It was obvious the situation was having a terrible effect on them.

We kissed Polina good-bye and bid farewell to the girls. Leaving Polina, we hoped that perhaps we had helped to raise her spirits, if only a little. The driver dropped Yuri off first at his building. Eugene was driven to the Metro, and Marty and I were then returned to our hotel. There I broke down and cried. We had never in our lives witnessed such despair and hopelessness. It was far worse than what we had anticipated.

The next morning, we took a taxi to the Chudnovskys' apartment. Eugene was waiting for us outside since he knew we would have difficulty finding the entrance at the rear of the building. We followed him to the apartment, where, once again, we met his wife, Marina, and daughter, Julia. Julia had been kept home from school to be with us. Hanging above Eugene's favorite chair in the living room was a poster of Albert Einstein, the scientist he most highly respected. Ironically, Eugene himself looked like a young version of Einstein.

Eugene handed us a sixteen-page document to be submitted for publication outside the USSR. Though a well-respected theoretical physicist, he was currently unemployed and spent most of his time reading at home. Marina tutored English on a private basis.

At thirty-three years old, Eugene was not a well man, but when Marina mentioned something about his heart condition, he quickly dismissed it. He admitted to having suffered two heart attacks over the past two years, which he suspected had been precipitated by KGB harassment. Living under constant surveillance and KGB threats caused mental torture. Yet he felt his health would be restored if he were allowed to emigrate.

We had to reconfirm our plans for Odessa. After some difficulty with the primitive Soviet phone system and our inability to speak Russian, we finally reached Moscow and got through to the Byalys. Leonid told us that everything was a "go" and not to worry.

Chapter IV

ODESSA

On the way to the hotel in Odessa, our Intourist guide informed us of a slight change in the timetable. We would be departing for Leningrad the following evening, one day ahead of schedule. I panicked. The meeting with the Rozental family had not been scheduled until the next day, and we had hoped to spend an entire day and evening together. This last-minute change, of course, was not an unusual occurrence on a Russian tour. We decided to take our chances and find the meeting place this afternoon in the hope that the Rozentals would arrive early. We recalled Lev's warning: "Don't go more than once. . . ."

Our hotel in Odessa was directly across the street from both the train depot and the city's largest department store. We went to the station to check the schedule of arriving trains from Kishinev and found one due in by late afternoon. We would have to stall for time to give the Rozentals a chance to arrive. Walking along the waterfront to the harbor, we found it easy to understand the picturesque description of Odessa in *Fodor's* travel guide: "the pearl of the Black Sea."

We walked through the main entrance of the apartment building where we were to meet the Rozentals and were confronted by a large, neglected courtyard--a sharp contrast to the beautiful shore we had just seen. Natasha had written down the address as 3/5 Ploschad Martinovskogo, but we could see only 3/4 Ploschad Martinovskogo. Although unsure whether we were in the correct place, we searched for apartment #71. Climbing to the second floor on an outdoor staircase, we spotted a tall, dark-haired man with prominent features who also appeared to be looking for something. I looked desperately at this man and quietly called out, "Jacov?" It was he. I fell into his arms, relieved to be at the right spot. "Jacov," I asked, "have you heard from Kishinev?" "*Yes*," he responded with a knowing grin as he ushered us into the apartment. Jacov Mesh and his wife, Marina, quickly told us that Era Rozental and her son were in town but had stepped out to get something to eat. Zigmund would be arriving by train in the morning.

Moments later Era and Roman appeared at the doorway, and we hugged and kissed and cried like long-lost friends. We noticed that Roman was wearing the tennis warm-up suit we had sent him for Chanukah. Sitting down, hands clasped, talking rapidly, at times consulting the dictionary for translation, we felt like one family trying to catch up on our lives after months of correspondence.

Finally we all exchanged gifts. Era, smiling broadly, removed a ring from her finger and handed it to me as a token of friendship. Tearfully I accepted the gift. Jacov, who had momentarily stepped out of the room, returned holding a package under his arm. A former professional boxer, he handed me two sets of boxing gloves for Steve and Rob. This overwhelming display of love and gratitude went far beyond our wildest expectations.

Marina then brought out dinner, although the Rozentals had politely eaten beforehand. I anguished over the meal, realizing the sacrifice that had been made for us. Their living quarters were unusually cramped and shabby even by Soviet "refusenik" standards. Nevertheless, we ate fish croquets for dinner, which were served with fresh vegetables, mashed potatoes, homemade bread, and wine. For dessert, chocolate eclairs!

After dinner, Jacov, in a halting voice because of his limited command of English, told us his apartment had been raided the previous winter by KGB. Books and equipment were taken, and he had been imprisoned for ten days for "hooliganism." One month later, he was rearrested and issued a "final" warning. The case was still pending.

Close ties to the West, particularly with UCSJ's group in Florida--the South Florida Conference on Soviet Jews headed by Hinda Cantor and Shirley Pollak--kept Jacov's hope alive. Joel Levin, a Miami plastic surgeon, had become the driving force in the campaign to free Jacov and after a visit to Odessa to meet with him had come up with the ingenious idea of staging a boxing match in Miami to draw attention to Mesh's plight. Joel trained for months before entering the ring with Hector "Macho" Camacho, a professional boxer. Miami headlines read: "Doctor Takes His Punishment in Hopes of Ending Another's."

In spite of warnings against it, we returned the next day to find Zigmund Rozental standing in the apartment doorway, waiting to greet us. Our delight in seeing him was diluted by the shock we felt at his appearance. A tall, thin man with a receding hairline, mustache, and beard, he looked gaunt--ill and old beyond his years. Separation from family can have a devastating effect, and the first thing Zigmund asked was for news about his parents. With Era acting as official translator, we offered him all the news we had received during our correspondence with them in Israel and described our meeting with them in Tel Aviv.

As the Rozentals prepared to return to Kishinev in midafternoon, we conveyed our fervent hope that we would see them again, the next time in Israel, when we returned there in two years for our younger son's bar mitzvah. Marty and I remained to meet with another group of refuseniks from the Odessa community, and at the end of the day we bid our gracious host and hostess farewell. Jacov escorted us outside, and Marty and I walked back to the hotel alone. We would soon be off again, heading for Leningrad, our final stop in the USSR.

Chapter V

LENINGRAD

"None of us will sleep comfortably until you, and all refuseniks, have been set free."

Leningrad, the "Venice of the North," was the last leg of our journey. We stayed at the Pulkovskaya Hotel, constructed by the Finns. It was the largest, most modern hotel in the Soviet Union, but it was inconvenient for us since it was far from the center of town.

After viewing the city's highlights with our Intourist guide, we split from the group once we had reached the downtown section. We contacted Boris Kelman by public telephone, and he gave us directions to their apartment.

A smiling Boris greeted us at the door. The apartment, slightly larger than others we had seen, had been cheerfully decorated. A former physicist, Boris was a warm and very proud man, a devoted husband and father, a true friend, and a leader in the refusenik community in Leningrad. Since applying for a visa three and a half years earlier, Boris had worked as a truck driver, had been in charge of caring for the ventilation system in a grocery store, and at the time of our meeting held a clerical desk position. Boris conducted English classes and seminars in his home, and his wife, Alla, a pediatrician, worked in a polyclinic. They had two sons, ages fourteen and four. The Kelmans lived with more privilege than most other refuseniks, owning a car and having the use of a summer dacha. Like the Byalys in Moscow, Boris used his car to chauffeur refusenik friends and foreign visitors, and their apartment was used as a meeting place.

One afternoon, while attending one of Boris's seminars, Marty was asked to deliver a lecture on the economic situation in the United States. A large crowd of refuseniks converged for the presentation. Marty spoke about inflation in the United States and the advantage of real estate as a good hedge against ballooning prices. The group was interested to learn that real estate generally increased at a higher rate than the consumer price index.

On an excursion to the Summer Palace of the Czars, located out in the country, we were required to check coats and even our shoes (so as not to scratch the parquet floors), but my large purse escaped detection. I had been hoping to avoid another episode like the one at the Pushkin Museum. The interior of the palace was a show of great splendor, and the beautiful gardens were reminiscent of Versailles.

At the Hermitage Museum, our guide warned the group to stick close together, because the building was large and it would be easy to get "lost in the shuffle." Marty thought she resembled a drill sergeant, and since it *was* our intent to get lost in the shuffle, we hurried past her. Carrying my purse, I was careful to protect it with my body as we passed the first set of security guards, but I neglected to guard it as we passed the second set of doors. In an instant a heavyset female guard came running up from behind, screaming, "Nyet, nyet!" As she pointed to the purse, I responded, "Sorry, I don't understand," and we quickly departed the scene. Large bags filled with contraband are risky in public places, but there appeared no alternative. Our "contraband" consisted of Hebrew books and cassettes, cigarettes, gum for the Kelmans' children, film, a small flashlight for Alla's medical practice, medication, and two sweaters. We could not leave things like books and recordings not earmarked for that particular day behind at the hotel, and we were trying to appear to be normal tourists. Though the museum is spectacular, we rushed to return to the Kelmans'.

When we arrived, Boris was in the middle of instructing an English class, and he asked us to speak so they could hear an American accent. The students were interested in knowing about family life in America, and we helped correct their grammar.

Alla had prepared a farewell meal in our honor, and several refuseniks had been invited to join us. It was Shabbat. Marty recited the Hebrew blessings over the bread and wine, and Alla lit the Sabbath candles. We toasted, "Next year in Jerusalem."

Facing us was the difficult task of preparing for customs the following morning. When we mentioned our concern about the scientific documents and Yuri's "Description of a Disease," Boris offered to help us protect them. He took the papers and, one by one, securely fitted them inside the folds of the Michelin maps we were carrying for our next stop, France. A few pages were also stapled into our trip itinerary.

Our mission was coming to a close, but before bidding us a final farewell Boris took us for a short drive and last look at Leningrad's "White Night." During the month of June the sun never sets in Leningrad. The calm waters of the Neva River belied the tumult felt by refuseniks. Ships were anchored at port, and from one side of the Kirov Bridge we saw the towers of a fortress; on the other side was a row of palaces. Looking at Boris, we promised, *"None of us will sleep comfortably until you, and all refuseniks, have been set free."* Good-byes were always painful.

Now the moment of truth was upon us. Although Marty and I were departing on a different flight from the rest of our group since we were going to France instead of Helsinki, we opted to drive to the airport with them. Our Intourist guide did not seem to understand and said we were "nuts" since their flight was eight hours earlier. Nevertheless, we hoped to blend in with the group as we passed through customs. Earlier that morning Marty asked the young man we had befriended on the tour if he would carry our film out with him. The man looked puzzled and asked, "Why?" Marty explained we were concerned about our film being confiscated because we were Jews and had heard stories about custom officials confiscating film from Jewish travelers. He understood and agreed.

At the airport, we were told it was impossible for us to enter customs with our group since their flight was considerably earlier and security guards maintained strict rules. Marty reclaimed our film, realizing there was no way our friend could return it to us after passing through the customs gate. With mounting anxiety we thought about the undeveloped film and scientific papers that we had to safeguard. Hundreds of pictures of refuseniks, as well as Yoffe's document, appeared on that film.

Seven agonizing hours later, it was our turn. Standing in the long line of people waiting to be processed, we had watched the line move slowly but steadily. Finally we were next. As we moved up, one of the guards pointed our way and said firmly, "You, over there." We had been singled out. Marty and I were being directed to a "special" line at the far end of the room at the back wall.

All our suitcases were opened, and everything was removed one by one. Articles of clothing were shaken out to make sure nothing had been concealed inside. Our pockets were searched, and our packages--even those gifts designated for our friends in France--were ripped open. Everything was dumped into a pile, and my purse was examined, object for object. Every piece of paper was studied, notebooks inspected, and the officials looked through the pages of our Berlitz book.

Discovered were three or four crumpled pieces of paper on which I had written down a few addresses in Cyrillic for taxi drivers, but there were no identifying apartment numbers. The discovery created a stir, and several more officials appeared on the scene. We waited until their backs were turned, and Marty whisked the small pieces of paper off the examining table. Ripping them into shreds, we disposed of "the evidence."

Marty was taken away for questioning and a "body search" conducted. I was interrogated on the spot and searched later. Marty's film was removed for "examining" in spite of his loud protests, and I watched them open our nested wooden Russian dolls, taking one out after another. They were empty.

And then . . . the Michelin maps were lifted off the table. My heart began to throb. What would happen to our friends if the papers were discovered? Where was Marty? Would we get out of here today? Tomorrow? Thoughts were spinning inside my head, which was pounding from the growing pressure, and perspiration beaded on my brow. My eyes focused on one of the guards, who began to shake the maps out . . . one by one. I panicked until I realized the papers had stuck within the folds of the maps, remaining concealed. Boris had done his work well.

When they were satisfied we were smuggling nothing, they released us. Relieved and exhausted, I saw Marty approaching. Our possessions and film were returned, and we hurriedly threw our things back inside the cases and fled from the room. Not a single word was uttered between us until we were safely aboard our Lufthansa flight and had lifted off the ground.

A thunderous burst of applause erupted from the passengers aboard the flight as the plane soared into the sky, leaving Russia behind. Our episode at customs had been a typical example of Russian-style harassment, unsettling for Americans, who are unaccustomed to such barbaric treatment. It only intensified our desire to return home and continue fighting for the freedom of our Soviet brothers and sisters.

After more than a few deep breaths Marty and I were able to settle back in our seats. We looked into each other's eyes and saw that each of us had undergone a metamorphosis. We had both been touched very deeply by our experiences, and our lives had changed forever. The very core of our system of values had been transformed. Newly aware and newly committed, we would never be able to concentrate on trivia again; home decorating projects could wait, and shopping sprees for the latest New York fashions seemed meaningless. Health and family relations remained high on the list, although petty squabbles among family or friends diminished in significance when contrasted with the dilemmas confronting refuseniks. *Our* problems jeopardized our creature comforts; *their* problems threatened their lives.

I knew I could never again be the person who had set foot on Russian soil just two weeks earlier, and yet incomprehensible was the notion that our path might one day cross the path of some of the dear people whose lives had left an indelible mark on us. Witnessing their plight firsthand had given us a new understanding of how far apart our worlds really were. In our hearts, at least, there was hardly any distance between us; their fate would rarely recede from our thoughts.

Would Lev be safe? If he remained the contact figure in Moscow, would he ever see the wife and children who had immigrated to America so long ago? What about Ida Nudel, a wellspring of support for the prisoners of conscience, and her cohorts Natasha Khassina and Mike Lumar? What would happen to Mark Nashpitz, the Moscow dentist befriended by Hetty?

We thought about Joseph Pekar and his musically talented children. Abe Stolar, the Chicago-born hostage held for fifty-two years in the Soviet Union because of his parents' misjudgment. Leonid Byaly and his wife, Judith, who would live with the tragic memories of that fateful automobile accident. Yuri Tarnopolsky. What was it about that man that made him so unforgettable? Would his penetrating eyes continue to haunt me? Would his wife, Olga, and young daughter, Irina, ever know the meaning of freedom?

What about Eugene Chudnovsky, so young to be stricken with a heart condition? Could we ever forget that evening at the Soloveichiks', where we had gathered together with Yuri's group of refusenik friends? The sad eyes of Liliya Zatuchnaya seem permanently implanted in front of my own eyes. Certainly we would *never* forget Polina Paritsky and her two daughters as they grieved for Alexander, who was serving his sentence in the Gulag.

The mixed joy and sadness at the meeting with the Rozentals will long be remembered. How could we ever thank our host and hostess, Jacov and Marina Mesh, who bravely went out of their way to make that occasion possible? Finally, had it not been for Boris Kelman's ingenuity in helping us camouflage our sensitive documents, we might not even be on this flight! Would Alla and their two beautiful boys ever taste freedom?

Soon we would be arriving in Paris. Within hours, we would contact Professor Paul Kessler to turn over Yoffe's filmed document; hopefully, it had not been x-rayed in customs. But even if the Soviet state had prevented us from taking the film out of the country unharmed, it could not excise all those new friends from our memory. It was their stories that we would carry back to the free world.

PART THREE: THE STRUGGLE

"Out of the depths have I cried unto thee."

Psalm 130:1

Chapter I

PLEA FOR HELP

"Entering the fourth year of the otkaz, everybody feels chilling terror."

Who were the other tourists traveling to the Soviet Union to meet with refuseniks? Why did they go? What kind of people left comfortable American homes to travel halfway around the world, sacrificing personal comfort, confronting Soviet harassment, and leaving behind their own personal freedom? It could not be described as a pleasure trip. Endless hours of studying and preparation were required, adherence to a full and strict agenda was demanded, and many hours were spent debriefing. It was also the responsibility of all returning tourists to do their part in educating others by joining the lecture circuit. These were not luxury European vacations at four-star Michelin hotels with daily maid service, gourmet dining, and a concierge to rely on for suggestions, directions, and reservations. American-style pampering could not be found in Soviet hotels, which offered "basic" lodging.

Daily maid service was provided, but the maids' function was to snoop through the personal belongings of "guests" rather than clean rooms. Plumbing was primitive in the dreary-looking rooms, and instead of a concierge there were "key ladies" posted on every floor to answer questions, offer "assistance," and take your key before leaving the hotel each day. All were KGB.

Gourmet dining? Hotel food was generally unappetizing, but American Jewish activists ate the majority of their meals in the apartments of refuseniks, since little time was left for anything but returning to the hotel to sleep. The few restaurants found outside hotels were seldom patronized by tourists because of the language barrier. Soviet restaurant employees were not motivated to learn another language since the USSR was not a popular vacation spot. Even if there had been a greater influx of foreign visitors, the vast majority of Russians spoke only their native tongue.

A trip to the USSR was not a fashion contest; good clothes and jewelry were left at home so as not to draw attention or offend modestly dressed Soviet Jews. Western tourists took few personal items, since suitcase space was at a premium and reserved for the needs of refuseniks.

Travelers requiring "R&R" did not sign up for Russia. Time restrictions precluded casual strolls through parks, attendance at theaters and nightclubs, or even a restful interlude at some cafe. For the duration of the trip there was no freedom of movement, no freedom of speech, and tourists were constantly on guard for KGB tails.

Within weeks after returning to Chicago I had prepared a simple program for tourists, "Russian, in One Easy Lesson." Understanding Cyrillic enabled tourists to navigate Soviet cities much more easily. We could read maps, street signs, and Metro stops and identify names of families on the entry walls of apartment buildings. There was no need to ask the local KGB for "service." Proficiency in writing Cyrillic facilitated our being able to transcribe addresses of refuseniks into Russian, for handing to taxi drivers, none of whom spoke or read English. Being able to speak a few Russian words and phrases was a matter of courtesy, a way to avoid appearing as the "Ugly American" in a foreign land.

It was acting as a new member of the briefing team, teaching Cyrillic to travelers for CASJ, that answered my questions about my fellow activists. Never shall I forget how intimidated I felt in front of my very first "student," a prominent Chicago rabbi.

The majority of the tourists were simply American Jews who were seasoned travelers and could afford the time and the cost of the trip. Most of them had volunteered to go abroad, but some were solicited by the organization because of their expertise.

Doctors were sent to treat the ill, to diagnose and administer drugs. Lawyers helped with difficult refusenik cases, even though their assistance was strictly unofficial. Rabbis were welcomed by the oppressed Jewish community, hungry for knowledge of their heritage and religion. There were grade school and high school teachers, college professors, and I even remember one university chancellor.   Politicians and journalists were desperately sought, but even politicians discovered that diplomatic immunity would not be honored behind the Iron Curtain. The wife of one Chicago congressman was humiliated by being strip-searched at Moscow customs and forced to undergo a gynecological examination before being permitted to exit the country. A number of students traveled to the USSR, some with their families and some alone. Businessmen and women offered to go, and they brought along their spouses. *Every* tourist was valuable, if for no other reason than to act as a courier.

What were some of their personal reasons for wanting to travel to the USSR? Families like ours, whose sons and daughters had held twinning bar and bat mitzvahs, were anxious to meet the Soviet families with whom their children had been twinned. Many of these people had been corresponding for a long time, and some had occasionally spoken by telephone and had sent material support.

Some American Jews were anxious to visit the cities from which their ancestors had originated, and a few simply found the idea of a trip behind the Iron

Curtain intriguing.

Those Americans who were already committed to their work with the Jewish community recognized the value of a serious mission to the Soviet Union, seeing it as a natural step toward deeper involvement.

Dominating the scene was a small group of "American housewives"[1] because we had the time, the desire, and the resources to give. Some of us accepted positions of leadership, while others worked supportively from behind the scenes. All were valuable. Coming from one-income families, we were not required to help out as breadwinners. Most of our husbands were busy with their careers, although some of them still found time to serve on an advisory committee. Most of us had older children, so we were no longer needed to fulfill the role of homemaker twenty-four hours a day. All of us were looking for substance in our lives, and we found a cause to which we were deeply committed. We were not interested in career changes, involving the return to college for advanced degrees, because it was not a position of monetary value that we were seeking. We found camaraderie as a group, and we formed our own sorority of American Jewish housewives. We joined forces, drew on each other's strength and expertise, and became a firmly united team.

Some of the more dedicated travelers returned to the Soviet Union for second and third trips, while others failed to obtain visas to do so.

Two months after Marty and I returned from the Soviet Union, a telegram arrived from Kishinev. It was dated July 31, 1982:

WE RECEIVED PERMISSION

Our hearts were filled with joy. Two weeks later Zigmund, Era, and Roman Rozental would be departing Kishinev to be reunited with Zigmund's parents in Israel. Political pressure had done its job. One more family had received permission, but thousands of other Soviet Jews remained behind the Iron Curtain, their lives in peril. I continued to work for those others through CASJ.

Toward the end of July, a postcard arrived from Kharkov from Yuri Tarnopolsky. He and his family remained in grave danger.

---

[1] Anatoly Sharansky once said that he was ridiculed by a prison official for having the support of only "a few American housewives." He had been shown a video in court of his wife, Avital, who was photographed in London with Rita Eker. Avital had flown to England to secure support from the British Soviet Jewry group.

Dear Nancy and Martin,   July 1, 1982

The repercussions of the great event have not ceased yet. Now I feel deep regrets while remembering all my slips and blunders and the lack of hospitality, and so on. To be taken by surprise is not an excuse. But, I believe that I will have chance to improve. . . .

Best regards from all your new friends.
Truly yours, Yuri

The "repercussions" from *our* experience had not ceased either. It seemed like moments ago that we had been sitting in the apartments of our refusenik friends. Barely two months had passed, and the effects of the mission were already reshaping our lives. The significance of our visit to the Kharkov community could be profoundly sensed by the sensitivity of Yuri's words.

The harsh reality, the ever-present danger, was clearly evident in Yuri's second postcard, which arrived one month later.

I received your letters and photographs. I am desperately groping for the English equivalents of the most emphatic expressions of joy and delight and gratitude in Russian, but in vain. I wouldn't find appropriate expressions even in Chinese. Your sons are absolutely wonderful boys. Stephen takes after his mother, and Robert takes after his father. The picture of the whole family emanates beauty, happiness and love, and our room is filled with them. . . .

Entering the fourth year of the otkaz, everybody feels chilling terror. Nevertheless, we shall overcome.

It did not take long to react to that urgent plea for help from Kharkov. Fate had led us to the Tarnopolskys' door, and their appeal would bring us back in focus. The depth of despair, so painfully felt during our meeting in the Ukraine, would never be erased from our memory.

The first step was to build a base of support, and the synagogue was the best place to begin. North Shore Congregation Israel is the largest Reform synagogue in the Chicago area with a membership of over two thousand families, some very politically prominent. After engaging support from the Social Action Committee, photographs of Kharkov refuseniks were placed in the entry of the building. Case histories of Kharkov families were publicized in the temple news bulletin, and information of their current status was reported periodically.

On October 1, when a telegram arrived from Yuri, we recognized the signal as a loud shout for help:

BEGINNING HUNGER STRIKE OCTOBER 1ST
TARNOPOLSKY

It was the time of Simcha Torah, the holiday symbolizing the rejoicing of the Torah, the most important holiday of the year for Soviet Jews. In Moscow twenty thousand Jews had gathered in front of Moscow Synagogue, in defiance of Soviet repression, to acknowledge their Judaism. As they danced and sang in the streets of Moscow, Kharkov refuseniks, isolated in the Ukraine, would not be celebrating. No synagogue existed in Kharkov, staged rituals were dangerous... there was a hunger strike. We recalled Yuri's first chilling public statement about the extermination of Soviet Jews.

A letter arrived from France. Jeannette Zupan was spearheading the French rescue drive for Tarnopolsky. A devout Catholic, she had studied Hebrew with the rabbi at a local synagogue. She began to take weekly lessons after learning about the desperate situation confronting Soviet Jews. In sadly recalling the horrors of World War II, she regretted that she had been only a child and unable to help during the Nazi atrocities. Like the righteous Christians who bravely sheltered Jews, she vowed to do her part as an adult to prevent history from being repeated. "Never again!" she said emphatically. Jeannette informed me that in France they were going to publicize the torment being suffered by refuseniks, citing the case of Yuri Tarnopolsky as an example. She urged me to join her in their struggle to free Tarnopolsky.

Chere Madame,
Yuri Tarnopolsky, with whom I have been corresponding for some months, informed me of his hunger strike beginning October 1st. He is asking me to make his situation known in France and to write.

Here in France, we are going to try and make known the existence of the torment suffered by the refuseniks, and very particularly the case of Yuri Tarnopolsky. At your end, you can do something also. He needs the manifestation of friendship and solidarity.

Since he asked me to warn you, it's because he counts you among his friends. As his friend, Chere Madame, I salute you cordially. . . .

Jeannette J. Zupan

As I put down the letter, I felt an immediate bond with this woman from France. We had never met, but we shared a common goal. Jeannette was in contact with Tarnopolsky and was reaching out for help and support. Her letter gave me strength and hope . . . Tarnopolsky's plight would be known in France. From now on, I had a partner in Paris.

The next day there was a telephone call from Yury Verlinsky, an emigre from Kharkov and a friend of Tarnopolsky's who had arrived in Chicago four years earlier with his wife, Luba, and son, Oleg. Yury was director of cytogenetics at Michael Reese Hospital, and Luba was in research at the Cardiovascular Institute at the same hospital. They were among the fortunate ones who had been able to emigrate before the door to freedom was closed. Both Yury and Luba were leaders in Chicago's Russian community. Yury had just received a letter from Tarnopolsky, who had requested he get in touch with me immediately.

Meanwhile, as refuseniks battled for their existence in Kharkov, the few Jews from other Soviet cities who had been released were starting new lives. In December, four months after we received the telegram from the Rozentals, Era Rozental was sent from Israel to the United States on a two-week tour. She spoke in seven cities throughout the country to Women's Plea Groups, under the auspices of the National Jewish Community Relations Advisory Council. CASJ brought her to Chicago, where she spent three days in our home. When Marty and I met Era and her family the previous May in Odessa, we never believed this day would come--and so soon! That the Rozentals would be waiting for us at Ben Gurion Airport in Tel Aviv only two years after that meeting in the Ukraine, as we all had wished together upon parting, was a dream come true.

A meeting for CASJ was held in our home, and many Soviet Jewry activists crowded into the living room to hear Era's story. As I sat next to her, I studied the faces of my friends and co-workers who were hearing Era's story for the first time. They appeared to be listening intently. It was a celebrated event when a refusenik family received visas, and a rare opportunity to share moments together in one of our homes. For me, personally, it was an evening to remember. Era had become a friend during the two years we spent corresponding from opposite sides of the Iron Curtain; now she was in my living room.

Referring to those left behind in the Soviet Union, Era said, "Everyone hopes. It's impossible to live without hope. And when we received permission, they received hope, because if it was possible for our family to leave, it made it possible for theirs, too." I had received the same hope. If political pressure generated by organizations like ours had helped to free the Rozentals, we concluded, Tarnopolsky and others could also be freed.

And so, the struggle began . . .

Chapter II

ESTABLISHING COMMUNICATION

It was October 1, the day Yuri Tarnopolsky was to begin his hunger strike. I waited with growing uneasiness before that first call placed to Kharkov to speak with him. I felt a little like a teenager again: out of my element, insecure. Would he be difficult to understand over the telephone? Would I be able to extract the necessary information from him and impart news from Chicago Action over the droning interference and the fear of revealing too much to the ever-present ears of the KGB? CASJ was anxious to monitor his condition during the strike.

"Do you speak Russian?" asked the Moscow operator, knowing my response would be an emphatic no.

"On your call to Kharkov, dear," continued the operator, "what is the serial number of that call?"

"Number 2621," I responded.

"Just a minute, dear, I'm checking."

CASJ had booked the call a week ahead of time with the international operator in New York, which was standard procedure for calling the Soviet Union. Direct phone calls from abroad were verboten to anyone within the refusenik community, so we arranged "messenger calls." One week in advance an American operator would transmit all information regarding the call to her Russian counterpart. If the call was approved, we would be issued a serial number that identified it. A messenger would then take a telegram to the apartment of our Soviet friends, apprising them of the forthcoming call. We too sent regular weekly telegrams through Western Union to make certain they knew to expect our calls. There was no guarantee either telegram would be delivered, and many were not. If an official telegram was not received, our friends wouldn't go to the post office, where all messenger calls came through, since there was no record of the call. Even if Tarnopolsky's telephone had not been disconnected in the KGB raid of 1981, we would not have attempted to reach him at home because it could have endangered his life.

"What time was your call scheduled for, dear?"

"One o'clock this afternoon, Moscow. It's thirty minutes late."

"I'm sorry, dear, but the circuits to Kharkov have been busy. Just a minute. I'll try it again."

Calling the Soviet Union was more challenging than telephoning anywhere else in the world. The waiting was frustrating and only intensified my anxiety.

"Hold on, dear." The Moscow operator had finally returned. "Your party is coming to the phone."

My fears soon dissipated. At the other end of the receiver was a calm, articulate, and forceful speaker who appeared unafraid of KGB antennas. These calls were to become a lifeline to the Kharkov community, and Yuri had, thankfully, taken the lead. Now I could do my part.

We had received his telegram pertaining to the hunger strike, I told Yuri, and we stood united in support of his efforts. Our only concern was for his personal welfare. He assured me he was feeling "OK" (at that point) and that he planned to continue with the hunger strike until November 9, when the Madrid conference reconvened.

"Don't worry about my health, Nancy. My decision to maintain the strike for forty days is firm. I don't want to press on the authorities, I only want to protest. This is my *only* tool."

To demonstrate the strength of our universal support, I informed him we would contact Washington and make the hunger strike known throughout the world.

Eventually, to ease the bureaucratic process, we limited calls to a specific day and time each week. For Yuri, we set Friday mornings at 9:00 a.m. Chicago time (6:00 p.m. Moscow time) for our weekly contacts.

Each call required hours of advance preparation. We needed to stay abreast of the latest political developments, be up-to-date on information from CASJ, and process news and requests from each call abroad.

Then there was the farcical call-booking process. This involved giving the name and address of the party we were calling to an American operator, who would repeat the information to Moscow while we remained on the phone. Invariably the Moscow operator would claim she did not understand or "there is no such address." Week after week the same game was played. Frequently such red tape necessitated several calls to and from New York just to schedule a single phone call.

Often we would be awakened in the middle of the night by some Moscow operator calling to check the information for accuracy. These "check calls" always came between midnight and 6:00 a.m. Chicago time, another example of Soviet-style harassment. Usually we would be awakened several times in one night just prior to an expected call.

On Friday mornings I would arise between 6:00 and 7:00 to set up my notebook of messages and connect a tape recorder to the telephone receiver for monitoring. The waiting game would begin, sometimes for hours, as calls seldom came through on time. One excuse after another was proffered: the circuits were busy, the Moscow operator wasn't answering, the line to Kharkov was "dead," and so on. Many times I reminded myself that at least I was waiting in comfort. Our refusenik friends were standing around at some uncomfortable post office during this waiting game, nervously preparing to speak English in a stuffy telephone booth.

Sometimes Moscow intentionally scheduled a call for the wrong day and time. The phone operators were all KGB. I would be awakened at 3:00 or 4:00 a.m. to hear a Russian operator gleefully announce that my party was "on the line!" There I was, drunk with sleep, without notes or tape recorder, to find that Yuri had been waiting on the line. I would dash out of bed to pick up another phone so as not to disturb the rest of the household. We usually had to scream into the receiver to overcome poor connections.

Not only were we compelled to watch every word, since calls were carefully monitored by the KGB, but we had to put up with annoying interference (jamming) in the form of loud static. The intensity of the interference was in direct proportion to the sensitivity of the messages being transmitted. Or the connection was cut altogether, and we would be left hanging in midsentence. Our charming Moscow operator would then explain, "I'm sorry, dear, but your party has gone home" or "I'm sorry, dear, but our lines to Kharkov are down." We would be forced to wait another week to reestablish contact. All that considered, it was always a relief when we made any real contact.

In time I, like my co-workers, was on a first-name basis with every New York supervisor handling calls to the Soviet Union. Through the Soviet Jewry movement we were able to place our calls directly with operators at the supervisory level. This was mandatory since regular operators did not possess the finesse necessary to complete these difficult calls. Later I would be setting up "contract" messenger calls to Kharkov, which meant that calls were automatically placed for me each week through New York. And so it was, week after week, then month after month and year after year. . . .

On October 10, following up on our monitoring of Yuri's hunger strike, CASJ sent three telegrams to Washington, D.C., addressed to President Ronald Reagan, the Honorable Charles Percy, and Elliott Abrams, Assistant Secretary of State for Human Relations and Humanitarian Affairs. The following message appeared on those wires:

YURI TARNOPOLSKY, A KHARKOV REFUSENIK SINCE 12/14/76, HAS BEEN ON A HUNGER STRIKE SINCE OCTOBER 1ST. URGE HIGH LEVEL INTERVENTION ON HIS BEHALF. HIS ADDRESS-- KRASNOZNAMENNY PER 2, APARTMENT 17, KHARKOV 310002 SINCERELY, NANCY ROSENFELD

CHICAGO ACTION FOR SOVIET JEWRY
474 CENTRAL AVENUE
HIGHLAND PARK, IL 60035

A fourth telegram was sent to Jeannette in Paris:

CHERE MADAM. RECEIVED LETTER. URGE YOU TO CONTACT
MITTERAND. USE ALL INFLUENCE TO ASK FOR SPECIAL
INTERVENTION ON YURI'S BEHALF. SINCERELY, NANCY
ROSENFELD

The next weeks saw a whirlwind of CASJ effort on Yuri's behalf, and I
found myself in the center of the vortex. Pamela contacted Congressman Sidney
Yates, urging him to write to Ambassador Anatoly Dobrynin. Congressman Yates
immediately appealed to the ambassador, focusing on the desperate conditions in
Kharkov and requesting his support for Tarnopolsky.
    Jeannette received a communique from Jean-Claude Colliard, the cabinet
director for the president of the republic. Monsieur Colliard said that President
Mitterand had given him Jeannette's urgent letter requesting immediate action on
behalf of Yuri. It was his intention to study the matter closely so he could help
draw attention to Yuri's plight.
    In November a letter arrived from Senator Percy confirming his active
support for Tarnopolsky. He raised Yuri's case with Soviet authorities in a new
appeal to ameliorate his treatment and grant him and his family permission to
emigrate. "I am hopeful that our combined efforts will be successful," wrote the
senator.
    When Yuri's long hunger strike concluded, we were greatly relieved. We
felt secure in reducing our telephone calls to once a month, initiating some
evening calls to include Yuri's friends and supporters who were unable to attend
the 9:00 a.m. Friday meetings. Yury and Luba Verlinsky amassed great support
and remained helpful throughout the long campaign to win Tarnopolsky's
freedom. There were also Misha and Elvina Berman, two other emigres from
Kharkov who had been friends of Yuri's. Like the Verlinskys, the Bermans had
also gotten out before 1979. Misha was a physician with a general practice in
Chicago, and Elvina was a psychiatrist at Michael Reese Hospital. These four
people were frequently present for calls.

In the midst of this flurry of activity, communications were beginning to break
down at home. I was not focusing on what my family was saying to me. As my
dedication to Soviet Jews grew more intense, I gradually became preoccupied with
my work. Little did I realize, at that time, how neglectful I was becoming at
home. The house was often a mess, dirty laundry piled up, trips to the market
were less frequent, and dinner was seldom on time. Sometimes the boys made

their own supper. When this began, Steve was in high school and Rob was in seventh grade.

Marty tried to warn me. "You are not around to help the boys with their homework. Where are your priorities?" he hollered one night. I stared back with a blank face. I thought the boys were doing fine. How could I concentrate on English papers when I was worried about hunger strikes?

Chapter III

DESPERATE LAST STAND

"We are burning the candles of our lives at both ends."

$\mathbf{T}$he day arrived when Yuri boldly decided to pull out all stops and immediately submit his manuscript "Description of a Disease" for publication. It was a calculated risk; he felt he needed to take this step if he and his family were to be free. Although worried, we followed his instructions. A newly edited version of the manuscript in which he graphically described the prolonged agony suffered by thousands of Jews waiting to emigrate was presented for publication. It first appeared in the December 31, 1982, *News Bulletin* published by the Scientists Committee of the Israel Public Council for Soviet Jewry.

We heard from Yuri again in December. All his correspondence was written openly and fearlessly on postcards, and the cards were numbered so we could easily determine if one got "lost." Mail took approximately three weeks to be delivered from portal to portal, and soon there was a regular flow of letters between Chicago and Kharkov. Letters from the United States were sent "registered return receipt," a procedure that had been suggested by our organization to *help* ensure the safety of the mail delivery. My letters were also numbered, but even registered, numbered letters did not all make it to the Tarnopolsky apartment, despite undoubtedly having arrived in Kharkov.

Yuri's December postcard number 3 stated that he would begin writing on the first and fifteenth of every month. Apparently he had made several aborted attempts to get through to us. "I am feeling well. My sight improved paradoxically during the last week of the H.S. (hunger strike)." Yuri had complained of blind spots in both eyes during the hunger strike. "There is only one remedy . . . to get rid of stress. The H.S. helped me do it. I hope it is not the only result in the long run. . . . Why did I do it? If one is incurably sick, and doctors refuse him help, he is ready to go to a sorcerer, to a shaman, to feed on snake eggs. . . . It is a gesture of helplessness, because we see we are perishing. . . ." These were words of despair wrenched out of a man who felt no hope, who was making a desperate last stand.

We received a request from Kharkov for books, "second-hand books of fiction and books for children, ages ten to fifteen." The Social Action Committee at North Shore Congregation Israel was quick to respond, and within two weeks books of all kinds were being sent to Kharkov. Few of these books were delivered, but a parcel of clothing from the committee did manage to slip through.

Concurrent with our activities in Chicago and Paris, help came from the San Francisco Bay Area. David Waksberg, director of the Bay Area Council for Soviet Jews, another branch of the UCSJ, had visited Yuri in Kharkov shortly after our visit, and he was quick to sign on. David began booking calls to Kharkov from California and sending telegrams and letters of support. *We were building a strong nucleus of support.* As more people joined the rescue effort, my confidence grew in proportion to the strength of the team.

In Kharkov, however, growing uneasiness prevailed as the weeks wore on with no news breaking through the Iron Curtain. We received the following letter from Yuri dated January 15, 1983.

> . . . I am literally gnawed by the mysterious lack of news about my manuscripts. . . . I suspect a kind of Bermuda triangle. . . a Black Hole, where all my anxiety and curiosity, on this, is lost without any tracks.... Listening to the radio, I have a feeling that something is happening between East and West. Some big old wheels are turning slowly, and with much squeak. We hope that the two gears will come into engagement. . . . However, I do *not* believe in a gesture of humanity, I *do* believe in a bargain. . . .

The weeks passed, and tension within the Kharkov community escalated. Our refusenik friends hung on every word from political commentators, which they were able to extract from infrequently broadcast news reports. They began to sense a "significant mutual desire" between the United States and the Soviet Union to find solutions to a series of problems during negotiations between the two heads of State. Yet they questioned whether their freedom was part of any possible agreement between the two nations. "What is going on in this direction seems to be behind a smoke screen . . . ," wrote Yuri. "Not a single bit of news on the radio has given us any indication of future prospects. . . ." He worried about being repetitive in his correspondence with friends abroad and felt he had lost some friends as a result. His concern persisted regarding papers he had sent out with couriers in 1979 and 1982. In addition, he was anxious about his manuscript, "Description of a Disease," entrusted to our care. "We all are waiting now, like fish under ice. We are waiting for spring."

Two weeks passed, and there was another postcard.

> I am writing you a letter a fortnight. . . . For about a year, I have been burning from inside out of anxiety and uncertainty about my papers. . . . Everyone is waiting for the result of the negotiations. However, our

question is completely clouded, and we have not a bit of information. . . .

Their heightened anxiety was due partially to a "forced" pause in communication for a few weeks, during which time many aborted attempts had been made to reach Kharkov by telephone.

Marillyn and Pamela went to Washington at the end of the year to hold a briefing with Congress and the State Department. Lynn Singer, who was then president of UCSJ, raised the issue of Soviet Jews with Secretary of State Shultz. Noise was being made at the highest level, but we were still waiting for results.

Continued desperation, exhaustion, and depression were the messages coming out of Kharkov. Eugene Chudnovsky wrote, "Most of our life, including our youth, has passed here." From David Soloveichik came "My heart is bleeding. I cannot get rid of fear for my daughter. What will be her destiny?" Jamming of telephone lines was worsening, increasing their frustration and anxiety. "I returned home with heavy heart," wrote Yuri in early February. "I heard the American operator quite well, but your voice was very weak. . . . Olga and I brought a special dull English novel to read while waiting for the call (if the book were more interesting, we would have read it long ago). We read for two hours, waiting. . . . Now, in the fourth year of our plight, we take it more seriously than a year ago. . . . *We are burning the candles of our lives at both ends.* . . ."

He persisted in expressing concern over his manuscripts. We tried to reassure him that "Description of a Disease" had been submitted for publication in October, was receiving good press coverage, and had appeared in an Israeli scientific journal during December. At the time, we did not understand that his primary anxiety was discovering the whereabouts of his poetry. In 1979 Tarnopolsky had given Yury Verlinsky a tube of toothpaste filled with "handmade" microfilm that contained all the poems. Verlinsky had smuggled the poetry out of the country when he immigrated to the United States. The fulfillment Yuri received from the birth of these poems was like a father's pride in the delivery of a child. They were his most prized creation, and his greatest hope was that they would survive long after he was gone. It was understandable that he was tormented over their fate. Verlinsky, along with his wife, Luba, continued his contribution to Tarnopolsky's cause in the United States.

On Friday evening, February 18, North Shore Congregation Israel held a special service, and the sanctuary was packed with congregants, including the Chicago contingent of the Russian community, led by Yury and Luba. The title of our presentation was

THE JEWISH COMMUNITY IN CRISIS:
REFUSENIKS OF THE SOVIET UNION

As I stood before the congregation, informing them of the current situation in the Soviet Union, Marty showed slides from our mission the preceding May. "It is not an exaggeration," I said, "to say that the lives of Soviet Jews are greatly dependent upon what we, as American Jews, are able to do in the way of help. We want to bring you closer to them. . . we are their lifeline of support."

Following our presentation, we were warmly greeted by both temple members and guests, many of whom promised to help. Support continued to expand.

Three weeks later, on March 9, a few friends--Misha and Elvina Berman and Gene Golan, a pen pal of Yuri's--were gathered with Marty and me at our Deerfield home to speak with Yuri. It was 6:00 p.m.

"These are dangerous times, Nancy. Something is happening here. We have some bad news. . . ."

Yuri told us that Eugene Chudnovsky had just been taken into KGB headquarters and warned about his scientific publications abroad. This was alarming news on two accounts: it signaled increased KGB activity but also made us all concerned about Eugene's cardiac condition.

"You know about his heart?" questioned Yuri.

"Yes, Yuri, we do know about his condition," I responded.

Yuri also had news about the Paritsky family, but its meaning was ambiguous. Sasha (Alexander) had sent Polina a telegram saying he was "alive and well," but a few days later a card with only a couple of words had said nothing about his health. Polina suspected that the telegram had been a "fake."

"Please, Nancy," asked Yuri, "if you could tell me, *what are our prospects?*"

"We are doing everything we can, Yuri. You know about the World Conference for Soviet Jewry, which is convening next week in Israel. Marillyn and Pamela will be attending that conference, representing Chicago. Do you have any messages for them to take along to the meeting?"

"I would like to say just a few words, Nancy. *The holocaust of Soviet Jews is a fait accompli, and nothing more!*"

"This will be relayed, Yuri. Remember, we are all working together every day. You are not alone. . . ."

When Yuri raised the subject of his poetry, I said that David Waksberg had a copy of the poems and had sent them to two publishing houses, both of which publish in Russian. David was waiting for a reply. Yuri was relieved to hear about it, although we didn't know then that David was missing a large selection of the poetry. When Yury Verlinsky arrived safely in America with the film, he gave it to a professional photographer in Chicago, who developed it and made prints. A few years later Misha Berman transcribed some of the poetry from photographs to paper. A collection of the transcribed work was mailed to France, where it was translated by the late Henny Kleiner, a Soviet Jewry activist and poet who was working with Jeannette. At the time, we had assumed that Misha had reproduced everything instead of submitting only a selection that represented Yuri's earliest work.[1]

". . . Nancy, I have one more thing to tell you, and it is very important. *I may have to reach you very quickly if something happens here. . . .*"

"I hear you," I replied. "We'll remain on alert. . . . Remember, we all love you, Yuri, and. . . ."

"Same here!"

". . . and, I'm sure we'll see one another again."

"I feel it too, Nancy . . . ," he responded emotionally.

As I replaced the receiver, the Bermans and I had a strong premonition of impending disaster.

"I'm afraid something terrible is going to happen to him," said Misha dismally.

I stared at Misha. My head would not permit me to think solely in negative terms.

"But Misha," I pleaded, "there have been other false alarms. Yuri's friends have been searched, several have been taken into KGB headquarters for questioning, but nothing further has happened to them . . . except. . . ."

"Yes, Nancy. Except for Sasha Paritsky! He's been imprisoned for almost two years."

Misha was right. We both wished that Yuri could be less aggressive in his public statements. We knew it would be far more difficult to help him, as well as his family and friends, if he were arrested.

"But courage, Misha, *not* silence or diplomacy, is the only thing which can save him in the end," I said, trying to sound convincing.

"Perhaps you're right, Nancy," he said softly. "We'll see."

Yuri's message to the World Conference was on the way to Israel to be presented at the meeting, along with a letter he had written in early March: "*I see the history of the Jews, and I see its last tragic chapter, the holocaust [moral holocaust]. . . . It's an extermination, well-camouflaged and slow . . . .*" He felt that the Soviets could do to the Jews what Stalin had had no time to accomplish. Although it seemed foolish to worry needlessly, we all felt a sense of foreboding.

We would not speak to or hear from Yuri Tarnopolsky again for over three years.

---

[1]In the spring of 1985, Yuri received an important literary award in France, Le Prix de la Liberte, for his newly published book, *La Clairiere dans la Pinede* (literally translated, *The Clearing in the Pine Forest*). This award was granted annually, by a jury chaired by Eugene Ionesco. To qualify for this honor, the recipient had to be a writer who, in his own country, had defended freedom of thought and expression. News of this award was published in three French newspapers: *Le Figaro, Le Monde,* and *La Croix.*

Chapter IV

URGENT CALL

$\mathbf{T}$he telephone was ringing. It was a chilly Sunday morning, and I was relaxing at home. The date was March 15, 1983.

I picked up the phone, and the operator said, "Israel calling." It was Pamela. Pam, together with many other worldwide Soviet Jewish leaders, was in Jerusalem attending an international conference for Soviet Jews. She was representing CASJ as co-chairman.

I was startled to hear her voice. "Pam, is something wrong?"

"Nancy," she said, "I have some bad news. Moments ago, an announcement was made over the loudspeaker system at the conference that Dr. Yuri Tarnopolsky had just been arrested in his native city of Kharkov."

I slumped in my chair. News of Yuri's arrest should have come as no great surprise. His 1979 application for emigration had been officially denied on the grounds of "insufficient kinship abroad," a typical argument used by the authorities to deny Soviet Jews their right to emigrate. Consequently, his only hope of leaving the country was through pressure, which he applied by being outspoken. He had made his protests widely known through statements issued to the press.

The prior November we had released his manuscript, "Description of a Disease," which he had finally approved for publication. Ten months earlier, my husband and I had carried this sensitive document out of the Soviet Union. I remembered the sleepless nights that followed our release of the paper that graphically described the prolonged agony of tens of thousands of refuseniks awaiting permission to emigrate.

Life stopped for us. We have lost everything we acquired during fifty years. We have lost our money, belongings, job, profession, skill. They call us traitors and double-crossers. We have neither past nor future. We don't plan anything, we don't strive for anything, we don't dream about anything except getting out of here. They keep us under the constant pressure of uncertainty. It is a real torture, indeed. . . .

We are the children and grandchildren of those who perished in the Tsarist pogroms, and the fascist shootings, who were skinned alive by the Petliura thugs, and who suffocated in the gas chambers. We are the descendants of two victimized generations. We don't want to be the third such generation. We wish for the same things as all the people in the world do: To live better, to work, to rejoice, to raise children, to be happy. Most of us have, however, a very specific goal: To escape anti-Semitism. . . .[1]

Would the public release of the manuscript have serious consequences for Yuri? I had asked myself. Would he be . . . ?

The harsh reality of this terrible news was still ringing in my ears. I had been personally responsible for having submitted "Description of a Disease" to the press. Had I responded too quickly to his request to let out all the stops and release the document? Should we not have been able to foresee this happening? Yet he had requested it, and we had complied with his wishes.

I suddenly realized that Pamela was still speaking. ". . . I know how upsetting this is for you, Nancy, but we need you to send out a press release immediately."

Yuri's arrest had been a warning from the KGB to the Jews. It was the sixth anniversary of the arrest of Anatoly Sharansky. The timing was perfect, and the message rang out loud and clear: being Jewish in the Soviet Union is a punishable offense; protest too loudly--attempt to leave--and you will be silenced.

The minute she received the news, Betty Kahn rushed into the office of CASJ to help me get out a press release. Another disciple of Marillyn's, Betty went on to teach her own classes in Jewish history. After being solicited by CASJ to go to the Soviet Union in 1980, she teamed up with a Highland Park attorney, Harvey Barnett, and went along as photographer. It was not the practice of the organization to permit tourists to travel alone to the USSR. Betty returned to the USSR in 1984 with Linda Opper.

Betty's tender black-and-white photos of refuseniks tell the story of the Soviet Jewry rescue movement in progress. After that first trip she incorporated them into a vivid slide presentation for CASJ; a second slide show was developed following her return in 1984. She is also responsible for developing a high school curriculum entitled "Let My People Go" that was used nationwide. The curriculum was designed to teach children the story of Jews in the USSR, from the first Jewish settlers to Sharansky. Her creative ability was seen everywhere, from postcards and fliers to songs and skits that she wrote for CASJ fund-raising benefits.

One hour after Betty's arrival on that frigid Sunday morning, the following message was sent across the nation and abroad.

---

[1]This passage was taken from Yuri's original manuscript of "Description of a Disease."

For Immediate Release
Dateline - March 15, 1983

YURI TARNOPOLSKY ARRESTED IN KHARKOV!

The Charge: Under Article 187/1 of the Ukrainian Criminal Code, "Anti-Soviet Agitation and Propaganda with the Intent to Defame the Soviet State". . . . News of Tarnopolsky's arrest horrified members of Chicago Action for Soviet Jewry. . . . And, now they are spending days and nights on the telephone, mobilizing protests against the arrest. . . . CASJ knows full well what a sentence of several years in duration can do to a man, even one who is not sick, as Tarnopolsky is. The prison conditions are harsh. The work load is reminiscent of Nazi labor camps; hard work, no warm clothes, little or no food. CASJ is worried about Yuri. They anguish for Olga and Irina. They are calling their representatives, senators, the President. They are begging all people of good will to send wires asking that these charges be dropped . . . that Yuri be allowed to return to his family.

Chicago Action needs your help now!

Chapter V

OUTPOURING OF SUPPORT

When they excavate the Russian Pompeii
out of the ashes of lies,
and display the findings in a museum,
and crowds will come rushing through the doors
with hum and hubbub,
who will believe that we were men
and not mere locusts?

Yuri Tarnopolsky

Pamela's call alerting us to Yuri Tarnopolsky's arrest set a formidable rescue machine in motion. He would not be alone; the West had heard his cry.

Following the initial press release, which was transmitted throughout the United States and abroad, CASJ placed hundreds of telephone calls and wrote letters informing people of Yuri's arrest. Among those contacted were senators, congressmen, the State Department, President Reagan, religious leaders, and scores of supporters. All offices of the Union of Councils for Soviet Jews throughout the United States immediately responded by activating telegram banks and fanning out thousands of wires to public officials, in both the USA and the USSR, on behalf of Yuri Tarnopolsky.

One of the most poignant letters was written by Yuri's twelve-year-old daughter, Irina, in which she addresses a heartfelt plea to the Soviet leader, Yuri Andropov. Nevertheless, unlike her American counterpart, Samantha Smith, she failed to move the Soviet president:

Respected Yuri Vladimirovich,

Not long ago, I came to know that an American schoolgirl, Samantha Smith, appealed to you in a letter, and you answered her. So, I decided to write you a letter, too.

My father, Yuri Ilyich Tarnopolsky, is in prison now. He is accused of slandering the Soviet system and soon he will be tried. But, my papa is an honest man. He has never lied. He is under arrest only because we are Jewish and want to leave for Israel.

Already four years we have waited for permission to leave. Now papa is arrested, and we don't know what will happen with us. I beg you to release my papa and let us leave for Israel.

That letter appeared in an article written by Robert Gillette and was syndicated in newspapers throughout the United States on June 13, 1983.

A major event was staged in the Bay Area: "A SOVIET WEDDING BY PROXY" was headlined in *The San Francisco Chronicle* on May 4, 1983. Ellen and David Waksberg, who were married three days earlier, held a proxy wedding on behalf of the Tarnopolskys to help publicize their plight. The Waksbergs repeated their vows in honor of Yuri and Olga, who had been deprived of a religious ceremony thirteen years ago. The event was officiated by Rabbi Sheldon Lewis in San Francisco's Union Square.

Our work continued. There were countless sleepless nights as we often worked up until dawn. We were constantly phoning Washington--the State Department, our senators and congressmen, the president. All efforts were coordinated with the UCSJ in the capital. Since I maintained a home office, which I referred to as the CASJ annex, I usually was not physically away from home. Nevertheless, during this period I neither saw nor heard what went on in my house. When I stayed up late to work, the boys came in to say good night and Marty went to bed. Night after night, this pattern was repeated.

Dozens of Yuri's supporters across the nation began phoning the office of CASJ, asking what they could do to help. These pen pals sent not only letters of support to Olga and Irina but parcels of clothing, books, and supplies. Not everything arrived.

One of Tarnopolsky's most ardent penpals was Lorna Adelman, a woman from Pennsylvania who initiated a mass mailing campaign of letters from her synagogue. Hundreds of letters were written from her area, many of which she sent personally.

Four months had passed since Yuri's arrest and barely two weeks since his sentencing. He smoldered in a Kharkov jail for two additional months before beginning the long, painful journey to a Siberian labor camp, where he was to be incarcerated for the next three years.

Yuri's arrest, trial, and sentencing were given maximum media coverage in Western Europe as well as the United States and Israel, with stories appearing in newspapers and on radio and television.

For several weeks we had tried unsuccessfully to reach Olga, booking messenger calls every two days, but the Moscow operator offered one excuse after another. "Dear, your party did not come to the post office" or "I'm sorry, dear, but she is not available." Then one day we heard Olga's voice for a few seconds before the connection was severed and the Moscow operator reported, "The line to Kharkov is out of order."

David Waksberg sent one of Yuri's chemistry papers to Professor Paul Flory of Stanford University, and it was handed to a scientist in Yuri's field of organic chemistry. Another copy was submitted to the scientific journal *Chemical and Engineering News*.

On the Fourth of July weekend, demonstrations were held in cities throughout the United States, and thousands of people came out in protest carrying signs "LET MY PEOPLE GO," "REUNITE SEPARATED FAMILIES" and "RELEASE PRISONERS OF CONSCIENCE." The demonstrations created public awareness as well as making a loud statement to the Soviets. Refuseniks were encouraged, but prisoners trapped behind the walls of the Gulag never learned about these events since news was forbidden.

In New York the Committee of Concerned Scientists was trying to learn whether Yuri had been stripped of his scientific degrees at the trial. This was a common action, and it relegated scientists to "nonpersons" by permanently removing them from the world of science.

Months passed, but still no word from Kharkov. Frequent attempts to reach Olga by telephone failed. Letters were written with no response. My anxiety increased; so did Jeannette's. Finally, a letter came from Eugene Chudnovsky. He wrote that he was greatly concerned about Yuri. He said that Yuri was a man of great intellectual and moral power, but that his health was not good and he could not endure several years in prison. Eugene added that many times he was surprised not only by Yuri's extensive knowledge but also by his ability to empathize with others. "He takes other people's troubles close to his heart," he wrote. "I can hardly imagine him in a criminal surrounding. It is even shocking that somebody takes the liberty of interrogating him."

Tragedy sometimes struck the rescuers as well as the victims. That summer Jeannette Zupan's nineteen-year-old son, Pierre, was killed instantly when he fell from the top of the Alps while mountain climbing. I was stunned. How could such a terrible thing happen to this gentle, caring person who had devoted her life to helping others?

In October hundreds of representatives from councils throughout the USA, Canada, England, France, and Israel arrived in the capital for the annual convention of UCSJ. There were think-tank sessions, talks by political figures and divided family members, and a panel of Nobel Peace Prize-winning scientists spoke about the importance of their relationship with Soviet Jewish scientists. Individual meetings with congressmen and senators took place as part of the lobbying effort in support of Soviet Jewry, and a vigil was staged in front of the Soviet Embassy.

Two more letters arrived within a few days from Kharkov. It had been seven months since Yuri's arrest, and his absence was felt keenly. "We can hardly express how depressed we feel," wrote Eugene. "Our hopes are lost, our friend has disappeared."

The second letter, from Liliya Zatuchnaya, demonstrated the generous spirit of the refuseniks, who gave support as well as received it. Liliya had been corresponding weekly with Jeannette and had been away from Kharkov when the accident occurred. When she returned home in September, a letter from Paris was waiting for her. Liliya immediately phoned Jeannette. "Her voice was full of pain and suffering," wrote Liliya. "It's been two months now since she has written. I still write every week and send cards. Her friend and neighbor wrote to me that she and her family are very brave, but you understand what it means to lose a dear son."

In November a letter finally arrived from Olga. She wrote that she had been out of touch because she had been preoccupied by "getting things for Yuri to help him survive. . . . He has arrived at his place of punishment . . . Chita. The climate is not good for him, and he needs warm dress and vitamins and many other things. I don't know how will he overcome all these difficulties, because his health is very poor. . . . I don't know when I'll see him . . . it has already been seven months. . . ."

After months of blocked calls to Kharkov, we reached Olga on December 8, but the connection was terrible and we could barely make out her voice. She seemed to be crying out from off in the distance, but it was impossible to discern what she was saying. We heard crackling sounds, static, but nothing intelligible. The refuseniks' isolation only seemed to grow.

There were rumors of a possible new hunger strike, and we were concerned about Yuri's well-being. We knew he would need a lot of strength in order to survive the harsh Siberian climate, the strenuous work he would be required to do, and the little sustenance provided. We feared his health would be permanently impaired. The grim details of prison life as told by Polina Paritsky kept returning. Sasha had been imprisoned for nearly three years, and there was little news of him. Who would be the next from Kharkov to be arrested?

In December our son Rob wrote a letter to Irina. For a year and a half he had seen me work night and day for the movement, and now he was reaching out to his new friend, the young girl in the Ukraine with whom he would be sharing his bar mitzvah. His youth and sheltered life made it difficult for him to grasp the magnitude of her desperate circumstances, but he was trying to understand, to be her friend.

Life continued. Our home life was normal (except for my compulsive activism). Theirs was not. Our family was intact. Theirs was broken. We were free. They were slaves. There was no symmetry. There was no equality.

Support for Tarnopolsky was beginning to mushroom as news of his worsening condition traveled around the world. We had international support and were beginning to build a machine, operated by thousands of hands, capable of "moving mountains." This machine functioned at different levels--political, academic, theological, legal--but it was managed and controlled at the grass-roots level. We, the volunteers, were at the helm. Day and night, week after week, year after year, the machine worked constantly with a single purpose.

At the theological level, we began by appealing to religious leaders throughout the country. On the home front, we had the support of many prominent rabbis, particularly Rabbi Bronstein from North Shore Congregation Israel.

I sent an appeal to the Archdiocese of Chicago and received a prompt response.

Dear Ms. Rosenfeld:

Thank you for your letter and information on Yuri Tarnopolsky. I receive many requests and reports concerning the lack of religious freedom in the Soviet Union. I am deeply moved by the faith of Jewish, Catholic and Protestant brothers and sisters in the climate of such severe persecution.

I have spoken to the mutual concerns of the Jewish and Christian community on several occasions since I have come to Chicago. Just recently, I participated in the Holocaust Remembrance at the Chicago Temple, lest we forget the terrible catastrophe of World War II. I hope this will create an ongoing dialogue in years to come.

I do share your concerns and have enclosed a copy of a letter which has been sent to Secretary of State Shultz calling attention to the case of Yuri Tarnopolsky and others whose civil and religious rights are being violated.

Please be assured of my support and prayers for our suffering brothers and sisters all over the world.

With cordial good wishes, I remain

Sincerely yours,
JOSEPH CARDINAL BERNARDIN
Archbishop of Chicago

On the political front, letters began to pour out of Washington at all levels of government. On June 27, 1983, just two days before the trial, Congressmen Morris Udall and Bill Archer initiated a letter to Ambassador Anatoly Dobrynin, urging him to appeal to his government to drop the case against Dr. Tarnopolsky and give him prompt medical care. "We request your attention to a matter of great urgency--the imminent trial of Dr. Yuri Tarnopolsky of Kharkov. . . . We address this appeal to you in the spirit of hope, justice, humanity, and peace."

This letter was countersigned by 97 other members of the United States Congress.

Scientists heard our plea and responded. Morris Pripstein, Chairman for the committee called Scientists for Sakharov, Orlov and Sharansky, wrote to Ambassador Dobrynin in May.

> In the name of justice and humanity, we urge the immediate release of Dr. Tarnopolsky and the prompt approval of his request for an exit visa.... We wish to stress that such a humane action on the part of the Soviet Government would certainly help restore the climate of scientific relations and exchanges between the United States and the Soviet Union, which has been so much harmed by arbitrary actions of the Soviet Government against members of its own scientific community.

Professor Paul Flory fanned out 129 telegrams throughout the USSR to Soviet officials, including Yuri Andropov and members of the Soviet Academy of Sciences. The message read: "I BEG YOU TO RELEASE PROFESSOR TARNOPOLSKY, AN IMPRISONED KHARKOV SCIENTIST. HE IS LOSING HIS EYESIGHT AND HIS LIFE IS IN GRAVE DANGER. COMPASSIONATE ACTION IS URGENT."

In May 1983, a prominent article appeared in *Chemical and Engineering News* entitled "SOVIET REPRESSION OF REFUSENIK SCIENTISTS UNABATED," written by Richard J. Seltzer, Associate Editor.

The Committee of Concerned Scientists, based in New York under the leadership of Dorothy Hirsch, issued an immediate release on July 29, 1983, following the Soviets' release of sixteen Pentacostals.

ANNUAL MEETING OF CLINICAL CHEMISTS
GENERATES SUPPORT FOR JAILED SOVIET COLLEAGUE

New York, July 29. . . . "The Soviets' release of the sixteen Pentacostals and indications from the Madrid CSCE conference that the emigration of other human rights activists may follow, infuses us with new hope. . . ." In their message to Soviet authorities, over 150 participants at the 35th Annual Meeting of the American Association for Clinical Chemistry, meeting in New York City, July 24-29, 1983, appealed for the release of the forty-seven-year-old chemist.

"Tarnopolsky's arrest and sentencing is particularly distressing against a backdrop of stepped-up harassment of Kharkov emigration activists, which began with the 1981 sentencing of acoustic physicist, Alexander Paritsky, to three years in a labor camp. Paritsky, along with Tarnopolsky and other Kharkov scientists, had established an unofficial university for Jewish students denied admittance to institutions of higher learning because of anti-semitic discrimination. Official opposition to the university resulted not only in the arrest of these two leaders, but also in its forced closing. . . ."

The attention of the media played a significant role throughout the campaign to free Tarnopolsky. It was important for the public to hear and see what was happening if we were to win their support. On April 25, 1983, NBC News aired a special report on the current situation in the USSR, focusing on the Tarnopolsky case. They filmed an attempted telephone call to Olga, but we never got through. Moscow blocked the call while the nation watched.

I was becoming a woman obsessed. What had begun as a few hours a week led to a few hours a day, and before long there was no time for anything else. Until then Marty had been supportive of my effort. As my obsession increased, his interest diminished. Gradually I became isolated from my family, and the boys began to harbor strong feelings of resentment as my attention was diverted away from them. Sometimes they wouldn't speak to me, other times they looked sullen, and once in a while we had screaming matches. They turned to Marty for help and sustenance. Although they still needed a mother, I was not always available.

Chapter VI

REPORT FROM THE GULAG

When the reveille bell rings my dreams fly away
with a cry,
like hunted birds fleeing the autumn branches.
The new day is wounded,
and writhing on the ground until night,
dying among hundreds of other shot down days.
I have incurred the unalterable fate of the tree,
sheathed myself with bark, grown hardened.
I am a tree without legs,
without a heart as to last,
to survive to the end without anguish.
But . . . that was yet another dream.
I awoke and stood up as a man.
A new day won't die if it turns into a poem.
Nothing and no-one on this earth
or in this cell
can take my place.
I am not a tree.
I am a man.
I am ready.

Yuri Tarnopolsky

In a letter dated April 2, 1984, Yuri graphically described conditions inside the labor camp to his wife in Kharkov. Undaunted by possible repercussions had its contents been discovered by prison authorities, he smuggled the letter out so the information could be disseminated in the West. As a scientist, Tarnopolsky clinically diagramed the hazardous conditions and deleterious effects. The following account of life inside the Gulag was documented largely from data obtained in that letter. Additional material was secured from studies done on other cases.

Within these forced-labor camps, inmates are exposed to routine humiliation and systematic abuse by tyrannical prison officials. Within the hierarchical stratification of inmates, some become stooges, compromising themselves for personal favors, and are dreaded even more than the official authority figures. Prisoners are plagued by terror, not knowing if they'll ever be permitted out of camp alive. They are kept in a state of permanent hunger while being forced to perform hard labor. UCSJ and its member councils receive frequent reports regarding merciless beatings of prisoners by guards on duty. Isolation from the outside world is absolute. Mail is confiscated, visitation is limited to wives and mothers twice a year, and there is little access to public news announcements. Sanitation does not exist. The camps are infested with mice, lice, and roaches.

"Chita is famous in the annals of the Russian penal system," said syndicated columnist Robert Gillette in 1983. "It was the place to which Czar Nicholas I banished most of the young army officers who took part in the Decembrist insurrection of 1825, an abortive attempt to replace Russian aristocracy with a constitutional government."

Gillette continued: "Sixty years later, when the American traveler George Kennan passed through Chita in 1885, it had become an established prison colony in the barren Siberian wilderness. . . ."[1]

In his letter to Olga, Yuri wrote:

The prisoners in the camp are being held in iron cages covered on the top by an iron net, like the ones used for animals in the zoo. Each cage is adjacent to living quarters, housing some three hundred men (two detachments). The cage is smaller than the living quarters, and there is scarcely enough space in which to stand. The construction of this "human zoo" started last year. Contacts between prisoners in different cages is strictly forbidden. There are a total of six cages, and inmates are forbidden to leave the cage except for meals or to go to work. The camp is infamous in the district for the harshness of its regime. . . .

Life seemed worlds away, and yet Yuri's mind remained active and his soul was free. In his heart he would never be enchained and forced into slavery. He wrote the following poem alluding to the prison labor, which was dedicated to the construction of the Trans-Siberian Railroad.

---

[1]Historical information on Chita and quotes and information about the denied prison visit come from "Dissident's Wife Denied Visit After Siberian Trek," a syndicated newspaper article by Robert Gillette, December 13, 1983.

The cell . . . a forgotten railway car
on the dead-end track.

Food
Waiting
and sleep -
and the rest is somewhere,
far away from here.

I cannot sleep.
I pursue my thoughts
among the snores of men
sleeping on their berths.
I think: I'm not a slave
among the slaves
from head to toe.

There are few beings here,
whose dream is like a groan,
whose thoughts--like fish on sand,
here in this land . . .
the forgotten railway car
on the dead-end track.

                                        Yuri Tarnopolsky

On November 7, 1983, six weeks after Yuri's arrival in the labor camp, Moscow sent a telegram instructing the prison administration to cancel a scheduled meeting with his wife. Olga traveled three thousand miles for six days by train to reach Chita. It was not until after she arrived at the gate of the prison that she was informed of the order barring her from seeing her husband. The real reason for the denial of the visit was not disclosed. "At first they would not tell me the reason," Olga explained. "Then, finally, they told me that it was because he had broken a rule. They had found a small notebook under his pillow." A camp official told her that "keeping a notebook is not expressly forbidden, but it should be kept on the bedside table, not under the pillow. . . ." According to labor camp rules, she was eligible to try again for permission in four months.

On February 1, 1984, Tarnopolsky declared a hunger strike after being denied permission to meet with his wife for a second time. In spite of weakness caused by the hunger strike, he was required to continue his work in the prison factory. By the fourth day he had to return to his "cage" after becoming violently ill.

The conditions at work are such that I did not feel well even when not on hunger strike. The crowded room is heated by a red-hot iron stove, while our feet are freezing. . . .

Suffocating from intense heat and lack of oxygen, he was forced to go outside during subzero weather to breathe.

On February 4th, I was sent to the punishment cell [solitary confinement] for having allegedly refused to go to work. The term of the punishment was seven days. Isolated in the punishment cell, I continued my hunger strike. The cell, a tiny concrete room with a concrete floor, had a powerful heater which was switched on each night, as the room temperature soared to unbearably hot degrees. No inflow of fresh air existed. During the day, the heater was turned off and the room temperature fell to 38 degrees fahrenheit. A wooden bunk was lowered just at night for sleeping. . . . A concrete pedestal was placed in the cell, but it was inclined in such a way to make it unusable for sitting. One could only lie down on the concrete floor during the day, in a layer of icy air. My warm underwear had been taken away, and I was only wearing a pajama top. . . .

The stench in the cell became increasingly overpowering as prisoners were caged amid their own filth. A funereal silence existed.

Since the first day of my incarceration in the punishment cell, I periodically felt like I was going to faint. I was compelled to lie down on the cold concrete floor, while waiting for my heartbeat to return to its normal pace. Then, I would begin to freeze and had to sit down until the moment when the weakness of my heart forced me to lie down again. This continued throughout the night because the hot air I was forced to breathe, when lying on the wooden bunk, made me suffocate. Each morning I had to fight for the right to receive hot water for my drinking cup, which the guards tried to take away. . . .

From the onset of the hunger-strike, I was subjected to daily psychological pressure by camp authorities. . . . On February 8th, I was visited by the camp director and a procurator. The director threatened to organize a beating for me by prisoners, and the warning was supported by the procurator.

On February 11th, the seventh and last day of my stay in solitary confinement, and the eleventh day of my hunger-strike, I learned about Andropov's death. Immediately, I declared the end of my hunger-strike.

I ate a piece of bread before being permitted to leave the cell. By this time, I had no strength left and was lying on the floor day and night....

A camaraderie of prisoners had been formed, and they did all they could to help me; I was washed and shaved (being too weak to do it myself), they prepared clean clothes and bed-clothes, they collected food and even some sweets. However, as a result of the hunger-strike, I was overcome by severe pains in my stomach and back, and remained nauseated for two weeks. Disorders in urination also persisted. On February 13th, I was ordered back to work.

I would like to request that the above testimony be considered my complaint addressed to the International Red Cross. I am protesting against cruel and inhuman treatment to which I have been subjected. . . .

In my statement, written to the director prior to the hunger-strike, I wrote that I protest against barbaric cruelty which was expressed by the denial of my wife's permission to visit me. This order was carried out in spite of the fact that she had travelled 6000 kilometers in order to see me, and for just two hours. . . .

After the hunger-strike, I sent a statement to the procurator in which I wrote the following: In response to my hunger-strike protesting against cruelty, I have been subjected to an even more cruel treatment, which could not be qualified as anything but torture. Everything that happened to me since 1979, after submission of my application for emigration from the USSR in accordance with Soviet and international law, completely contradicted legality, humanism and common sense. What followed was a series of actions of increased cruelty, arbitrariness and absurdity, which threatened my very extinction.

. . . On March 21st, I informed the procurator that I would resume my hunger-strike if the question regarding the visit with my wife was not be resolved in the near future. . . . The resumption of my hunger-strike would pursue the following purpose: To clarify whether the policy of cruel repression is continuing to exist, which has been directed against Jews wishing to leave the USSR in accordance with Soviet and international law.

. . . Based upon my own experience, cruelty by Soviet authorities regarding repressions against Jews has no limit. If this is to be my fate, I would like to be of assistance to the world public by increasing public awareness and understanding. It is my hope that conditions can be reversed in the USSR after the formation of new leadership.

> I appeal to the world public with the above-mentioned statements, and request that everything possible be done in order to put an end to the shameful and barbarian refusal [denial of emigration]. I appeal for assistance in the reunification with my wife and daughter, from whom I remain separated [which refers to the principle of "reunification of families"]. My crime consisted of having told the truth about the "state of refusal" and the dangers of mass moral destruction. . . . I appeal to the world public for help in preventing another tragedy like the Holocaust. . . . I intend to resume the hunger-strike on April 25th.

Our concern for Yuri's welfare escalated. Enraged leaders around the world listened in horror to Tarnopolsky's bitter account of prison life in Chita after receiving the press release we sent from CASJ. Their response was immediate:

The Committee of Concerned Scientists, which was continuing to monitor the Tarnopolsky case, issued the following press release, following news of Yuri's letter to his wife:

FOR IMMEDIATE RELEASE:
CHEMISTS AT NATIONAL PARLEY REGISTER DISTRESS OVER
COLLEAGUE MALTREATED

> April 13, 1984 . . . The maltreatment of Soviet organic chemist, Yuri Tarnopolsky, necessitating his hospitalization in a forced labor camp, roused the concern of colleagues in St. Louis for the National Meeting of the American Chemical Society, April 8-13. More than 300 chemists signed petitions to Soviet officials, invoking humane considerations in appealing for Tarnopolsky's early release. . . .

A message was drafted by the American Chemical Society and submitted to the procurator general of the USSR, the president of the Soviet Academy of Sciences, the camp commandant at the Chita labor camp, and Soviet Ambassador Anatoly Dobrynin.

A roster of thirty-three chemists, in a variety of specialties including organic, inorganic, physical, electrochemistry, biochemistry and chemical engineering, signed their names to the petitioning letter:

> We, participants at the National Meeting of the American Chemical Society, convening April 8-13 in St. Louis, Missouri, wish to relay our concern for our colleague Dr. Yuri Tarnopolsky, 47 year old organic chemist from Kharkov now serving a three year labor camp sentence. A former emigration activist, Dr. Tarnopolsky has been seeking to emigrate

to Israel for over seven years.

Knowing of Dr. Tarnopolsky's chronic heart and gallbladder conditions, we were particularly distressed to learn that he undertook a hunger strike in February, necessitating his hospitalization within the labor camp. He took this drastic step to protest cancellation of scheduled visits from his wife--punishment for his physical inability to perform the arduous work assigned to him.

In light of his poor health, we ask that Dr. Tarnopolsky be granted early release. At the least, we hope that humanitarian motives will impel you to allow him family visits and assign him work commensurate with his capability.

Amnesty International, which is based in London, responded at once to Yuri's outcry, issuing recommendations that letters be sent to specific Soviet officials. They also expressed concern over the state of Tarnopolsky's health and reports that he had been forced to work beyond his capacity and had been punished for failing to adhere to the strict work load. Amnesty International further requested that Yuri be given work, diet, and medical treatment commensurate with his state of health.

In France, the freedom movement for both Yuri Tarnopolsky and Alexander Paritsky was also gaining momentum. Paritsky was finally released from prison in August 1984. The same year, a committee of prominent French scientists had formed under the name of Comite Youri Tarnopolski. This committee was directed by Dr. Michel Che, from the Universite Pierre et Marie Curie in Paris, and my dear friend Jeannette, who served as executive secretary. They formed a strong front and worked political wonders. Letters and telegrams were sent out weekly to both French and Soviet officials, and all were followed up by telephone. News articles frequently appeared in all major French newspapers and magazines thanks to the effort of the French "machine" overseen by Jeannette Zupan.

Through weekly correspondence and phone calls between Jeannette and me all efforts in France were carefully coordinated with our work in the United States. Any major story released in Paris was automatically wired to the United States and appeared practically simultaneously in our own press. The system also worked in reverse. We were up to date on everything concerning the Tarnopolsky case that was transpiring politically in both the USA and France. As with CASJ, we formed our own think tank by coming up with new approaches to problems and feeding on each other's ideas. Less than a year had passed since the death of Jeannette's son. Though I could feel her pain, she remained steadfast in her effort to rescue our friends. We never spoke about Pierre.

Nancy with Yuri
Tarnopolsky. Kharkov,
May 1982.

Nancy with Jeannette Zupan.
Paris, May 1991.

Annual conference of UCSJ. Alan Dershowitz,
Lynn Singer, unidentified scientist. Poster
of Sharansky. Washington, D.C., October 1980.

Seated: Co-chairmen of Chicago Action for Soviet Jewry (CASJ) Marillyn Tallman and Pamela Cohen, also president of the Union of Councils of Soviet Jews (UCSJ). Standing in the middle is Nancy Rosenfeld. June 1991. Photo by Betty Kahn.

"A SOVIET WEDDING BY PROXY." The proxy wedding of Ellen and David Waksberg on behalf of the Tarnopolskys. Union Square, San Francisco, May 4, 1983. Photo by Jo Fielder.

Tarnopolsky on first day of hunger strike, (top right) October 1, 1982. Final day of hunger strike (left), November 9, 1982. Tarnopolsky family, December 1982.

Moscow demonstration. Fifteen dissidents were arrested. May 17, 1987.

Congressman John Porter at CASJ.
1986. Photo by Peggy Pollard.

Senator Paul Simon calling
Tarnopolsky, October 31, 1986.

CASJ demonstration in Chicago. Activists carrying posters of Ida Nudel and other prisoners of conscience. Circa 1980.

Moscow demonstration. Signs reading "Margaret Thatcher, don't believe the Communists." Winter 1989.

Mayor Harold Washington's office. Phoning to Vienna to welcome Tarnopolsky to freedom (left to right): CASJ activists Ken Ross, Jean Freed, Pamela Cohen, Shmuel Azarkh; Jane Ramsey, director of community relations; Mayor Washington; Robert Mednick (CASJ). Absent from photo is Alderman Martin Oberman. Chicago, February 1987.

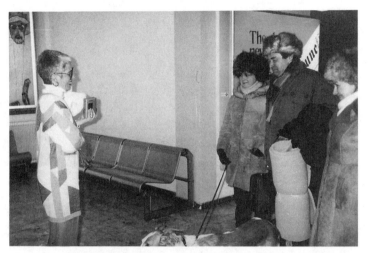

Tarnopolsky family arrives in Vienna, greeted by
Nancy. February 1, 1987.

CSCE Ambassador Warren
Zimmerman calling Mayor
Washington. Tarnopolsky
in background. Vienna,
February 4, 1987.

Mayor Harold Washington
and Yuri Tarnopolsky.
Chicago, March 19, 1987.

Yuri on steps of U.S. Capitol. Washington, D.C., October 1987.

Illinois Congressman John Porter's office. First row (left to right): unidentified woman, Avital Sharansky, Tanya Zunshine. Back row (left to right): Yuri Tarnopolsky, unidentified man, Congressman Porter, Kathryn Porter, and Zachar Zunshine. Washington, D.C., October 1987.

Tarnopolsky addressing CASJ rally in Highland Park, Illinois, for Ari Volvovsky. June 1987.

Avital Sharansky. CASJ office, 1983. Photo by Betty Kahn.

UCSJ delegation meeting with President Askar Akayev of Kyraghyzstan during first Human Rights Conference in Central Asia. Pictured: Abdumanob Pulatov (Uzbek human rights activist kidnapped and arrested during conference), Tursunbek Akhunov (Kyrghyz human rights leader), Micah Naftalin (national director, UCSJ), Valery Abramkin (Moscow Helsinki Group), Ambassador Ed Horwitz, President Askar Akayev, Pamela Cohen (president, UCSJ, and co-chair, CASJ), Leonid Stonov (Human Rights Bureau director). December 1992.

Pamela Cohen seated at her desk at CASJ. Photos of refuseniks and prisoners of conscience line the wall. 1983. Photo by Betty Kahn.

Marillyn Tallman, Congressman John Porter, Pamela Cohen. Highland Park, Illinois, 1983.

(—Let's work to build a prison camp like this example.)

JUNE 1983

This widely distributed Soviet poster describes Jews studying plans of Nazi death camps to be constructed in Lebanon. The word "СiОНi3М" translated into English reads Zionism and the camps listed are Auschwitz, Majdanek, and Buchenwald.

Chicago Action for Soviet Jewry

This flier was distributed by Pamyat during its raid on the liberal Moscow newspaper *Moscovsky Komsomolets* on October 13, 1992.

It will be we who act tomorrow!

Enemy wait!

All pederast sons of Kosomol bitches they will soon snuff out.

J e w i s h   S o d o m y newspaper

NOTE: MK is of the newspaper. No Star of David is around the original.

Masonic Komsomolkikes

Masonic brainwashers

Masonic sons of Komsomobitches- It is the main pederast of Moscow.

Terrible punishment awaits every worker of this paper for synagogue toilets.

Ten thousand postcards with Yuri's photograph, designed by CASJ, were sent out in 1986. Five thousand were addressed to Gorbachev, the other five thousand to Yuri. These cards were widely distributed in the United States, Europe, and Israel and began to flood the post offices in Moscow and Kharkov.

Dear Yuri,

You are always in our thoughts and in our
hearts. We will never stop working for you
until you are free!

We condemn the inhumane treatment to
which you are being subjected. Keep up
your courage. We will keep up our work
on your behalf.

Name _____

Address _____

_____

Dr. Yuri Tarnopolsky
Krasnoznamenny Per. 2
Apt. 17
Kharkov, 310002, USSR

Dear General Secretary Gorbachev:

We ask for immediate emigration visas for
Dr. Yuri Tarnopolsky, his wife and
daughter, whose cases are provided for by
the Helsinki Accords.

Dr. Tarnopolsky's health is failing. The
family's emigration will not only be an
acknowledgement of their legal rights but
a humanitarian gesture.

Name _____

Address _____

_____

Secretary General
    Mikhail Grobachev
The Kremlin
Moscow, RSFSR, USSR

Dear Nancy and Martin,   July 1, 1982

The repercussions of the great event have not ceased yet. Now
I feel deep regrets while remembering all my slips and blunders
and the lack of hospitality, and so on. To be taken by surprise
is not an excuse. But I believe that I will have chance to
improve.
   We are glad to know that your trip has been a success. We
have got this information from our new guests from Bay Area.
We all admire you and are charmed with the brave couple.
I'd like to tell you a lot of things, but I have to restrain
myself in this first postcard.
   I am staying in Kharkov for the summer. I will be happy to
hear from you. Best regards from all your new friends.

                              שלום ולהתראות

       Truly yours   Yury

First postcard from Yuri

Dear Nancy and Martin,

I have come home. I am rather well. My eyesight has suffered most of all. Now I am reading piles of letters including yours. I am unable to find words to express my gratitude for your steady support.

Now I need some time for reconnaissance and adaptation after my 3 year Antarctic explorations. However you should be sure that my will to leave this country is uncompromised.

Give my love to your wonderful sons.

My wife sends you best wishes.

Yuri

March 24, 1986

First postcard from Yuri following his three years in the Gulag

Anatoly Scharansky Public Forum plaque in Lincoln Park. Chicago, 1982.

PART FOUR: THE STRUGGLE ESCALATES

"Don't fear, don't believe, and don't hope. Don't believe words from the outside; believe your own heart. Believe in that meaning which was revealed to you in this life, and hope that you will succeed in guarding it."

Natan Sharansky

Chapter I

ISRAEL REVISITED

Three years had passed since we were last in Israel, and now we were returning for our younger son's bar mitzvah. The date was June 15, 1984. Although we were the same group of seven--Marty, Steve, Rob, my parents, Jane, and me--our lives had changed; the issue of Soviet Jews was in the forefront.

En route to Israel we had a three-hour layover in Paris, where Jeannette met us to map out new strategy for the coming weeks.

Waiting for us in Tel Aviv were the Rozentals: Zigmund, Era, Roman, Blima, and Blima's sister-in-law. How far we had come since our first meeting in Odessa. Then neither Era nor Zigmund had much hope of emigrating. Now, as I looked from one to the other, I saw happiness instead of the despair that I had seen in their eyes two years earlier. Yet they were not completely happy, nor did they feel peace. The family had been broken by the death of Misha shortly after their arrival in Israel. Left behind in the Soviet Union were relatives and friends, many of whom they feared would never be seen again. Now they were starting to rebuild their lives in a strange country with a new language and customs. They were learning to be Jewish. They were "home"--but it would take time.

The following evening we were guests for dinner at their apartment in Rehovot. Marty and I went with the boys, but Mom and Dad remained at the hotel to rest following the long trip from Chicago. Jane stayed with them.

Era met the four of us in front of the building and guided us upstairs to their flat. The apartment, large enough for a family of three, was sparsely furnished with a few pieces brought from Kishinev. The entire family was there to greet us, and Era had prepared a dinner that reminded me of the Russian meals we had sampled, but with the bounty of Israel. Platters of cucumber salad, egg salad, and herring served with onions were passed first, followed by steaming trays of chicken with rice and stuffed cabbage. We spoke about mutual friends left behind and discussed the forthcoming bar mitzvah celebration. Finally Era brought out a variety of cheese for dessert, which we ate along with fresh fruit, ice cream, and Jell-O for the children.

The evening was meaningful for Marty and me, bringing back memories of similar meetings spent with refusenik friends. For Steve and Rob, however, it was painful. They had no such memories, and their youth and privileged life prevented them from sharing my involvement; they felt uncomfortable and bored. The language barrier made communication impossible, so our boys and Roman Rozental sat without speaking, finally fidgeting and giggling with embarrassment.

Our second evening in Tel Aviv was spent with relatives of Alexander Yoffe. We shared photos of Alex's family from Moscow and took additional ones to send to him. Alex's cousin, Shulamit, was working with new immigrants in the process of resettlement, and her husband, Yulna, was employed as an Israeli tour leader.

On the way to Jerusalem we recalled the story of David Marcus, an American Jew who flew to Israel in 1948 during the siege of Jerusalem to help the Jewish state. Through his brilliant engineering feat, the "Burma Road" was quickly constructed. Built with dirt and gravel, it was named after a highway connecting the jungles of Burma with the mountains of China. The new Burma Road bypassed the main artery between Tel Aviv and Jerusalem to bring food and supplies by special convoy to the besieged city.

The faces of Mother and Dad were glowing with joy, and our hearts were bursting with songs of thanks for the blessing of being able to share these moments together once again. From the Pale of Settlement, to Chicago's North Shore . . . to the land of Israel.

As Diaspora Jews from America, we proudly reminisced over our rich heritage. After the birth of the State of Israel on May 14, 1948, David Ben Gurion proclaimed, "The land of Israel is the birthplace of the Jewish people.... The State of Israel will be open to Jewish immigration and for the ingathering of the exiles. . . . We hereby proclaim the State of Israel."

Following the proclamation, the Arabs declared war against the new state, and fifty thousand troops began firing against the Haganah, Israel's infant army. Yet the combined effort of Egypt, Trans-Jordan, Syria, Lebanon, and Iraq proved no match for Israel's nearly forty thousand trained soldiers. Although the Arabs managed to capture the Old City, the Jews held on to their land. On November 30, 1948, an agreement for a cease-fire was signed under the supervision of the United Nations.[1]

After Israel's sweeping Six Day victory in June, 1967, the gates of the Old City of Jerusalem were reopened to Jews, and the barbed wire fences were torn down.

Henry Kissinger, the "miracle man of peace" during the 1970s, engineered shuttle diplomacy in the Middle East, which eventually led to the Camp David Agreement. On September 17, 1978, a pact was signed between Prime Minister Begin, President Sadat, and President Carter.

---

[1]Statistical information regarding the War of Liberation was obtained from *The Course of Modern Jewish History* by Howard Morley Sachar (New York: Dell Publishing, 1977).

On the eve of Shabbat, the day before Rob's bar mitzvah, we returned to the Old City and the Western Wall. Our thoughts and prayers were with our refusenik friends left behind in the Soviet Union. I was grateful, however, to be with my family at this holy shrine. Our life had become complex, but here we were together as we shared these wondrous moments. The boys' ambivalent feelings toward me seemed to melt away. I felt their love, and Marty's too.

As the rabbi opened the ark the next morning, he handed the Torah to my mother, who passed it to Blima, who gave it to me. I in turn handed it down to Rob. "From Russia and generation to generation . . . ," quoted Rabbi Ben Chorin.

The faces of the Rozentals matched the sparkling gleam in the eyes of our family, as Rob began to address the congregation. . . .

"Now that I have finished reciting the Torah and Haftorah portions, my thoughts are focused on Irina Tarnopolsky from the Soviet Union. . . .

"Now that I am thirteen, I want to fulfill my responsibility as a Jew by performing a mitzvot. I have decided to share my bar mitzvah with my friend, Irina, even though she is in the Soviet Union and I am here in Israel.

". . . At the same time I recited my blessings this morning, Irina recited hers in Kharkov, privately with her family, which symbolically united us in a 'twinning ceremony.' . . . Perhaps one day we can meet. Miracles can happen, because my brother's 'twin,' Roman Rozental, from Kishinev, is here with his family today.

"After the ceremony, we are telephoning Kharkov so I can speak with Irina. . . .

"One week ago, my mother, father, brother, grandparents, and aunt left Chicago for Tel Aviv, and the Rozental family met us at the airport. . . . I pray, one day in the future, the Tarnopolsky family will be freed, at last, and be able to immigrate to Israel, which is their dream. To the Tarnopolskys, I say, 'L'shana haba a'bi-y-rushalayim.'"

At the King David Hotel we waited for the call to Kharkov, but it never went through, so we had to go on with the celebration without that contact with the Tarnopolskys. Still, we felt they were with us. Placed on a table in the hotel dining room was a centerpiece with an Israeli flag, an American flag, and a photograph of the Tarnopolsky family. Toasts were made in English, Russian, and Hebrew.

Before we knew it, our visit had come to an end. Aboard El Al once again from Tel Aviv, we kept our eyes glued on Israel until the country was no longer in sight. As with our first "homecoming," we left with our hearts filled with new impressions, and again we had been enriched by experiencing this together as a family.

Like America, Israel was founded by immigrants seeking religious freedom, and it continues to be a haven for Jewish refugees throughout the world, despite the many challenges it faces. Since our first trip to Israel, the Rozentals had arrived here to begin a new life in freedom. We left for home hopeful that we would be reunited with more Soviet Jewish friends on our next visit.

Chapter II

AMERICAN REFUSENIKS AT THE BERLIN WALL

The year 1984 was drawing to a close. Alexander Paritsky had returned to Kharkov after having been released from prison in August, and Yuri Tarnopolsky remained incarcerated after a year and a half. The international rescue machine was still working around the clock.

Preparations were under way for us to make a return trip to the Soviet Union. Marty and I would be bringing in material support, moral support, and detailed news of the rescue effort and hoped to return to the United States with information and requests from three cities: Leningrad, Kharkov, Moscow.

We had been briefed and were packed and ready to go. Then, two weeks before departure, the American Embassy in Moscow delivered the news: our applications for visas had been denied. Although tourists were seldom refused entry, and we had applied for visas as a family since we were planning to take the boys, we were unequivocally refused. No "official" reasons were ever given. Our family received a dubious distinction from the USSR. We became "American refuseniks."

We could not get back into the Soviet Union, and our refusenik friends could not get out.

After waiting a full year before trying again to obtain visas, we hoped to succeed by applying through a third country. Le Comite des Quinze, a Soviet activist group in Paris, arranged for a French tour of Moscow and Leningrad so we would stay clear of the Ukraine. Olga Tarnopolsky was sent a message through tourists about our plans to visit Russia. She had been preparing to meet us in Moscow when the response to our visa application arrived from Paris. The Soviet Embassy contacted the French travel agent, informing him that Marty and I had been refused visas, but Steve and Rob, aged sixteen and thirteen, had been cleared to travel--alone. There was no mistake. The Soviets had seen through the ruse.

Unable to return to Russia, but still insistent on showing our sons "life beyond suburbia," we headed for Germany. En route, we stopped off in London to meet with Rita Eker from the London 35's, an independent Soviet Jewish group affiliated with UCSJ. Tourists from London were waiting to take a small suitcase, which we had carefully prepared, into Kharkov. The case included warm clothes to help sustain our friends for the winter, as well as a few books. We continued on to Paris to meet with Jeannette and Henny Kleiner, the woman who had translated Yuri's poetry from Russian to French for the 1985 publication of his book of poems.

Jeannette had invited Marty, the boys, and me to join her family for dinner. She also invited Henny, who related how her family had fled Hitler and gone to live in Israel and then immigrated to France in 1951. Now retired, she was working full-time with Jeannette on the Tarnopolsky case. As we sat down for dinner, Jeannette brought out one course after another as we struggled to converse in a mixture of English and French, with Steve and Rob trying hard to follow.

What a pleasure it was to have some time to spend with Jeannette. A diminutive woman in her fifties, she bustled with energy, her eyes sparkling with warmth. When she spoke of Yuri, the smile that so often crossed her gentle face gave way to a furrowed brow, and her eyes would get misty. Two years had passed since we first began working together, and the better we came to know one another, the more sharply and instinctively we acted on each other's signals.

All too soon it was time to leave, but the boys and Marty and I would always remember this evening.

To our amazement this pleasant sojourn was followed by another refusal, Soviet style, in Paris. There were two lines between Paris and Berlin, an express train and a local that made every stop between the two capitals. Our family was denied permission to board the express train because it was operated by Intourist, which ran between Paris and Moscow, with a stop in Berlin.

In Germany we were struck by the imposing Berlin Wall separating East from West. Like the Iron Curtain, the wall was impenetrable. Stories of captive East Berliners hurling themselves over the wall or trying to tunnel out stuck vividly in our minds. It was a chilling sensation to view buildings so closely abutting both sides of the wall, dividing freedom from Soviet control. How difficult it must have been to be on the East side, looking at freedom just across the street and yet unattainable. We found the contrast--the West alive, colorful, and full of smiling people, the East drab, monotonous, and grim--so obvious as to be macabre.

That microcosmic representation of the differences between the Eastern and Western worlds was carried even further once we explored some of East Berlin. In an old Jewish neighborhood full of crumbling buildings, for example, we saw a strong similarity to parts of the Soviet Union that we had visited. The local grocery store, crowded with shabbily dressed residents, had little food on the shelves and absolutely no bread. We remembered peasant women in Moscow queuing up to buy a loaf before the supply ran out.

The synagogue was a large old structure, but it was closed. We rang the bell of an adjacent apartment, hoping to find a caretaker. A woman answered, and when we told her we were Juden (Jewish) Americans, she ran to get the keys. She explained that there were only five hundred Jewish families remaining in East Berlin as a result of the Holocaust--little need for the large temple before us.

Our next stop was more difficult for all of us. As we faced the gate at Dachau, we fell silent. We walked the grounds, saw the barracks, the crematoriums, the gas chamber, the guards' watchtowers.

The Holocaust had taken the lives of six million Jews. Had the world learned from the mistakes of the past? Could history repeat itself? Would Soviet Jews be doomed? Would the international rescue effort save them?

As I looked at Marty and then the boys, and saw our sons' young faces grow dim and pale, I knew we could never stop fighting for the release of our friends. I could see that all of us were committed to do our part.

Never again.

Chapter III

RELEASE FROM IMPRISONMENT

"Freedom didn't impress me. Release from the camp was only a change from one camp to another."

$\mathbf{F}$ifteen days before Yuri Tarnopolsky was due to be released from the labor camp, he was returned to a punishment cell without explanation. Psychologically, he was prepared for an extension of his prison term. Nevertheless, because the end of his term was approaching, he refrained from petitioning or asking for release. Since he wanted neither to dignify nor to acknowledge the legality of his punishment, he clarified his position by refusing to put his signature on any paper or legal document. Appealing for money to cover his expenses for the trip home or petitioning for a propiska (residence permit), he felt, would be an admission of guilt. For the same reason, he refused to sign a request for permission to work after his release. He was mentally prepared for anything that could befall him.

The normal procedure for inmates about to be discharged is to allow them to let their hair grow out three months prior to being released. Instead Tarnopolsky's head was shaved just twenty-five days before his expected release. After his return to the punishment cell his head was shaved again "since they couldn't find anything better to punish me with. They couldn't change anything inside of my head, they could only change the outside appearance of my head . . . and so they did."

It is a struggle to maintain one's strength and honor after being wrenched from life and everything meaningful, especially in the face of unrelenting danger: ". . . the meaning of life can be discovered only when you challenge fate and destiny. . . ."[1] Five days before his release, Yuri was freed from the cell. Suffering from inertia and frozen in spirit, he said, "I felt nothing." To his wife and a friend who met him, it appeared as if all blood had been drained from his veins. This friend, a former inmate, had been released earlier. He and Yuri

---

[1]Quoted from Sharansky's book *Fear No Evil.*

would maintain a lifelong friendship, staying in contact even after Yuri's emigration.

"Freedom didn't impress me," said Yuri upon his release. *"Release from the camp was only a change from one camp to another . . . bigger in size, a little more comfortable, but I still felt like a prisoner of the country. . . .* Barbed wires, metal cells, and Chita camp cannot do anything to change my feelings about being free."

March 15, 1986: Tarnopolsky was released from Chita exactly three years from the date of his arrest.

March 28: What do you say to a man who has just spent the last three years of his life in a concentration camp? My heart was pounding with anxiety as I sat, groping for the right words to express my feelings, while waiting for the call to go through. Yuri had been missed. We had all felt the void, and we could never be certain of the state of his health or the severity of the treatment he was receiving. It was a constant worry.

Jumping up as the telephone rang, I nervously grabbed the receiver and was told he was on the line. When he began to speak, the weariness in his voice was painfully audible. His voice lacked color and cadence. I welcomed him home. "How are you feeling, Yuri?" He responded softly, saying he felt ill and was quite weak. He hoped to visit a doctor in Kharkov and then, if necessary, go to Moscow for further tests and treatment.

"Our situation hasn't changed. Everything remains the same as three years ago. The only important thing is to leave the USSR and be free. Nothing else matters except freedom."

I hung up the telephone in tears, relieved to hear his voice but saddened by the dull, listless tone. In three years Yuri had been through hell and back, and his voice reflected it. His position remained the same. Physically he had suffered, but his spirit and resolve to leave the country had not been broken. The Soviet authorities had failed in their attempt to "rehabilitate" him. His soul had remained free.

One week later we spoke again, and this time he sounded stronger. He had recently been informed by the militia that he could be retried if he could not find a job. Nevertheless, in his predicament it was impossible to find a position. He had tried unsuccessfully for several years, and after a stint in the labor camp it would be much more difficult.

"It is hopeless," said Yuri. On the positive side, he had just reapplied that day for an exit permit and was waiting for a reply.

He mentioned the letter he had written two years ago documenting his experiences at Chita. He said it was impossible to relate all the details. "They are shocking. Nevertheless, I think you know what it is like to be imprisoned in a place like Chita. . . ."

He was very worried that his heart had been damaged in the labor camp since for some time he had been experiencing discomfort and shortness of breath. Because he had not yet received the propiska, he was ineligible to be examined by a doctor. "My only goal is to leave this country. I have no legal obstacles and have never dealt with secrets. Hundreds of letters were sent to me at Chita, but I only received four of them. My situation is the same . . . but what are my prospects?"

Misha Berman had joined me for this second call. After speaking with Yuri, Misha sat with his head in his hands. Shaking his head from side to side, he spoke and his voice cracked. "This meant so much to me to hear his voice. He's my friend, and we have missed him so much."

On February 11, Anatoly Sharansky had been released from Chistopol prison following nine years in captivity. The world saw this dramatic liberation on television; we watched Sharansky's plane from Moscow swiftly touch down in East Berlin. Haggard and thin, with ill-fitting clothes, a bewildered Sharansky emerged from the plane clutching his famous book of psalms. He was met by an East German policeman, who pointed to a waiting car and instructed him to walk over at once without any detours. Breathlessly, we watched our television screen as Anatoly Sharansky walked to freedom, from East to West Berlin. Later that day Anatoly was reunited with his wife, Avital, whom he had not seen in twelve years. They were put on a plane and flown to Israel, where he made aliyah.

In a less dramatic but no less important rescue, the well-known activist from Leningrad, Yacov Gorodetsky, had recently arrived in Israel. As political pressure continued to mount, a few others would also be liberated. Yet there was no denying that the road ahead of us would be both treacherous and difficult. To rescue Yuri Tarnopolsky, we still needed a miracle.

The first mail to arrive from Yuri was a postcard dated March 24, 1986. He had not lost his sense of humor:

Dear Nancy and Martin,

I have come home. I am rather well. My eyesight has suffered most of all. Now I am reading piles of letters, including yours. I am unable to find words to express my gratitude for your steady support.

I need some time for reconnaissance and adaptation after my 3 year Antarctic explorations. However, you should be sure that my will to leave this country is uncompromised.

Give my love to your wonderful sons.
My wife sends you best wishes.
     Yuri

One week later, a letter arrived.

Dear Nancy   March 31, 1986

It was wonderful to hear your voice, although the sound was very weak. I came to the conclusion that my ear suffered just like my eyesight. . . .

I should stress that the three years, even in those conditions, were part of my life and not mere existence or stagnation. That hard period has given me a line I am going to follow, connected with scientific reflections. . . .

Three years of confinement had left Yuri starved for material in his field of study, and he felt a strong compulsion to return to his work. His head had amassed a preponderance of ideas during his prison term; he had had endless time to do nothing but think. Now he burned to put his thoughts on paper and continue research. He was searching for a list of the most recent scientific works on pattern theory, by Professor Ulf Grenander of Brown University, which had not been included in his original monograph, *Lectures in Pattern Theory*, Volumes I-III. Yuri had the monograph in Russian translation, but the study, which had been completed after the monograph, was unavailable to him. If he could obtain the list, he would be able to request specific reprints from the professor.

Upon contacting the Applied Mathematics Department at Brown University, I found that Professor Grenander was out of the country on leave, but his secretary, Mrs. Fenseca, promised to send the requested material right away. After the first package failed to reach Yuri, she continued to send packages of the same material until he ultimately received it. Once again the scientific community had stepped in with support, forging another link in the chain connecting Yuri with the West.

On April 11, we spoke to Yuri again. "I feel good, but only to some degree. . . . My worst complaint, right now, is my vision, which has badly deteriorated in three years away. . . . I think that people who left in the seventies don't understand the real situation now, and I have to decide for myself [what's right to do]. I won't sit quietly. . . . During the last three years, I had a lot of time to sort out my feelings and to think. I felt very calm. I understood what I was doing and what I was fighting for. I feel that my chances of obtaining a job right now are zero. I'm not going to beg like a dog; it's up to them to put me in prison if they want. I will only accept a job in my professional field, but I refuse to beg anybody. . . . I'm not going to run around in this circus. If they choose to return me to prison, they may do so, but if they offer me a job in my field, I'll take it. I'm doing what I'm doing and that's it. I don't know if they'll ever let me go, but I maintain my principled position. . . .

"Right now, I'm going to continue with my work and research in my field of science as I have been planning. I think I have discovered a new area in this field, which I'll write about, but it will take some time. . . . I'm also going to write down everything concerning my medical data. My heart seems to be improving since I can run up to the fourth floor during cool weather, but it will be harder in the heat. I'll write down everything, although it could be used against me if I go to prison again. Nevertheless, I need to write it down. . . . I remain very calm. I am not nervous. I always felt that the authorities could have extended my prison term or exiled me afterwards if they wanted."

I realized that the road ahead would be long and arduous, but at least Yuri was out of prison. We could deal with the rest.

In April we contacted his relatives in New York. I spoke with Yuri's cousin, Yelena Rabinovich, who sent a message to Yuri from the family: "We are waiting for you, and we feel in our hearts that you'll be here soon." In a letter, I relayed this message back to Yuri. Yelena gave us the address of his relatives in Israel, and we wrote to them immediately. This was all transmitted back to Kharkov.

An appeal for support was made to Frank Press, president of the National Academy of Sciences in Washington, D.C. Three weeks later we had a reply from his office:

May 7, 1986
Dear Ms. Rosenfeld:

The concern of Chicago Action for Soviet Jewry over the plight of Soviet chemist, Dr. Yuri Tarnopolsky, as expressed in your letter of April 14, is shared by many members of the National Academy of Sciences. Our Committee on Human Rights, which has been given a copy of your letter, undertook Dr. Tarnopolsky's case at the time of his arrest in March, 1983, and has worked on his behalf since then. In consequence, the Committee was aware of Dr. Tarnopolsky's release from labor camp last March and of the danger of his being rearrested on charges of "parasitism." The Committee was pleased to receive your update and to know that Dr. Tarnopolsky has requested scientific literature in his field. Articles and/or journals, of possible interest, will be sent to Dr. Tarnopolsky by the Committee as they become available.

Yours sincerely,
Frank Press
President

On May 9, Rabbi Bronstein spoke with Yuri. ". . . I wanted to have the joy and privilege of speaking a few words to you today. I look forward to meeting you face to face."

"I am looking forward, too," said Yuri, "but there is no hope for that."

"We must keep up our hope, Yuri. As you know, we're working in many directions, and we must keep working on it."

"I understand. Thank you, Rabbi."

"I read your poetry in French translation, and it was very moving and deep and wonderful poetry. The essay you wrote at the end [Description of a Disease], I also had the privilege of reading. . . ."

The day following his talk with the rabbi, Yuri wrote that he had been deeply touched by the conversation. He asked if it were possible for the rabbi to give him his address and permit him to ask some questions. ". . . It is a shame, but I don't know how to address a rabbi. I am not sure that 'Dear Sir' would be in place."

At the end of May, news arrived from Tarnopolsky's cousin in Haifa, Yacov Weissberg. After receiving my second letter on April 30, his wife took a day off from work and went to the Jewish Agency to send Yuri and his family an invitation (a vizov). The Weissbergs had just received a letter from Yuri's cousins in New York and were worried.

Dear Nancy,   May 20, 1986
                               Haifa

. . . They say the Soviet authorities are pressuring Yuri to take a job in a classified and top secret factory. Of course, if he were to take such a job, he would never be allowed to leave Russia. . . .

The Weissbergs hoped our joint efforts would be effective in achieving our mutual goal: freedom for Yuri and his family. They also had received a letter from Jeannette, in which she had enclosed letters of several prominent professors from the Comite Youri Tarnopolski. She urged them to send an invitation to Yuri immediately.

Weekly calls monitoring the situation for Tarnopolsky, his family, and friends continued on schedule, and copies of all taped conversations were sent to Paris for Jeannette's evaluation. The information extracted from these tapes was useful to both of us. Frequently, one or more of Yuri's supporters participated in the calls. Milton Glaser, a retired Chicago area chemist, came several times to speak with him. Milton was responsible for sending Yuri information on the latest developments in the field of continuous chromatography. This field would be significantly important to Yuri in the future.

Before each phone call, we had to do our homework carefully to be sure those calls were productive. After keeping abreast of all news from the Chicago papers as well as *The New York Times* and *The Jerusalem Post*, we had stories to follow up on, letters to write, and daily information to look over. Packets of material continued to arrive from Jeannette each week--newspaper articles from the French papers, political correspondence, and copies of letters from Kharkov. Weekly calls were made to Washington to confer with representatives at the Union of Councils on the latest developments. Frequent communication was maintained with Dorothy Hirsch at the Committee of Concerned Scientists in New York.

At the end of each day I would fall into bed completely drained and exhausted. But I could not sleep. As I tossed and turned, my mind was thousands of miles away. Already I was planning our strategy for the following day.

Each call to Kharkov represented a lifeline to freedom. All available information needed to be transmitted to our friends in the Soviet Union, not only for their ears but also for the eager ones of the ever-present KGB. It was their official duty to monitor phone calls from "subversive Western agents."

This was a game, a stupid one, forced on us by tyrannical Soviet officials. We knew the KGB was listening, and they knew that we knew. Whenever the whole charade seemed absurd I reminded myself that this eavesdropping at least ensured that the KGB knew the world would not forget our friends caught behind the Iron Curtain. Our imprisoned friends would never be isolated as long as we maintained communication. And without the willingness of these dauntless souls to speak out openly against repression, the world would not hear the truth that would move it to act.

As my involvement in the movement deepened in intensity and the heartbeat of our struggle quickened its pace, feelings of inadequacy would return to haunt me as weakness turned into strength. When the task and responsibilities became overwhelming, I thought about Rita in London, who before his release had worked day and night on Sharansky's case and had made him her "mission in life." Ruth Newman in Washington, D.C., had also focused her energy on Sharansky; the Washington Committee for Soviet Jewry had originated an annual Sharansky birthday, anniversary of his arrest, and anniversary of trial vigils at the Soviet Embassy, among other events. Lynn Singer in New York did a yeoman's job working for Sharansky's release. Hinda Cantor and Shirley Pollak in Florida were fighting for Alec Zelichenok, a prisoner of conscience, as were Lillian Hoffman, Rhoda Friedman, and Phyllis Daniels in Colorado. Concurrently, Joyce Gilbert in Houston was working for Anatoly Genis, a long-term refusenik from Moscow; and Judy Patkin and Sheila Galland were involved in Boston with Moscow's Ida Nudel and Alex Yoffe. These women gave meaning to the word *activist*.

In the beginning I had felt somewhat intimidated by both Marillyn and Pam because of their position in the organization. I was the "new kid on the block," and almost immediately I had assumed a role of leadership without having had any prior experience. I looked to them as role models and always stood slightly in awe of their vast knowledge and ability. As time went on, I gained confidence.

Chapter IV

NEW KGB WARNING

"I feel, myself, like a link in the chain that began millennia ago, but I think like a chain, not like a link."

As Yuri began to regain his strength, he plunged into his scientific work with new fervor, intent on making up for lost time. He worked at home without an "official" job or access to a scientific laboratory.

He wrote to Professor Michel Che, chairman of the Comite Youri Tarnopolski in France. The committee had expanded from an initial base of twelve prominent scientists to a growing list of worldwide Nobel laureates. As they mobilized their efforts to help win his release, Yuri appealed to the professor for help in obtaining scientific literature that addressed his wide scope of interests:

1. New trends in solvent extraction of metals
2. Industrial applications of membrane technology in separation
3. Continuous chromatography
4. Origin of life and molecular evolution
5. Artificial intelligence
6. Pattern theory

Professor Rolfe Herber, chairman of the Chemistry Department at Rutgers University, sent Yuri books in advanced organic chemistry in an effort to help support him.

After being absent from Kharkov for three years, Yuri noticed regrettable signs of disintegration among some refuseniks within the community. He wrote:

After long years of the refusal, and without any light at the end of the tunnel, differences between people are coming to the foreground. . . .
There are people here whom I don't want to see and people who don't want to see me.

It is very difficult, if not impossible, to resist the laws of nature. It is unnatural to resist them. But, when the conditions of human existence are totally unnatural, it comes as no surprise, when we see a queer, dubious and mysterious behavior of people, under such conditions, because decent behavior demands great strength to resist one's own nature, to resist the erosion of personality, an entropy increase, as physicists say. . . .

I discovered that a lot of people helped Olga after my arrest and she acquired many friends in several cities here. If we have lost one or two friends, it means that the friendship was not genuine. Nevertheless, they are suffering people who need compassion.

It is not easy to decide if all truth deserves revealing. However, my three years have taught me a lesson; the whole truth is better than a half truth, and a half truth is better than ignorance. Here in the USSR, it is not done to inform a patient of his cancer. As far as I know, the custom is contrary in the USA. It is evident, all the more, that our caring relatives should know our diseases, or the symptoms of the general disease. This is my half truth.

Support for Tarnopolsky was mounting, and new groups were jumping on the bandwagon. Cincinnati Council for Soviet Jews, under the leadership of Sandy Spinner, had been actively working for over a year when Sandy and I began to coordinate our efforts, conferring daily. She was also deeply involved in the Paritsky case.

Yuri held firm to his position, seeing himself as a "link in a chain" in history.

People lived on earth long before me and I hope will live long after me. We know what is good and what is evil, only because of our Lord's commandments. We also use our reason to distinguish good from evil. . . . If there are no people who are willing to sacrifice their physical comfort, well-being, health and even life for what they consider good, then the value of the Good drops like the price of gold, if it can be too easily extracted out of the earth. . . .

There has always been an insolvable paradox. If one wants to be free, how could he sacrifice his freedom . . . ? If one wants to live, how could he sacrifice his life? It makes no sense. However, only in this way can other people, in similar situations, live freely.

Does it mean that I love other people more than myself? No, my wife and my daughter, who are the most dear people to me, suffered from my absence, and I see how much my absence has damaged them. To be intrepid may mean to be cruel, which is why I feel uneasy when I am praised. It is not to my credit, that history and humanity mean so much for me. It is my fate. . . . *I feel, myself, like a link in the chain that began millennia ago, but I think like a chain, not like a link.*

Yuri understood that we all fight our battles in our own way, so in the midst of his struggle to release himself from bondage, he brought to our attention a number of refuseniks unknown to the movement because they had maintained a low profile. Yuri felt these were good, deserving people despite their decision to remain quiet.

By the end of June, the long-secret document, along with an accompanying letter, arrived in the diplomatic pouch.

Dear Nancy,   #6   June 1, 1986
Enclosed are two of my letters, sent to you earlier in a roundabout way, which I have just reproduced from memory. First, the last letter, written on March 16, 1986. . . .

Having failed to change what was inside my head [by shaving it], my tormentors took revenge upon what was on the surface of it.

. . . Both shaven or hairy, my head keeps rejecting all this sinister absurdity, which people, claiming to be civilized, want to nail into it.

My job proposal [offered by the authorities, after his release from prison] was canceled. There was no threat concerning the future. However, I see distant signs of a secret fuss around me. I think something is going to happen. No idea what.

I am sending you, with this letter, a short matter-of-fact description, in Russian, of my three years in prison, reduced to eight pages. I am doing that because I don't know what awaits me tomorrow, and I wish to leave my evidence. It was written in a few hours, but I have no time to edit it. We shall decide later what to do with it.
Love, Yuri

After reading this letter, I was filled with growing admiration and deepening concern. Would this lead to a second arrest? The thought was terrifying for me. I immediately contacted Yury Verlinsky to help translate the document. We then awaited further instructions from Tarnopolsky about what to do with the material.

In the meantime, Yacov Gorodetsky came to the United States from Israel for an extended visit. He wanted to do his part in helping to further the struggle for Soviet Jewish emigration. Working directly with the Union of Councils and CASJ, he moved into our home, taking an active part in the campaign to free Tarnopolsky.

Yuri sent pictures of himself and his family, which were taken in a forest outside Kharkov. He wrote, "I enclose four photographs, taken in the early spring. I am going to make new photos next week. You will see more vegetation in the forest and on my head." As I gazed at the photos, I saw how severely prison life had aged him. There was deep pain in his eyes.

As he began to regain his health, though, both his mood and tone seemed to improve steadily. It was a relief to hear the lightness and sparkle begin returning to his voice.

We too had reasons for optimism. *The New York Times* printed an article about a "step-by-step" easing of U.S. trade restrictions on the USSR that would be considered if Moscow would begin to relax its curbs on Jewish emigration. This proposed policy supported the twelve-year-old Jackson-Vanik Amendment, which would be on the agenda at year end, when the summit convened between Reagan and Gorbachev.

Attention was focused even more strongly on the dissident movement when Yelena Bonner, wife of noted activist Andrei Sakharov, captured the spotlight during her six-month stay in the United States.

The news that 119 Soviet citizens would soon be permitted to join relatives in the United States was described by Senator Paul Simon as "a *small* step forward, but a hopeful sign."

During weekly phone calls to Kharkov, renewed once Yuri was released from prison, we relayed all news events to him and made sure he received accurate quotations from the sources. He continued to report on the ever-changing situation in the city. This close monitoring of events proceeded uninterrupted except for some of the usual delays, jamming, and a few blocked calls. Now Sandy Spinner in Cincinnati was making regular calls as well, and we compared notes. It was comforting having a partner on American soil as well as one in France.

It was also enlightening to have Yuri's perspective on political realities. We maintained close communication with Yuri's relatives from New York, but Yuri made it known that they would have no bearing on his situation. "May I warn you," said Yuri, "against possible groundless hopes that this might enhance our release? . . . It [family connections] is the only right way, in some specific cases, but, I am afraid, this specificity is difficult to understand." For less prominent refuseniks, or Soviet Jews applying for the first time to emigrate, American relatives were a valuable asset, but not for a former prisoner of conscience and outspoken political activists. Tarnopolsky had other relatives living in California, but we were not in touch with them. The point was that continued political pressure at the highest level was our only hope of obtaining freedom for those isolated within the walls of the Ukraine.

Yuri also expressed concern over the possibility of trade advances between our two countries and warned us to be "vigilant." "What I am afraid to prophesy about are the new trade advances, which may lead to an increase in quantity, not in quality, of emigration. It is highly important for this system to intimidate, to punish, to crush and to terrorize those who dared to be people, who didn't want to be mere domestic animals or even a thing. You could take my anxiety as my self-interest. But, believe me, I don't look at the situation from this point of view. I call upon you to be vigilant, and I hope to escape the Cassandra fate."

At the end of June, Tarnopolsky took his family to the country for a needed and well-deserved three-week vacation. They swam in the lake and took long walks. Yuri wrote:

You should have seen Nika, when she first found herself among trees, grass and field flowers with no concrete buildings in sight. My feelings were the same, but I couldn't allow myself to express my joy with the same running, jumping and sniffing around. What we have in common, though, is that we both are not used to barking. . . .

Now, I am working at home, with the same enthusiasm and with apparent progress, but I am still not sure that I am doing anything new. However, after reading a lot of literature in Russian, I am almost sure that it is new. I hope to find the possibility to look through current foreign journals, in this field, in the future. I should tell you, that this work was inspired by Eugene's [Chudnovsky] published theoretical work. You know that every person stores, in his or her head, a huge amount of information. But, at every single moment, we think only about a limited number of things. We can jump from one topic to another, but we are able, as well, to concentrate upon a few topics for a long time. How come? How do ideas come to our mind? This is the question I am trying to answer, and the answer is connected with the general theory of evolution, which is a hot spot, in modern science, and with Eugene's published theoretical work. . . .

Regarding my poetry, I am afraid that someone wished to overprotect me [by not publishing them in Russian]. I myself had only wished when I sent them out of the country several years ago that they would be published in Russian and not perish with me here. If you, Nancy, personally believe in me and trust me, you should share my belief, that these poems will someday take their place in what is written in Russian, because they are a necessary link in a chain of Russian poetry. Time and again, an axe fell down on this chain in this century, as well as the preceding one. I doubt that my poetry is of interest to other nations. I ask you only to present them to Russian publishers in the USA or in Europe, and not to lobby too much.

"We do believe in you," I responded during our next call, "and we shall follow through."

Still unresolved was the issue of what to do with his document, written June 1 and sent through diplomatic channels.

"That letter is constantly on our minds, Yuri," I told him one day in late July. "It is deeply troubling information, and we all ache for you because of your horrifying ordeal. The translation of the material is completely finished now. What would you like us to do with it?"

"You have my permission to go ahead and publish it," he replied.

Everyone concerned was uneasy about those instructions. The last time he had sought publication of a sensitive paper, "Description of a Disease," it had led to his arrest and three years in a labor camp. That experience, our awareness of the possible consequences of such actions, made us exercise extra caution. Marillyn, Pamela, and I conferred. The matter was discussed with the State Department, and we followed their advice to proceed with publication but to do it anonymously.

The plan was conveyed to Yuri on August 6. We told him that we had sent his paper to Washington to be carefully processed and distributed. Yury Verlinsky and Misha Berman had collaborated on the translation, and the material read quite well. We felt that he would be pleased with the new version. Yuri was grateful.

Then he abruptly returned to the issue of the poetry. After receiving a copy of his published book from Jeannette, he was shocked to discover that a major portion of his poems was missing. I too was shocked to learn of the omission. Although the poetry was significantly less important than the document in terms of his freedom, it was of extreme importance to him. As part of his legacy, the poems dramatically depicted notable times in Russian history. I promised that we would try to solve the riddle and would check back with Russian publishers in the United States even though the first attempt at publishing in Russian had failed three years ago. What followed were several frantic calls between France and Chicago to try to resolve the mystery.[1]

The more critical matter of the document was again brought up on August 15. We told Yuri we had been informed by Washington that his paper was being widely circulated--anonymously. Amnesty International had also been apprised of its contents.

"No!" exclaimed Yuri indignantly. "It should *not* have been released

---

[1]A large selection of Yuri's poetry, containing some of his most treasured poems, was never published.

anonymously."

It had been sent unsigned, we explained, because of the consequences of publicity in the past. We knew that he was master of his own fate, but we wanted to be very certain that nothing would happen to him this time. We asked Yuri if he wanted us to resubmit it with his name on it. He emphatically responded that it should be done at once and that we should not overprotect him. He admitted the possibility of being rearrested as a result of the publication, but he was willing to take that chance.

"I have to leave something behind with my name. It is very important. My fate depends upon higher authorities, and if we don't want anything to happen again, we must be more decisive. . . ." Yuri said that the general situation had remained unchanged since three years earlier and that there had been no apparent progress since before his arrest. Therefore, his decision to make a public statement *with* his name was firm.

That conversation left no doubt about how the document was to be handled, and I promised to abide by his wishes.

"Do you have more time?" asked Yuri.

"Of course," I responded.

"I'd like to tell you," he continued, "that what has happened with us here is now a fact of history, but your behavior, the behavior of American Jews, is also a fact of history. It is a very bright and good page in Jewish history. We [Soviet Jews] don't stand alone. This is an historical time. American Jews care very much, not only by their words but by their actions."

We discussed the importance of the next few months. At a meeting in Helsinki between Moscow and Israel, possible concessions and consular exchanges between the two nations were being discussed. In November a Helsinki review meeting that would last several weeks would be held in Geneva, and in December Gorbachev and Reagan would be holding a summit.

After that call I realized the implications of our agreement to republish the document with Yuri's name on it were incalculable. In spite of lingering concern regarding his personal welfare, we finally realized there was no alternative but to abide by his decision. Yuri was obviously aware of the potential consequences. He knew the document would be read by both friend and foe.

We addressed the issue again at the end of August. "Your request has been honored, Yuri. The paper has been recirculated, with your name, in Washington, Paris, London, and Jerusalem. Copies of the revised document were also forwarded to Amnesty International and the Committee of Concerned Scientists. Interest in the contents of the document has been escalating, but I am not at liberty to discuss it with you. Trust us. The material will be presented as evidence at the Helsinki review meeting in Vienna this November, at which time a tribunal will be set up to put the Soviets on trial."

Yuri listened intently before reaffirming his strong belief in his actions, stressing the importance of leaving behind well-documented evidence of a crime.

He related what had happened three days earlier:

"On August 19th, I was summoned to the militia and was told that I would never leave the USSR. They told me that I could be rearrested and put into prison again on the grounds of 'parasitism.' I could be arrested on the street at any time, without warning, and I could be thrown into prison for ten days without trial. This all could be followed by two years' or more imprisonment. I would have little hope of getting out alive after the second time, because now I know the conditions and my state of health. But I'd like to say that if I'm in prison for the second time, I won't write letters to anybody, even to my family. . . . I will maintain complete silence. I would not ask for any meeting with my family. Maybe you think I am very cruel, but this way would be much easier for my wife. It [details of prison] has very grave effects on her, and so it is better for her not to know. . . . For me, this would be a new form of protest. I know that some refuseniks now are leaving the USSR, in Kishinev and Riga . . . it is strange, very strange. I think that we should take it seriously. In my letter #8, you can better understand what this does mean."[2]

After informing us of the new KGB threat, he paused before continuing. "I am now absolutely calm," he said, "and I'm going to wait patiently until the end of the year. . . . I'm doing nothing that could prompt such threats. This was not an *official* warning. Between an official warning and imprisonment, there is a month, according to Soviet law. But they would permit me to be captured, without warning, in the street, and they would throw me into prison for ten days without trial."

Strong and immediate action on our part was crucial if we were to help prevent a new arrest.

For Immediate Release
Dateline - August 22, 1986

TARNOPOLSKY RECEIVES WARNING FROM KGB

Congressmen John Porter and Tom Lantos, co-chairmen of the Congressional Human Rights Caucus, immediately sent Gorbachev a telegram expressing the concern of the United States Congress regarding the life of Tarnopolsky. They pleaded for the chairman's intervention. On August 22 a copy of the telegram and a letter were sent by Porter and Lantos to Soviet Ambassador Yuri Dubinin:

---

[2]Letter #8: "The new trade advances may lead to an increase in quantity, not quality of emigration. . . ."

His Excellency Mikhail Gorbachev
General Secretary of the CPSU Central Committee
The Kremlin, Moscow

Dear General Secretary Gorbachev:

We as Co-Chairmen of the Congressional Human Rights Caucus, representing over 150 Members of Congress, are very concerned about the well-being of Dr. Yuri Tarnopolsky of Kharkov. We are concerned that he is in imminent danger of detainment and arrest and are worried that, having just completed three years in a labor camp, he would not survive an additional term. In the spirit of international cooperation, we urge you to intervene on his behalf to prevent impending imprisonment and to grant him an exit visa. We are monitoring his case closely.

Tom Lantos
John Porter
Co-Chairs, Congressional Human Rights Caucus

The Honorable Yuri Dubinin
Ambassador
Embassy of the USSR
1125 16th Street, NW
Washington, DC 20036

Dear Ambassador Dubinin:

In this time of increased understanding between our countries, when the prospect of a second summit meeting between our two leaders seems to be becoming more of a reality, we are extremely alarmed to find out about severe new threats to the life and well-being of Dr. Yuri Tarnopolsky of Kharkov.

Enclosed is a copy of a telegram sent this afternoon to General Secretary Mikhail Gorbachev regarding Dr. Tarnopolsky. We understand Dr. Tarnopolsky was summoned to the militia August 19, 1986, told that he would never be allowed to emigrate from the Soviet Union and warned that he could be arrested for "parasitism" at any time.

Dr. Tarnopolsky has already served more than three years in prison and labor camps as a result of his request for an exit visa. We ask that you do everything in your power to see that he does not have to spend additional time incarcerated and that he is given immediate permission to emigrate.

We are monitoring this case very closely. Your help in this matter would help strengthen the mutual understanding between our two countries and improve the prospects for world peace.

Tom Lantos   John Porter
Member of Congress   Member of Congress

THE NEW YORK TIMES, SUNDAY, AUGUST 31, 1986:
SOVIET DISSIDENT REPORTS KGB THREAT TO JAIL HIM

Newspapers around the world carried the story of Tarnopolsky's new KGB warning, and scientists from major institutions were solicited for help. Sandy Spinner's assistance had become essential to the rescue effort. She was incredibly resourceful and creative, and we began to collaborate on the drafting of important letters.

August 25, 1986

Dr. Donald Ciappenelli
Director of Chemistry Lab
Harvard University
12 Oxford Street
Cambridge, Massachusetts 02138

Dear Dr. Ciappenelli:

It was a pleasure speaking with you today regarding the case of Dr. Yuri Tarnopolsky, an organic chemist from Kharkov, and we are hoping to gain your help and support so we may be able to save the life of this wonderful, courageous, and intellectually gifted man. We are asking that an invitation be sent from the Chemistry Department of Harvard University, requesting that Dr. Tarnopolsky be granted a visiting fellowship at Harvard for the academic year of 1986-87. . . .

An appointment for Dr. Tarnopolsky is urgent at this time, since he has been recently threatened with prosecution for the charge of "parasitism," a charge which stems from being unemployed. Dr. Tarnopolsky is unable to find professional employment (or any employment) because of his refusenik status and his status of ex-prisoner of conscience. Obtaining a job offer from the West would make it more difficult for the Soviets to legally prosecute him on these charges.

In addition to legal protection an invitation would provide, it would offer tremendous moral support for Dr. Tarnopolsky to know that fellow chemists abroad remember him. In the spirit of collegiality, we urge you to facilitate an appointment for Dr. Tarnopolsky at Harvard. Dr. Tarnopolsky will undoubtedly be unable to accept the offer, but the important thing is that the offer will have been made, and it is an official offer, as far as the Soviet authorities are concerned.

I look forward to hearing from you soon. We hope that you can help us with this case so that the talents of this multi-faceted man will not be lost to the free world.

Sincerely yours,
Nancy Rosenfeld
Chairperson for the Committee to Help Free Tarnopolsky

Similar letters were sent to many colleges and universities. Dr. Ciappenelli, as well as department heads at other prominent institutions, enthusiastically and actively joined the battle for the life of Yuri Tarnopolsky by writing letters and sending telegrams to public officials both in Washington and in Moscow.

All available information was relayed to Yuri during our next call, on August 29, and he had news for us. The militia in Kharkov had promised to find him work, and Yuri's security depended on this type of action.

"Yesterday a militia man, Rachupain, called me on the phone and promised to find me a job. We should not believe any words. I think they are planning the ending, but my security depends upon the policy in general, not on promises of militia in power. I'm not scared. Yesterday's call was the result of worldwide outrage from concerned friends who are supportive of me. I am very grateful to senators, congressmen, and all my friends abroad. My security depends upon political changes, but our present policy is ridiculous. Right now, we should all wait and see."

Paris radio aired a report of Tarnopolsky's new KGB threat and talked about the worsening conditions threatening all Soviet Jews. An account of the broadcast was relayed back to Yuri.

Danger continued to fill the lives of Jews who were trapped in the Soviet Union. There was widespread fear that rioting would break out, which could lead to a new era of deportation and pogroms. Anti-Semitic articles increasingly appeared in *Pravda* and *Izvestia*, while simultaneously anti-Semitic posters were being sold throughout the USSR. Emigration was practically at a standstill.

The Red Army was being used as a punitive measure. Boris Vainerman, from Leningrad, was ordered to report for duty on September 4 and was told that he was being reinducted because he had helped the wife of a prisoner of conscience. Refuseniks were being drafted into the Soviet army, which would make them ineligible for emigration for many years following active duty.

Ex-prisoners were being rearrested, and they were being brutalized and mutilated in the camps. Joseph Berenshtein had his eye put out in prison, and Yuli Edelshtein mysteriously fell and was seriously injured.

At the beginning of September a long letter arrived from Yuri in which he addressed the merits of publishing the document with his name. "Your proposal of anonymity gives me pause," he said. "I see how it is difficult for normal people to get used to an abnormality. Anonymity does not make sense. It does not make sense to hide, to wriggle out, to dodge, to appeal to logic or justice, to resort to roundabout ways. . . ."

On the local front Yuri's case was beginning to attract increasing attention. WBBM radio in Chicago contacted me early on the morning of September 2 to ask if I would agree to be interviewed that morning with Sherman Kaplan. I was given one hour to prepare. During the broadcast I was given full opportunity to explain Tarnopolsky's degenerating circumstances. I reported on the recently released document about Yuri's prison experiences, the new threat of arrest, and the worsening conditions generally affecting all Soviet Jews.

Three days later WGN-TV arrived to interview Yuri during our scheduled call. I found it particularly satisfying to know that the world would be watching a documented broadcast of the KGB telephone game. New York had been informed in advance that the call would be televised and that extra caution was therefore to be taken in dealing with Moscow.

"I'm sorry, dear, but no calls except to Moscow can be put through this morning. The lines are down to all other cities in the Soviet Union," reported the Moscow operator mockingly.

"I cannot believe this," I replied to Miss Winner, our New York telephone supervisor. "It is absolutely incredible."

"I don't believe it either," she replied. "I've been sitting on the circuit myself with the operator, and she just returned to the line to report the problem. The Moscow operator repeated the serial number of our call and said she would continue to hold it, but we can do nothing more than wait for the lines to clear up." A few minutes passed while we waited for information.

"Just a moment, Nancy," said Miss Winner. "The Moscow operator just returned to the line. Yuri's on the phone."

"Yuri!" I screamed.

"Yes. I'm here," said Yuri calmly.

"We're on television, Yuri, in Chicago. Tell us the latest news." I was careful to enunciate each word so Yuri would understand, especially through the usual "interference."

"No news, Nancy. No job, no job proposal. I have no hope to find work. There is no income at all. Now there are new regulations restricting Olga from giving private English lessons."

"I hear you. We have news."

"I'm listening," replied Yuri.

"We are receiving maximum publicity. Last Sunday, *The New York Times* published an article about you in the front section, the Associated Press picked it up, and major newspapers throughout the country and abroad reprinted the story. Tuesday, it was reprinted on page one of the Russian-language newspaper *Novoye Russkoye Slovo*. The Voice of America broadcast news of the article into the Soviet Union over the weekend, and on Tuesday I was interviewed on Chicago radio. Can you hear me?"

"Yes. I hear you perfectly," said Yuri.

"I spoke with Jeannette, and your story was aired last week on Paris radio for twenty minutes. The Comite Scientifique sent Gorbachev telegrams requesting intervention and appealing for your visas, and Henny is going to Israel this month with your poetry to contact an Israeli publisher. Next week the American Chemical Society is meeting in Anaheim, California, and your case is being presented as a test case to create a Human Rights Subcommittee. This action is being spearheaded by Dr. Melvin Pomerantz, a physicist with IBM in New York, and Dr. Tom Spiro, from Princeton University. I spoke with your family in New York, and they read about you in the Russian-language newspaper. They send their love."

"I received a letter from them," Yuri replied.

"Yuri, I would like you to speak with the reporter from WGN News."

"Nancy, one moment. We received the bar mitzvah cassette from Moscow, and you can't imagine how pleased I was. Rob read beautifully from the Torah, and his message was very moving. I am very moved."

"I'm deeply touched, Yura."[3] A short pause followed as I reflected on how Rob's cassette had so affected Yuri that he had interjected a little humanism in the middle of a television broadcast. The cassette had been sent to Moscow with tourists and delivered to Alexander Yoffe. ". . . Here is Christine Negroni, the reporter from WGN News."

"Dr. Tarnopolsky, I would like to ask you how you feel about all the publicity which Mrs. Rosenfeld has just informed you about."

"I would say, truthfully, that I don't look forward to publicity. I'm looking for visas. But I think it was very good."

"Do you think that one will result in the other?" asked Ms. Negroni.

"I don't think there is any connection now. I don't see any change in the policy."

"How do you think you're going to accomplish getting visas?"

"It doesn't depend upon me. I think it depends upon the American position."

"Can you explain that to me?"

---

[3]Yura is the familiar form of the name Yuri.

"I'm afraid it could take too much time to explain. I believe that people in America now understand our situation, and I have nothing to add. Yesterday I received a letter from Senator Howard Metzenbaum, and I feel he understands the situation very clearly."

"Don't you think this might help you?"

"I believe that a better understanding of the general situation confronting Soviet refuseniks is what can help us."

"Can you give me a short explanation about that situation so people in Chicago can understand it?"

"I returned after three years of imprisonment, and I noticed no change in policy. . . . I am not referring to my personal situation; I am referring to the situation of Soviet refuseniks in general."

"What is that situation?"

"The situation is a crime, a catastrophe. . . . I am unable to give you the details over the telephone."

"I was told the Soviet government informed you that you would never be allowed to emigrate."

"Yes, I was told recently that I would never leave the USSR. But I think that *words are one thing and actions quite another.*"

"And so you still have hope?"

"Of course I have hope. . . ."

At the end of the call the cameramen packed up their equipment and prepared to leave, and I expected them to rush out to their next assignment. But instead they stayed to ask questions about Soviet Jews. The reporter, Ms. Negroni, lingered to learn more about Yuri. She had been touched by her conversation with him, and it would be the featured story on the evening news. CNN News rebroadcast the interview throughout the weekend.

So much had transpired since a week earlier, when Yuri had dropped the bomb of his latest KGB warning. Our frenetic around-the-clock efforts reminded me of the period following his arrest. This time we hoped to forestall police action.

Tarnopolsky, however, feared that the televised call would backfire, having the opposite effect from what we had intended. He could, he warned, be cut off from the West, which would mean total isolation. We would no longer have a means of monitoring the situation in Kharkov. We tried to reassure him that high-level publicity was advantageous to the refuseniks' cause and that every measure would be taken to prevent communication from being severed.

The call had been productive. It was good for viewers to witness problems confronted in dealing with Moscow. Information had been transmitted on both sides, and all of it had been recorded by the television cameras. Yuri hated the spotlight, but he trusted our judgment concerning the value of good coverage.

In Paris the Comite Youri Tarnopolski wrote a letter to Anatoly Sharansky on the eve of his visit to France.

September 8, 1986

Dear Anatoly Sharansky,
We are very happy you are coming to Paris, and we trust you will inspire, with a new breath of life, actions of solidarity with the Jews in the USSR.

The colleague for whom we have been multiplying our interventions, Yuri Tarnopolsky, has just been threatened with another arrest. In order to avoid this tragedy, we need every kind of support. We are, once more, requesting that of Mr. Pierre Mauroy, the former Prime Minister and present Mayor of Lille,[4] which is a town associated with Kharkov.

Mr. Pierre Mauroy is expected to attend the meeting of the Presidium on September 11th and is to go to Kharkov next month, within the framework of the "twin cities Lille-Kharkov." He has always replied politely to our requests, and those of the Jewish community, but we are aware of his delicate position. . . .

Could you speak with him on behalf of the refuseniks of Kharkov? No single exit visa has been granted in that town during the last five years, and the militia is exercising absolutely terrifying blackmail. "You will never leave the USSR," they told Yuri Tarnopolsky on August 19th. "You can be rearrested and put into prison again on the grounds of 'parasitism'. . . ."

Intervention, by Mr. Pierre Mauroy, is urgently needed to prevent this, and we are instantly requesting him to act.

One word, to him from you, would make all the difference. Thank you for keeping up the necessary struggle and best wishes.

Sincerely,
Jeannette Zupan, Secretaire Executive

Two days later the *comite* wrote to Gorbachev after sending one hundred protesting telegrams from prominent scientists worldwide:

---

[4]Pierre Mauroy was the prime minister of France from 1983 to 1985.

September 10, 1986

Mr. Mikhail Gorbachev
General Secretary of the Communist Party
The Kremlin
Moscow 103132, USSR

Mr. General Secretary,

We trust the one hundred additional appeals will enable you to realize how greatly worried the scientific community feels about our colleague. We are shocked at the threatening language and attitude of the Kharkov militia, and we are requesting you to put a stop to this hostility by granting exit visas to Yuri Tarnopolsky and to his wife and daughter.

Thanking you in anticipation, we remain,

Yours faithfully,
E. Nakache
Physico-chimiste, France

Copies of that letter were sent to President Francois Mitterand; Jean-Bernard Raimond, minister of foreign affairs; Pierre Mauroy, mayor of Lille; the Committee of Justice for Men of the Academy of Science, Paris; the Soviet Academy of Science; and the ambassador of the USSR, Paris.

While we were preparing for the next call to Kharkov, Peter Shaw, a retired English professor from the State University of New York in Stony Brook, phoned to request a book of Yuri's poetry be sent to him. Professor Shaw had corresponded with Olga for two years during Yuri's imprisonment and had sent several books to Kharkov. He was anxious to be of assistance in the fight to free Tarnopolsky. We sensed his compassion and sensitivity and knew we could count on Peter for advice and support. He offered to help edit manuscripts and to assist us in any other way he could.

At the beginning of the second week in September I had an opportunity to speak alone with Yuri. We were becoming real friends as we struggled toward our mutual goal: his right to emigrate. I noticed a warmth in his voice that I suspected was reserved for those he felt close to. Our conversations had become more natural with time, and suddenly I realized that I was calling Yuri "Yura." Right from the beginning, we had felt a deep affinity for each other. It was something unspoken. A perfect match between two people from two different worlds had been created on an intellectual level. The electricity of that bond became the energy that propelled us throughout the difficult years of the campaign.

As pressures continued to mount, we were both being driven deeper into an obsession with vanquishing our enemy. It was a crazy, chaotic world where people could be driven to the brink of madness by tyrannical powers that threatened life itself. This insanity forced world leaders, politicians, scientists, academicians, and housewives to join forces to save one life. It was idiocy, but there was a method to the madness, and it worked. One life saved led to the rescue of many others. So Yuri and I and all the many other kindred souls united in this battle went on. Through our calls we continued to monitor the general situation in Kharkov and at the same time incessantly reminded the Soviets that the West was watching--closely.

I told Yuri about a long article that had just appeared in *The Jerusalem Post*, entitled "Isolated Life in Kharkov." It depicted their entire situation, beginning with the history of the city dating back to the seventeenth century. The article focused on stories of Yuri and his friends Alexander Paritsky, Eugene Chudnovsky, and David Soloveichik.

As the weeks went by, we were engulfed by the mounting urgency of these contacts. The fight intensified on both sides of the Iron Curtain.

SEPTEMBER 19:

"Go ahead, dear, your party is on the line," said Moscow.

"Another package from Professor Grenander's office was sent registered mail to you yesterday."

"That's very important for me, Nancy. I've been busy with scientific research, and it seems to be going well. I'm working at home from morning until night. For the next couple weeks, it will be difficult for me to write letters because of my work. Please explain this to our mutual friends."

"I understand. I'm glad about your work. I realize how important it is for you. By the way, your letter #11 arrived with the photographs and the drawing by Irina. Irina is beautiful, but the pain in her eyes is apparent. Her drawing of a man with the thin, anguished-looking face appears to be her perception of you during the hunger strike. Am I right?"

"I'm not sure."

"Olga looks exhausted. Is she physically tired or depressed?"

"Both. But there's nothing you can do to help her."

". . . [Foreign Minister Eduard] Shevardnadze arrived in Washington to meet with Shultz today. Soviet Jewry is on the agenda, and your name is on the State Department list."

"I heard that prospects for the summit are bleak."

"That's not correct. We are hopeful. A couple obstacles remain that need to be cleared up before the summit can proceed."

"I know. . . ."

Later I spoke with Yuri's family in New York. "Nancy," said Yelena excitedly, "it felt as if Yuri had entered our living room when we saw his face on

the television screen and listened to the interview."
Congressman Porter wrote again to Ambassador Dubinin:

> Mr. Ambassador, the Soviet Union is a signatory to such documents as the Universal Declaration of Human Rights and the 1975 Helsinki Accords. The right to free emigration is guaranteed under both these documents, therefore I am asking you to use your influence to allow the Tarnopolsky family to emigrate. . . .

SEPTEMBER 26:
"Yuri, a colleague of yours is here who has just returned from West Berlin. One moment."

"This is Jim Snyder,[5] Yuri. I spent last week in Berlin at the IXth International Conference, where many ideas of the kind you worry about were discussed. In addition, we had an opportunity to bring your situation to the attention of the chemists and alert them of the difficulties you've been facing in the Soviet Union. We circulated a petition to the body at large, and not only managed to gain support of a large number of chemists but also the organizers of the symposium. We appealed for your immediate release. People were outraged to learn of your plight."

"Thank you very much. I'm listening."

"We intend to send these documents to President Gorbachev and Ambassador Dubinin. The conference was attended by five hundred scientists from all over the world, including most countries from Western European and a few from Asia, primarily Japan. I understand you are interested in computers."

"Yes, but not in connection with chemistry, because I have no possibility to work and affect policy. I'm interested in the application of computers, in their ability to think. I'm an experimental chemist, so I'm looking for another field to apply my brain, which is why I was interested in them."

Such contacts gave Yuri hope as well as some outside contact in his professional wilderness.

We informed Yuri that Eduard Shevardnadze was still in town, conferring quietly with Secretary of State Shultz, and both men, as well as the president, were optimistic about a new date being set for the summit. Behind-the-scenes negotiations were under way for a new settlement, which was to be reached before Shevardnadze would leave for Canada the following week. The foreign minister struck a positive note at the United Nations when he said, "Encouraging outlines of meaningful agreement have been emerging lately."

OCTOBER 3:

---

[5]Jim Snyder is a senior chemist at G. D. Searle and Company.

"L'Shana Tova [Happy New Year], Yura. As we usher in the new Jewish year, I am surrounded by friends and supporters of yours from North Shore Congregation Israel, who join me in wishing you and your family a happy new year."

"Thank you, Nancy. We wish you the same."

"Rabbi Bronstein has invited me to address the congregation on the morning of Yom Kippur, and I want to bring them closer to you by letting them hear your voice. My speech begins with the first two lines of one of your poems:

When the reveille bell rings my dreams fly away with a cry,
like hunted birds fleeing the autumn branches . . . .

Have you a message for the congregation, Yura?"

"I have strong hope that my family and I will be released, but it is not because there is a shift to humanity, but rather it is due to the determination and understanding of Jews and other people around the world. As my family and I celebrate the new year, we'll be thinking about our friends in America. We will have a modest celebration at home as a family, and we will dip apples in honey with the hope that our lives will be as sweet as the taste of the honey."

"That was wonderful, Yura," I replied softly. "It will be delivered. Now, a little business before you speak with Rabbi Hart. The annual meeting for the Union of Councils was held this week in Washington, and Pamela Cohen was elected president. Sandy conferred with a representative from the Committee on Security and Cooperation in Europe regarding nondelivery of your telegrams (sent following the latest KGB threat), and the matter will be raised at the Helsinki review in Vienna next month. The Union of Councils will be represented next weekend in Iceland for the presummit. How do you feel about it?"

"It is a very important meeting. It seems to me that events are going in the right direction, but I'm afraid to be an optimist. I think that every Jew in his soul is an optimist."

"Perhaps."

"L'Shana Tova, Yuri. It's Rabbi Hart."

"I'm very glad to hear you," responded Yuri.

"All of us in the congregation are thinking of you throughout the High Holy Days."

"Thank you very much, Rabbi," said Yuri in a voice filled with emotion.

". . . We are also very happy and excited that on Yom Kippur, Nancy is going to be addressing the congregation. Everyone present will be informed about your situation, and we hope this new Jewish year brings freedom for you and your family and friends."

"Thank you, Rabbi. This evening my family will be thinking about all of our friends in America as we celebrate Rosh Hashanah. It is important that we are alive, something hard to imagine. . . ."

Saying good-bye was very painful, and we all had tears in our eyes by the end of the call.   Besides Rabbi Hart, three members of the Social Action Committee of the synagogue were present: Cecile Levy, Ed Kooperman, and Pat Nisenholz.   As we sat together in the kitchen of our Deerfield home, we too were dipping apples in honey in celebration of the new year.   We were deeply moved to think that Yuri would soon be doing the same with his family in Kharkov.   It seemed to bring us all closer together.

Representatives of the Union of Councils were in Reykjavik preparing for the presummit; Yuri's name was on a list of refuseniks to be raised with the Soviets.   Soviet Jewry was a major issue on the agenda.   Before President Reagan departed for the meeting he delivered a critical speech: ". . . The ultimate goal of our foreign policy remains the extension of freedom across the world."

OCTOBER 10:

"Hello, Yura?" asked Yury Verlinsky.

"*Da.*"

"*Dobriy vyehchyeer* [good evening]."

"Yura?" responded Tarnopolsky.

"*Da*, Yurochka." He handed me the phone.

"Yura, it's Nancy. Yura? Yura, can you hear me? . . . Oh, damn, they're blocking. Stay on the line, Yura!" I screamed.

Several minutes passed. "Nancy?" replied Yuri.

"Thank God," I replied with relief. "We waited for one hour and fifteen minutes for this call to go through, and then they cut the line. Happy fiftieth birthday!"

"Thank you, Nancy. I'm OK. No need for alarm."

"I spoke with Dr. Harold Friedman, from New York, and Dr. John Endicott at Wayne State University. Both men were pleased to know you received the material. I've been invited to attend a meeting of the American Association for the Advancement of Science this February in Chicago, and they asked me to present your case."

"I'm very glad, Nancy."

"Our friends are already in Reykjavik, preparing for this weekend's meeting. Your name is being raised. Before President Reagan left, he gave a major speech. . . ."

"Yes, I know. I heard the speech on the radio."

I was relieved to know that it had been transmitted since it would certainly be a boost to the refusenik community. "Good!" I replied emphatically. "Today on the Associated Press they said that Soviet officials would give close consideration to the complaints of demonstrators for Soviet Jews. Pam Cohen went on national television to inform the public that we have questions to put to the Soviets regarding Soviet Jews."

"I understand."

"The Soviets are unhappy with our President in Reykjavik. They said we're trying to cause problems, and they've implied we are trying to put a wedge in negotiations. Our representatives, of the UCSJ, held a press conference yesterday in Reykjavik."

"Yes, I know."

"Professor Julian Heicklen [Penn State] wants you to know he has written a review article dedicated to you, which will appear in *Advances of Photochemistry* at the end of 1987."

"Very interesting. Nancy, I have a message from Sasha Paritsky. He was just released from the hospital, but feels he was misdiagnosed and would like to obtain help from Dr. Bernard Lown at Harvard Medical School."

"We'll look into it. Here's Yury. *Minoot, pahzhahloostah* [minute, please], Yura."

When Yury Verlinsky spoke with him, he obtained all the details regarding Paritsky. Yury was also able to speak with his friend Slava Burdein, who had accompanied Tarnopolsky to the post office. The Burdeins, also refuseniks, had been waiting several years for permission to emigrate, and the Verlinskys were sponsoring them as "nearest of kin."

". . . a celebration, in honor of your fiftieth, will be held tonight, and the Verlinskys and Bermans will be here to help wish you a happy birthday."

"I'm very touched," he replied with sincerity.

"We have a cake which says, 'Happy Birthday Yuri,' and we'll send you the photos."

"I'm very glad, Nancy," responded Yuri softly.

"Hello, hello--" beep, beep--"Yura, can you hear me?" No answer. There was a series of continuous beeps on the line, but no voice. The line had been severed.

Yacov Gorodetsky returned to Chicago for an extended visit, and he moved back into our home. Gorodetsky spent every day at Chicago Action, phoning Moscow and Leningrad day and night in an attempt to maintain support and coordinate actions with the UCSJ. All news was then relayed back to the Information Center in Jerusalem. In addition, he continued to offer strong support and considerable time to the Tarnopolsky case.

After having been cut off abruptly during our call to Kharkov last week, we were quite worried when our next call failed to go through after three hours of efforts to place it. It was the first completely blocked phone call since Yuri's return from prison, and we suspected he probably had been waiting at the post office while subjected to harassment from the authorities. Another possibility was that something could have happened to him, and Yasha felt it advisable to contact

Yuri's friend, Professor Yacov Alpert,[6] in Moscow to determine what may have transpired. It was possible to make a direct call to Professor Alpert's apartment, and an emergency call was placed immediately. Gorodetsky spoke with Alpert. We were relieved to learn that Yuri was not in danger and had returned to Kharkov after having spent two days in Moscow with the professor and his wife in honor of Yuri's birthday. He had left in a hurry to return to Kharkov so as not to miss our call. He *had* been there waiting. . . .

Dear Nancy   October 17, 1986   #12

I have finished my work, at last. I have been to Moscow on October 13-16, and, on my birthday I saw off Tanya Bogomolny with her husband and dog. My second goal, during my trip to Moscow, was to read current scientific literature. Now I have a more grounded hope that my work is new. . . . Today we had no call from you. I hope it is mere chance. But, all this is meaningful. . . .

---

[6]Yacov Alpert, a prominent seventy-five-year-old theoretical physicist and former professor of physics and mathematics, had been seeking to emigrate from the Soviet Union for almost twelve years but had been refused repeatedly on the grounds of "secrecy." Since 1980, Yacov had been one of the leading organizers of scientific seminars held in Moscow for refuseniks unable to engage in professional work and research because of their refusenik status.

Chapter V

APPEAL TO GROMYKO

OCTOBER 21:

As I groped in the dark for the ringing phone, I saw the clock face: it was 3:00 a.m. I whispered into the receiver to avoid disturbing Marty. I assumed it was the usual harassment from Moscow, calling at this ungodly hour to verify our scheduled call set for 9:00.

"Hello, dear, on your call to Russia, your party is on the line," mocked the Russian operator.

"My party? No, there must be some mistake. My call is for 9:00," I retorted.

"I'm sorry, dear, but he's on the line now. Go ahead."

"Just a moment, Moscow." I flew out of the room and knocked on Yacov's door.

"Wake up, Yasha, Yuri's on the line. I'm not prepared. I need help."

In an instant, he was at the door. We ran to the phone, and I grabbed my notebook and tape recorder as I picked up the receiver. Out of breath, I began speaking.

"Yurochka?" My voice sounded unnaturally shrill.

"Nancy, I don't know what happened on Friday. I received no telegram, no [official] invitation for the call. I think the call was deliberately prevented."

"I was frantic, Yura. I don't know what happened today either because it's only 3:00 in the morning here in Chicago. But it does seem to be a very clear connection at this hour," I said, laughing.

"Yes, it is clear, but I'm sorry I awoke you," he responded softly.

"It's OK. I'm glad to hear your voice." It was better than no call.

"Nancy, I have a message. On October 17th, I wrote a letter to Gromyko asking him for his assistance in receiving our permission to emigrate. Simultaneously, I also sent a new application to OVIR. I ask you and all of my supporters to give full support and write to Mr. Gromyko, being very insistent, and not to be satisfied until you receive an answer."

"Of course, Yura. It will be done."

"I can read you this letter."

"*Pahzhahloostah* [please], Yura."
"It was written on October 17, 1986, addressed to:

President of the Supreme Soviet
Andrei A. Gromyko
The Kremlin
Moscow 103132
RSFS, USSR

Dear President Gromyko:

For more than seven years I have been waiting for the permission to leave
the USSR in accordance with Soviet and International laws. There is no
legal reason for refusing exit visas for my family and for myself. Because
of my legal reason to emigrate from the USSR, I spent three years in the
labor camp where I was treated with uncivilized cruelty. Now I am
without any job and means for subsistence. However, I am determined to
continue the struggle for my legal rights, and I am ready to face new
repressions.

I ask you for the assistance in restoring my legal rights and granting me
the permission to leave the USSR.

Sincerely,
Yuri Tarnopolsky
Krasnoznamenny Per 2, Apartment 17
Kharkov 310002
USSR

"OK, Yura, I have it. Yura, can you hear me? Yura . . . ?"
The line was cut. Yasha rushed to my side and grabbed the phone.
"Allo, allo," demanded Yasha.
"Are you finished?" quizzed the Moscow operator.
"*Nyet*," responded Yasha. "We've been disconnected."
My heart was racing and my head began to pound as we waited for the
line to be restored. It seemed like hours.
". . . Nancy, it's Yuri. What happened?"
"No idea. They cut the line. Please continue," I stammered.
"When I returned from Moscow on October 16th, I was visited by three
branch officials from Lille, France, and one of them was Jacques Gonnay."
"It must have given you satisfaction, meeting them in Kharkov." I realized
that this incident could have brought us to another turning point.
"Yes, of course."

"I have a letter to read to you from Northwestern University. This one was dated October 13, 1986:

Dear Dr. Tarnopolsky,

I am pleased to let you know that your appointment as Visiting Scholar in the Department of Chemistry for the term January 1, 1987, through December 31, 1987, has been approved by the Vice President for research.

We are delighted that you will be pursuing your research at Northwestern University.

Sincerely yours,
Stephen Bates
Associate Dean

cc: Joseph Lambert, Professor and Chairperson,
         Department of Chemistry

"I am very grateful, Nancy. It is a great pleasure."

"Yasha is here, Yuri. He has just returned from Reykjavik and will give you a firsthand report." Yasha reported news of the presummit in detail.

"Yura, Pamela had an interesting encounter on the plane from Reykjavik. She had an 'unofficial' chance meeting with Ambassador Yuri Dubinin. . . ."

"Yes, I heard about it over the radio on the BBC. They related the conversation in detail but did not mention Pamela's name." I was startled to hear that it had been broadcast.

"Nancy, I want to caution you about calling our apartment. You have the number. Our phone was recently reconnected because my mother, who is living in Siberia, is very ill and it is necessary for her to be able to reach us. Please, use it only in an emergency."

"Of course, we know that. Last week, when our call didn't go through, we were worried that something might have happened, and we phoned Yacov Alpert."

"I know, and that's why I'm mentioning it, because the treatment of refuseniks is all the same. I don't know how long it will be before I am again thrown into prison."

A second prison term was unthinkable. I gathered my thoughts again. "It's outrageous. . . . How was your birthday?"

"There were two celebrations. One in Moscow, and the second one was at home in Kharkov with a couple friends, Eugene and Lev."

"Two celebrations. That's interesting, Yura, because we also celebrated your birthday twice. The first time we had your friends for dinner, there was a birthday cake, and we sang happy birthday. We took wonderful photographs ...

and then I dropped the camera and the film was destroyed."

"Oh no, Nancy."

"Yes," I laughed. "I called everybody back, we reordered the cake, and we sang happy birthday all over again. This time the pictures turned out, and I'm sending them to you."

"I think there is a special meaning. In Russia, when something is broken, they say it is for happiness. Nancy, I miss you as my most dear friend, and now I think it is the right time to meet."

"I feel the same, Yura."

"I have strong hope, but I just don't know when."

"We do too. We're hoping it will be soon, and we're working hard to achieve that goal. You're a treasured and beloved friend."

"Yes, Nancy. We love you, too. . . ."

Being a CASJ volunteer took seven days a week, twenty-four hours a day, fifty-two weeks a year, with almost no time for myself or my family. Two months had passed since Steve had departed for college, and I was barely aware of his absence. My mind was always occupied with Soviet Jewry matters, and I was *never* "free." Although I slept very little, I seldom felt tired, because I was running on nervous energy.

Even when a good night's sleep was possible, I had to rise early and set up the day's schedule. The agenda did not include breakfast, marketing, social outings with friends, household chores, or dinner preparation. Frequently Marty would return home from work to find that no dinner was on the table and I was still working on the case. He would explode. "Where the hell is dinner? I'm sick of this! You spend all your time taking care of Soviet Jews, but you forget you have a family."

Each week I went into the office of CASJ, timing my visits to coincide with weekly staff meetings. In times of crisis I was at Chicago Action on a daily basis, even at ungodly hours. Usually I preferred to work at home, where it was quiet and easier to concentrate. Though close to my family there, I remained in my own world.

Three days later we spoke again.

"We've hardly slept in the last three days, Yura," I commented jovially. "We contacted Erik Mueller at UCLA, and he's sending you two manuscripts, *Daydreaming in Humans and Computers* and *Towards a Computational Theory of Human Daydreaming*."

"Ah, that is absolutely exciting. He is the only scientist who is working close to my field."

"Jeannette wants you to know that the mayor of Lille, Pierre Mauroy, met in Moscow with Geydar Aliyevich Aliyev[1] to request visas for you, Paritsky, and both of your families. The response was rather good."

". . . I believe only action, but nevertheless, this is something new."

"Your letter to Gromyko has been transcribed, and we moved on it at the highest level. I'm going to read another letter, written three days ago, and if anything happens to our connection, stay right there and we'll restore communication."

"OK. I understand."

"The letter is addressed to:

His Excellency Yuri V. Dubinin
Ambassador
Embassy of the USSR
1125 16th Street
Washington, DC 20036

Dear Ambassador Dubinin:

We are enclosing a copy of a letter from Dr. Tarnopolsky, our good friend and colleague. Dr. Tarnopolsky sent this letter to President Andrei A. Gromyko and OVIR on October 17th.

Our esteemed colleague, Dr. Tarnopolsky, has already served three years' hard labor in a prison camp. We feel that it is time that the authorities exceed to his wish to emigrate with his family so that they may be reunited with their relatives in Israel.

In the spirit of brotherhood among colleagues, no matter where they may live, and the brotherhood of men of good will, we urge you to intervene on Dr. Tarnopolsky's behalf.

Very respectfully yours,

Dr. Donald J. Ciappenelli, Ph.D

Dr. Ulf Grenander
Professor of Applied Mathematics
Brown University

---

[1]Aliyev was the first deputy chairman of the Council of Ministers and a full member of the Central Committee, the Politburo, and the Presidium.

Dr. Julien Heicklin
Professor of Chemistry
Pennsylvania State University

Dr. Rolfe Herber
Professor of Chemistry
Rutgers University

Dr. Joseph B. Lambert
Professor and Chairman of Chemistry
Northwestern University

Dr. Melvin Pomerantz
Fellow of American Physical Society

Dr. Thomas G. Spiro
Professor of Chemistry
Princeton University

cc: Secretary General Mikhail Gorbachev
      President Ronald Reagan
      Secretary of State George Shultz
      Admiral John Poindexter

"It is a very good letter," responded Yuri.

"Another letter was addressed to President Reagan on October 21st, and similar ones were mailed to Secretary of State George Shultz, Admiral John Poindexter, and Dr. Bernard Lown. I'll read it:

President Ronald Reagan
The White House
1600 Pennsylvania Avenue
Washington, DC 20500

Dear President Reagan,

We want to bring to your immediate attention the case of Dr. Yuri Tarnopolsky, an organic chemist from Kharkov, who is a long-term refusenik and ex-prisoner of conscience. . . .

Since we have been able to closely monitor Yuri's situation by telephone, we learned of a new threat by the KGB to rearrest and imprison him. . . .

Recently, he sent us a paper, at great personal risk,
which documents his arrest, trial and imprisonment. . . .

We are appealing for your immediate intervention so that Dr. Tarnopolsky
may receive a visa and be allowed to emigrate with his family to Israel.
Due to his impaired health and dangerous situation, we feel it necessary
to act at once on this case.

Respectfully submitted,
Nancy Rosenfeld
Chairperson for the Committee to Help Free Tarnopolsky

"My reaction is that this is also a very fine letter," said Yuri warmly.

"Yura, you requested we contact Dr. Bernard Lown at Harvard Medical
School on behalf of Paritsky. However, since we can only approach Dr. Lown for
one case at a time, we made a decision to approach the American doctor for Sasha
in the future because first we are going to him for you."

"Nancy, all the records regarding Sasha's health are with his brother in
Israel. You can obtain the reports from him."

I was thankful for his approval. "We'll do that. Yura, we are halfway
home. Do you read me?"

"Yes, Nancy. But the general air in Kharkov is one of terror. . . . Marina
Chudnovsky was warned she can be imprisoned because she doesn't work, foreign
tourists were prevented from meeting Kharkov refuseniks just eight days ago . . .
it's just as terrifying as before my arrest almost four years ago."

"I know. This is why we're so closely monitoring."

"I fear something is going to happen . . . I don't know what. There are
other signs, too."

"What other signs, Yura?" I asked with alarm.

"This kind of activity is increasing."

"We'll do everything possible to help from this end, Yura."

"Nancy, I have the impression that you are at the heart of all this activity."

Smiling, I responded, "We are all working together, Yura. We have a big
investment. We want you out, and we want you out now."

"I hope to see you soon, Nancy," Yuri responded softly.

"I hope so, too. . . ."

A postcard with Yuri's picture on the front was designed by CASJ--a
common practice at that time for high-visibility cases. Five thousand of the cards
were addressed to Secretary General Mikhail Gorbachev, another five thousand to
Yuri:

Dear General Secretary Gorbachev:

We ask for immediate emigration visas for Dr. Yuri Tarnopolsky, his wife and daughter, whose cases are provided for by the Helsinki Accords.

Dr. Tarnopolsky's health is failing. The family's emigration will not only be an acknowledgement of their legal rights but a humanitarian gesture.

Dear Yuri,

You are always in our thoughts and in our hearts. We will never stop working for you until you are free!

We condemn the inhumane treatment to which you are being subjected. Keep up your courage. We will keep up our work on your behalf.

After the cards had been distributed among groups and individuals throughout the United States, Europe, and Israel, post offices in Moscow and Kharkov were inundated with postcards. Although Tarnopolsky never received one because they were seized by the authorities, he knew of their existence. Whether they reached his apartment was unimportant; what counted was the flood of cards pouring into the USSR on his behalf.

A long and moving letter was written three days after our last phone call:

Dearest Nancy,   #13   Oct. 27, 1986

I perfectly understand what titanic work you have been doing. It is not only a fight for three captives. We may not be worth such gigantic efforts. This is also a fight for principles of humanity and justice which are vital for the human race. I can categorize this only in secular terms because I have no religious education to judge your activity from the point of view of religious duty. In my heart, I am sure that this is highly Jewish. I am watching this breathtaking fight, not only as its object, but also as an admiring spectator. I myself am not passive, but am constantly thinking about what else might be done.

You are a real treasure from all points of view. I feel sorry taking a part of your attention which you could give to Martin and your sons. May God bless you, and may he give success to both of us. . . .

Shalom! Yuri, Olga, Irene

Chapter VI

DIGGING A TUNNEL

"We are like two people digging a tunnel from two different sides, and I think we will meet in the middle."

OCTOBER 31. SENATOR PAUL SIMON'S OFFICE:
Pamela, Yasha, and I arrived at the senator's office early in the morning to prepare for the call to Kharkov. It would be televised on three major networks.

"Hello, Moscow, this is the United States operator. Will you please ring a number for me in Kharkov?"

"Yes."

"The number at the post office is 310001."

"I want to speak with the Russian," demanded the Moscow operator.

"Allo," said Yasha.

In Russian, he repeated the number of the Kharkov post office, but the Moscow operator denied that such a number existed. Yasha continued to argue with her.

". . . Allo, there is no such number, so don't call back," snapped Moscow. She hung up.

"You must do something," pleaded Yasha with the American operator.

"We know this number is correct because it is the one we use each week to pass your calls to Kharkov. Apparently the operator in Kharkov does not want to help us," responded Miss Winner.

Suddenly the Moscow operator returned to the line. "Go ahead; your party is on the line."

"Yuri, we are calling from Senator Paul Simon's office, and we're on television. I'm putting the senator on the line immediately."

"Dr. Tarnopolsky?"

"Yes, I'm here." Yuri sounded very calm.

"This is Paul Simon. How are you doing?"

"Not badly."

"But we understand you are being threatened with the possibility of being returned to prison. Is that correct?"

"Exactly, and I've had another call from the militia. It was a warning."

"We want you to know that we in the United States are interested. I have contacted the Soviet ambassador and have written to Secretary Gorbachev, and there is interest in your situation and in your plight. We hope that we can get Soviet officials to modify their stand so you and your family can come here."

"Thank you very much for your support. I am very grateful."

"We are grateful for your courage, and we want to help in any way we can. What is your job situation now?"

"I have no job, so I am constantly under the threat of another imprisonment. Nothing has changed in our situation in Kharkov."

"We want you to know we are doing everything on our part to try and be of help, and we'll continue to keep in touch with Soviet officials on this."

"I know that, and I'm continuing with my struggle."

"If at any point you have suggestions of anything we can do, we would appreciate your getting the word across to us."

"I know that, and thank you very much. Many friends have been faithfully helping."

"Thank you, and our very best to you. Here is Nancy," the senator concluded.

"Thank you, Senator Simon," I replied. "Yura, there are other people here who would like to speak with you. I'm putting Pamela on the line."

"This is Pamela Cohen, Yuri. I am kept fully informed about every single move you are making by Nancy. All of us across the United States, our sixty thousand members and thirty-five councils, the United States Congress and Senate, all are fully aware of what is happening in the Soviet Union."

"I must say that your support gives us strength to endure."

"I understand. Next week, when we meet in Vienna, we'll have an office and full delegation. We'll be meeting with the congressional delegation of the United States as well as delegations of other Western countries. We will raise your situation. Would you like to make a statement for the Vienna meeting?"

"I know that Soviet officials now have agreed to discuss the problems of Jewish refuseniks, but I'm afraid that such discussions may last another seven years. *You should believe only actions and not words and not promises and some discussions*," said Yuri.

"You're right, Yuri, and that is our position. When I met with the Soviet ambassador, I gave him this message:

We are happy with the efforts on the part of the Soviets, but rhetoric and language alone will be insufficient for us, if we are to proceed with any kind of bilateral support.

"This is the message we are bringing to the Soviets, as well as to the countries of the free world. We further understand that a case-by-case approach, by liberating one prisoner or one or two families, is no evidence of any real change in Soviet policy. We won't settle for a few token releases. We're all with you, Yuri, and we'll do our best."

"Thank you, Pamela. You seem to have a good understanding of the problem."

"Did you hear the press conference in Moscow?"

"No."

"The Soviets said there was no problem with emigration or human rights. Unfortunately, we have evidence to the contrary. The American delegation and American Congress know the real situation."

"Yes, I know that American congressmen are aware of our condition. I can judge by letters I have received from senators."

"We wish you well, Yuri, and we're with you. Yasha Gorodetsky is here. One moment."

"Thank you, Pamela."

"Hello, it's Yacov. You have heard everything, and I know you understand the strong support you are receiving from Senator Simon. I wish you good luck and hope to see you soon. Since I'm leaving for Toronto, I'm going to put Nancy back on the phone."

"Yuri, Yasha was scheduled to speak in Toronto this morning, but he changed his plans to be with us at the senator's office. Congressman John Porter, who had also hoped to be here, asked me to tell you that he recently wrote again to Ambassador Dubinin requesting the ambassador's influence in helping to secure visas for you and your family."

"I am very glad, Nancy. Now the only thing we need is to be able to look each other in the eye. Nothing could be compared with that."

Grinning, I replied, "I agree. Yuri, I have a telegram, which was sent yesterday by Senator Simon to Gorbachev. It was handed to Ambassador Dubinin at the Soviet Embassy in Washington:

> I am aware that Soviet officials are building a fabricated case against Yuri Tarnopolsky to re-sentence him to prison. Due to the impaired health of Mr. Tarnopolsky, I urge you to act immediately to cease the threat of prison and grant him and his family permission to emigrate to Israel."

"Nancy, there is no great difference for me between imprisonment and life in the refusal."

"We all understand that, Yura. Frankly, I hope it won't be too long before you are free, because I can tell you that patience is *not* one of my greatest virtues."

He laughed. "So, you are like me. I think, Nancy, that in this situation, only impatient and persistent people can win."

"Since we are both persistent and impatient, we shall triumph. We just won't take no for an answer."

"*. . . We are like two people digging a tunnel from two different sides, and I think we will meet in the middle.*"

"Dig a little faster."

"I'll try. . . ."

When Pamela and I left the office, we felt bolstered by the support from the senator, and we knew it would have a similar effect on Yuri. He also knew that his message would soon be aired to the delegates at the Helsinki review in Vienna.

It was fortunate that Yasha had changed his plans to be with us, because without his assistance the call might have been aborted. Once again the nation had been a witness. Personally, I felt the bonds of friendship deepening as we persisted in trying to dig out of a long, dark tunnel.

A feeling of electricity was in the air; there was definite movement. Political support was increasing at the highest level, and Yuri was digging aggressively. With the driving force of our freedom struggle, which was fanning out in all directions, we realized the need for legal counsel. The activists unanimously agreed to solicit the aid of Professor Irwin Cotler, a prominent international attorney from McGill University in Montreal, Canada. Professor Cotler, who was well versed in the cause of Soviet Jewry, worked closely with Chicago Action and the Union of Councils. He had represented Anatoly Sharansky, and he was the counselor for the American delegation in Vienna. We contacted him upon his return to Canada from Vienna.

Professor Cotler was familiar with the Tarnopolsky case and requested Yuri's portfolio. He phoned immediately after receiving the material. "It's a very interesting case," said Cotler. "I'll be happy to represent him as legal counsel. The fact that Yuri was arrested on the sixth anniversary of Anatoly Sharansky's arrest is something not to be taken lightly." Professor Cotler would be meeting with Yasha Gorodetsky that evening and would confer with him in detail.

NOVEMBER 7:

". . . Your message was delivered in Vienna this week. Several former refuseniks were there: Slepak, Brodsky, Ida Nudel's sister, Lana Friedman, and the Bogomolnys[1] . . . . The Union of Councils is holding their first press conference today with divided family members, and the Bogomolnys were there until yesterday, when they left for New York. I spoke with Tanya last night, and she wanted you to know that everything went well. She talked with a lot of

---

[1]Long-term refuseniks Tanya and Benjamin Bogomolny had just arrived from Moscow, where Yuri had seen them off at the airport. As of 1986, Benjamin was the longest-term refusenik and was noted in the *Guinness Book of World Records* as the "most patient refusenik." Tanya, a cancer patient, in April of 1986 was the founder of the Refusenik Cancer Patient Group. This group, which was based in Moscow, served as a vehicle to help expedite visas for cancer patients.

people about your case, including Professor Cotler. She and Benjamin will be arriving in San Francisco tomorrow, where they plan to live, since Tanya's family is in California."

"This is very interesting, Nancy."

"I'll be speaking with Tanya tomorrow. Do you have any messages for her?"

"I wish her good health, and I wish her to *use her strong arm*. Do you understand me?"

"Of course."

"Tell her not to forget us. I remained with them those very last minutes before their departure, and I followed them with my eyes as they left."

"Tanya told me your freedom is her priority. It is also the priority of your other friends, who feel that you should be next to receive a visa."

"You have told me something very important, Nancy. How is Tanya feeling?"

"I don't know. I was going to ask you that question. How did she appear when you saw her in Moscow that last day?"

"She did not look well, but she had very strong hope of avoiding further recurrences of the cancer."

"She told me how much it meant to her that you accompanied them to the airport."

"Tanya speaks English perfectly and could be of great help to other refuseniks."

"I know that. Yasha is flying to New York this morning to meet with Tanya, and then he'll return to us in Chicago for two to three more weeks."

"Could you tell me the results of the American election?"

"The most active supporters of Soviet Jews retained seats in office. . . . Another important issue: we have been advised to seek legal counsel for advice and guidance, and the man we have chosen is one with tremendous experience in this area. I'll tell you more about it later."

"When I hear anything about the discussion of law, I have strong doubts, because law does not exist. There is no justice."

"I know, but this person is fully aware and has handled some prominent cases. We are hopeful."

"This is very different. It is the first time you have chosen this way."

"It's because we are not leaving a stone unturned, Yura. . . . Early next week there will be things waiting for you in Moscow from Paris. Check on Monday."

"Thank you, Nancy."

"Regarding your struggle, Yura. You see yourself as a 'link in the total chain,' and you inquired about my position. I see myself the same way because I am just one of many people involved with your case. Your struggle, like many others, is being carried out on an international level involving friends, politicians, academia, and the media. It is being carried out at the highest level, and I represent just one small part of this operation. Can you hear me?"

"Yes, with great attention. I understand, Nancy."

"At the same time, Yura, I wouldn't feel the impatience and I wouldn't be so insistent if it weren't for the strength of our bond."

"I know, Nancy," he replied pensively.

"Is there anything else you'd like to ask or tell us, Yura?"

"No, Nancy, there is no news. Our life is monotonous, and yet we are not depressed. My work keeps me going."

"We're all working hard and are constantly busy. We shall not rest until you are home free. Keep on digging that tunnel, and we'll work as hard as we can from this end."

"I promise. I'm thinking of a new tool for digging, but I don't want to use dynamite."

"So are we, and I feel we're getting closer to the middle of that tunnel. . . ."

Dearest Nancy,   #14   November 6, 1986

This week has been rich of mail. I have before my eyes 19 staggering photos and the letters up to #27, and also the birthday napkin, the invitation from Northwestern University as well as your Yom Kippur speech from North Shore Congregation Israel. . . . The photos gave me the full effect of my presence in your house at my own birthday party. I am delighted to also see your parents in the photos. It seems to me that all these wonderful and kind people, in the photos, have been my good friends or relatives for a long time. The most amazing thing is that with some of them, including you, I once spoke face-to-face. Nancy, you outshine everything, even the fire of the candles.

What I am thinking about more and more is what drives people, like you, to help people like us; to spend your time, energy, and money; to jump up in the middle of the night, when the phone rings, to bother with the gloomy, sleepy, heartless boss of the animal farm (and he doesn't budge); to have a repeat performance of a birthday celebration, in order to send photographs (and they are worth all the troubles). . . . This passion and warmth could melt down the Antarctic ice, and it certainly melts down all the layers of ice deposited in our hearts. . . .

How incredible it seemed that our chance meeting of so long ago could result in an international rescue and a meaningful relationship. When I finished reading, there were tears in my eyes.

On November 10, Senator Edward Kennedy wrote a letter to Gorbachev on behalf of Tarnopolsky.

Dear Secretary General Gorbachev:

I am writing to express my profound concern and interest on behalf of Dr. Yuri Tarnopolsky of Kharkov. As you know, I have only spoken out on a select number of Jewish refusenik cases, and I believe this to be one of equal importance. . . .

I appreciate your responsiveness to my request. The freedom of the Tarnopolsky family would help to prove the sincerity of your government's hope for peace between our nations as expressed in Reykjavik.

Sincerely,

Edward M. Kennedy
United States Senator

A large crowd of well-wishers was waiting at the airport to greet the Bogomolnys when they arrived in San Francisco. During a press conference held at the airport, Tanya reported that their reception was "as warm as the weather." Yuri was relieved to learn that Tanya was feeling better and was anxious to get to work. Tanya understood Yuri's message that he wanted her to use her strong arm. She had been politically active in Moscow on behalf of refusenik cancer patients, and she was anxious to remain active in the United States. She wanted to continue her work by helping these refuseniks receive permission to emigrate, and she was also eager to help close friends like Tarnopolsky. With her command of English, she could be a powerful spokesperson.

The Vienna meeting, adjourned until January, emphasized the Soviets' position versus reality. The United States delegation, which was headed by Lynn Singer, former president of the UCSJ, received good press coverage, and CSCE Ambassador Warren Zimmerman lambasted the dual policy of the Soviets. Western nations would not be fooled by what the Soviets were proclaiming, and the world would not ignore the issue of Soviet Jewry. A long fight was envisioned.

The 55th Annual General Assembly Meeting of the Jewish Federation met in Chicago, and four thousand leaders from all over the country arrived to hold symposia. A Soviet Jewry rally was held during the week, and several thousand marchers joined in solidarity with Soviet Jews to send a clear message to the USSR: "Now is the time to grant exit visas to all refuseniks and prisoners of conscience." Speakers at the rally included Mayor Harold Washington, Pamela Cohen, Israeli Prime Minister Shimon Peres, and Alexander Kushner, a recent emigre from Odessa.

A special meeting was held in support of Tarnopolsky, and members of the Russian Jewish community in Chicago came out to attend. Yasha Gorodetsky was the featured speaker, and he delivered a message from Yuri:

> Such things as arms control and regional conflicts, they are very complex and intricate things needing much discussion, conferences, etc. But, the question of human rights, and especially Jewish emigration, is as clear as day. There is no room for any discussions because there are documents at the United Nations and there is a Declaration on Human Rights, etc. Any discussion can only detract from the attention to our plight.

"Your message was delivered," I informed Yuri. "Remember that we are no further away than a telephone call, and you can always reach us by calling collect."

Tarnopolsky's mood, reflecting hope and caution, was revealed through letters as well as his through his tone of voice. His many followers searched for ways of demonstrating their love and support. They returned this message: "*Just remember that there are NO walls high enough to keep out the concern and the love of ALL of your friends all over the world.*"

"Keep digging that tunnel," I added. "Continue your internal letters (like the one to Gromyko) and look for new tools. We are maintaining a positive mental attitude supported by hard work, persistence and impatience, and the efforts of many talented and important people who have joined forces in support of your struggle. *We shall succeed!*"

> Dear Nancy,	#15	November 15, 1986
>
> I am writing you the next day after the call. I feel more and more delighted and satisfied that I have found in you not only a distant supporter, well-wisher and benefactor, but also a close friend, sympathizer, companion and comrade in common work. You are a friend as close as you are geographically distant. . . . It took some time to realize that I have been favored such a rare gift of God as real friendship. . . .

Preparations were being made for a major press conference that would be televised from San Francisco, including a call to Yuri, on November 21, and I was planning to stay with the Bogomolnys. Before I left for the West Coast, CASJ decided to approach a second international attorney, giving us a stronger base of support and counsel. Before drafting a letter to Professor Alan Dershowitz, Sandy Spinner reminded me to emphasize the Bogomolnys since Dershowitz was familiar with their case.

November 17, 1986

Professor Alan Dershowitz
Harvard Law school
Cambridge, Massachusetts 02138

Dear Professor Dershowitz,

We want to bring to your immediate attention the case of Dr. Yuri
Tarnopolsky. . . . We understand that Professor Cotler has already spoken
to you about Yuri, and, as you know, has agreed to represent him as legal
counsel. We know you are inundated with similar requests, and we are
reluctant to impose upon you. However, since Tarnopolsky's situation has
become desperate, we are hoping to gain your help and support on this
case. . . .

I am leaving for San Francisco on Thursday and will be spending the
week-end with Tanya and Benjamin Bogomolny, who are close friends of
the Tarnopolsky family. Tarnopolsky accompanied the Bogomolnys to the
airport in Moscow on October 14th, and they are eager to join the
campaign to help free their friends. Tanya and Benjamin will be joining
David Waksberg and me this Friday with our weekly telephone call to
Yuri, and we are hoping to have good press coverage. We are further
expecting to be joined by Senators Cranston and Wilson.

We feel this case has gained tremendous momentum over the last few
months, due to the increasingly dangerous situation in which Tarnopolsky
finds himself. We are appealing for your immediate support because we
feel your help would be most valuable. . . .   Through the strong
international campaign on Tarnopolsky's behalf, and by his high degree of
visibility, we are hoping he and his family may soon receive visas to
immigrate to Israel. Yuri could never survive another prison sentence!

I look forward to speaking with you Wednesday before my departure for
California.

Very truly yours,
Nancy Rosenfeld
Chairperson for the Committee to Help Free Tarnopolsky

A letter from the State Department arrived expressing concern over the
latest threats to reimprison Dr. Tarnopolsky. It pledged its support and declared
that the Department of State would "continue to press the Soviets to honor their

human rights commitments under the Helsinki Final Act and other agreements. Human rights and Soviet Jewish emigration will remain an issue of the highest priority to the U.S. government."

Chapter VII

SAN FRANCISCO

"When the cannons are speaking, the muses are silent."

I was greeted by Tanya and Benjamin at the apartment building of Tanya's sister, where they were all staying together. Barely two weeks had passed since their arrival from Vienna, and both appeared exhausted, the strain clearly visible on their faces. "It's doctors in the morning and reporters in the afternoon," said Tanya. Yuri had been right; she did not look well. Her concern about the cancer was somewhat alleviated due only to the knowledge that she would be receiving good medical attention in the United States.

The night before the press conference, I could not sleep well. I had stayed up late working on notes for the early-morning call. It had been set for 7:00 in the morning--9:00 Chicago time--to avoid tipping off the Moscow operator to any change in our regularly scheduled Friday call. As far as she knew, it would be originating from Chicago, not San Francisco.

At 1:00 a.m. I managed to crawl into bed, but by 3:00 I realized I was no longer alone. Tanya's dog, Moonie, had jumped into bed with me. Too groggy to care, and filled with anticipation as the minutes ticked away, I dozed off for another few hours.

Reporters began streaming into the building at 6:30, and soon the apartment was filled to capacity. The phone began to ring at exactly 7:00.

"Go ahead, Nancy," said Miss Winner. "I have Yuri on the line."

". . . I'm in San Francisco, Yuri, and we're on television and radio. I'm with David Waksberg and the Bogomolnys. A lot of people are here from the press: television, radio, and newspaper reporters. Can you hear me?"

"Yes, Nancy, I'm listening."

"First, I want to tell you that Professor Irwin Cotler, from McGill University in Montreal, Canada, will be representing your case as legal counsel. He was Sharansky's attorney. Professor Cotler will be leading a massive international effort on your behalf, which he has already begun as of last weekend while attending a symposium on human rights at Harvard University. He has also raised your case at Columbia University in New York and will be working very hard on your behalf."

"I have some news for Professor Cotler, Nancy. Tell him I was refused again today."

"I hear you, Yura. Tanya's sitting next to me and wants to speak with you right away."

"I'm very glad."

"Yurochka, it's Tanya. I'm all right. Other people are in the Soviet Union, so I should feel well, you see? I must."

"I'm very happy to hear you, Tanya. I understand. I received another refusal, but it made no impression upon me."

"Yuri, it's David. We have a big campaign for you, and I hope and pray it will have success."

"Yes, I hope too."

"The KGB has taken steps to keep us apart, Yuri, but it doesn't matter, because one way or another we will remain in contact," continued David. "We don't stop for a minute. Nancy has been such a leader and is doing everything."

"Yes, I know that. She is a wonderful woman."

"I speak to Nancy every week, Yuri, because she calls me in an effort to keep us informed."

"She is a miracle," replied Yuri.

"Yes, and another miracle occurred with the arrival of Tanya and Benji."

"Ah, yes," exclaimed Yuri.

"The first thing Tanya and Benji told me when they arrived was 'Now we must get Yuri and Olga.'"

"I'm very grateful to all of you, and also for arranging this call."

"Yuri, do you have a message for the reporters who are here today? Or, if they have any questions, would you be prepared to answer them?"

"Yes, I'll try my best, although I'm not prepared. I regard, as the first priority, the freeing of all political prisoners. I've heard that representatives of the West German party, who recently traveled to the Soviet Union, arrived at an agreement in Moscow when they addressed the Soviet government on the issue of human rights. *I consider human rights as important as fresh air, pure water, and the absence of pollution.*"

"Yuri, a reporter from ABC News asked what you think about the Daniloff affair[1] and the release of Daniloff, Orlov, and David Goldfarb. . . . Do you believe it will help your situation and that of others?"

---

[1]On August 31, 1986, Nicholas Daniloff, Moscow correspondent for *US News and World Report*, was arrested by KGB and charged with espionage. Daniloff's arrest was in retaliation for the capture of suspected Soviet spy Gennadi Zakharov, who had been working in New York at the United Nations. He, too, was charged with espionage. He was later released along with other Soviet dissidents, including Yuri Orlov. This affair touched off a series of expulsions involving both American and Soviet diplomats.

"I think the presence of such people in the world may help us, because they can reveal the truth about our situation. Nevertheless, it was an isolated episode, unconnected with the whole issue."

"A reporter from the *Jewish Bulletin* wants to know what you think will happen next, what is happening now, and what will be happening in the future."

"I am afraid that the answer is *nothing*. . . . Do you understand me?"

"Yes. A TV reporter asked if you believe the Daniloff situation can hurt your case and that of others."

"No, by no means."

"We have a question: if you are spending more time on science or poetry?"

"There is a proverb: *When the cannons are speaking, the muses are silent.* It is not the time for poetry. I am unable to write, but I have been concentrating on scientific work."

"A reporter wishes to know the conditions of your life in Kharkov now and the activities of the KGB."

"I could quote the conditions as 'stagnation,' but the KGB doesn't bother me. Now they don't harass me."

"All the reporters want to know why you wish to leave the USSR."

"Because my personal experience has demonstrated that it is very dangerous for me to live in this country."

"Thank you, Yuri," replied David. "I'm going to put Tanya back on the phone."

"Yuri, it is very difficult for reporters and the public at large to understand our situation. It is impossible for them to grasp how you are being harassed, how the KGB has its heels after you, and how you are living in a sort of railway station all your life. Am I right, Yuri?"

"Thank you, Tanya. It is absolutely correct. I am under constant threat of a second imprisonment."

"If that happens, we'll lose a poet and a very capable scientist. Yuri is writing an original book, which he began in prison and is finishing in Kharkov."

"I have sent my work to Nancy," responded Yuri.

"Thank you, Yuri. I'll put Nancy back on."

"We're coming to the end of the call, Yura," I responded. "*Remember, we shall never run short of impatience, so keep digging that tunnel. We are hoping to see the light at the end of the tunnel very soon.*"

"I hope so too, but I'm afraid to use dynamite because I don't want to blow myself up."

"No! We must dig carefully."

"But, I'm not passive, Nancy. Regarding internal letters, like the one to Gromyko, I received my answer today in the form of another refusal."

"I understand, but that only makes us work harder."

"Nancy, I recently advised you to read the book *The Oppermans* by

Feuchtwanger. I read this book in a prison cell in Sverdlovsk, and I saw a very close parallel to my situation. I identified with the main character of the book. It is a close description of my own fate."

"I read it. However, Martin Kruger was a success only after he died, since his work was not recognized until after his death. You should understand that we are not interested in your postmortem."

"Of course, but there is a very important message."

"I know. . . ."

". . . Don't forget *The Oppermans*. . . ."

The press conference was a major event in California, broadcast on every television and radio station and covered in several leading newspapers. Voice of America transmitted the news coverage back into the Soviet Union a few days later. There was a feeling, shared by many at the time, that this event would have a significant impact on Tarnopolsky's case.

His last message to me, "Don't forget *The Oppermans*," was reverberating in my ears. Of course I understood. To be successful in moving against injustice and evil, we needed to employ our professional tools while maintaining a personal commitment. At the same time, it was important to Yuri that he leave something valuable behind. To achieve that end, he would stop at nothing. He was, as he had said, only a "link in the total chain."

Chapter VIII

DELHI DECLARATION

"I have just used dynamite, and I expect reprisals."

I had just completed my November 28 call to Yuri, and he had indeed dropped a bomb--one whose aftershocks I was still feeling as I reviewed our conversation. The call had begun with my relating significantly good news to Yuri:

"I spoke with Professor Alan Dershowitz at Harvard University, and he feels you have a powerful case. He asked me to tell you that he will be happy to represent you as legal counsel and will work in tandem with Professor Irwin Cotler from Montreal. These two men worked synergistically on the Sharansky case."

"It sounds good. Now, I have a statement concerning the *Delhi Declaration*--" There were several clicks, then the line went dead.

"Yura . . . Yura!" I screamed. "I can't hear you." There was no sound-- then the dial tone. Frantically I dialed the international operator. Moments later Yuri was back on the line.

"I don't know what happened, Nancy, but let's continue:

The *Delhi Declaration* has called for a nonviolent world. However, in my opinion, the seven-year-long refusal for Soviet Jews to emigrate contradicts this declaration. I denounce the refusal as a manifestation of violence, hate, and injustice because it increases distrust between people. As one of many Jewish victims of the violence of Soviet authorities, I appeal to all the Jewish adherents of nonviolence and all people of goodwill who support justice and tolerance, including Mr. Gandhi, in order to ask the Soviet government to back this excellent declaration by immediate action.

"After I'm arrested, it will be too late to raise Cain. It will be useless. I'm giving you a rare opportunity, and everything depends upon you and upon our friends. This is the only way to eliminate the refusals. Without new sacrifices, I believe it will be impossible. That's all." For a moment, the line that connected our distant worlds was silent.

"That's a powerful statement, Yuri," I said hesitantly. "I'm scared, but we shall deliver your message immediately. You can rely upon our doing everything possible to make certain your statement is publicly aired and has wide circulation."

"Thank you, Nancy. I don't expect miracles."

I, on the other hand, didn't know what to expect. I knew that just a week ago Yuri had said his intention was not to blow himself up. Since then he had changed his mind. Now he was voluntarily putting his life on the line, for himself as well as others, to attain freedom. He was desperate, and it was obvious there wasn't a moment to waste.

CASJ immediately made calls to Montreal and Boston: "I strongly urge you to identify Tarnopolsky with the official Soviet line in his statement," said Professor Cotler. "The problem is that official Soviet practice is a mockery of its policy."

Professor Dershowitz: "There could be reprisals if the State Department is not informed at once. I will personally contact Washington right away."

That afternoon, Yuri's position was announced via press release:

For Immediate Release
November 28, 1986

FORMER PRISONER OF CONSCIENCE APPLAUDS PRINCIPLES OF DELHI DECLARATION

> Former prisoner of conscience, Dr. Yuri Tarnopolsky from Kharkov, in a statement today to friends in the West, called upon General Secretary Mikhail Gorbachev to extend the principles set forth in the newly created declaration of non-violence to all Soviet citizens. This declaration was signed yesterday in New Delhi between India and the Soviet Union. Although Dr. Tarnopolsky applauds Mr. Gorbachev's concepts of a non-violent world, he has noted by his own experience that these principles have been abused and often not observed when relating to his life as a refusenik.

> The text of Tarnopolsky's statement is released by Chicago Action for Soviet Jewry.

Within hours, Tarnopolsky's statement was being broadcast all over the world. In addition, it was picked up by the Voice of America and aired in the Soviet Union.

We were on the warpath.

PART FIVE: JOURNEY CONTINUES

"There are two cardinal sins from which all the others spring: impatience and laziness."

Franz Kafka

Chapter I

ACTIONS SPEAK LOUDER
THAN WORDS

The telephone was ringing. It was 4:00 a.m. on December 4, 1986. I fumbled for the phone, then heard the operator say, "France calling." It was Jeannette.

"Nancy, Pierre Mauroy has just concluded a meeting in Paris with the Soviet ambassador. *The Tarnopolskys have been granted visas.*" I gasped. Was I dreaming? I could scarcely believe my ears.

Fifteen minutes later I was on the phone with Pamela. "Pam!" I shrieked hysterically. "I just received a call from Paris that the Tarnopolskys have been granted visas. I'm calling Yuri immediately at his apartment, but I wanted to let you know before I phone international."

"Go ahead, Nancy. You have my blessings," responded Pam lightheartedly.

Within seconds the international operator was on the line. "This is an emergency," I declared. "I must get through to Tarnopolsky right away." I was informed of fifty other emergency calls waiting to be placed that morning, but my response was "Please, give this priority."

In less than half an hour the telephone was ringing at the Tarnopolskys' apartment.

"Yuri, is it true?" I stammered breathlessly into the phone.

"Is what true?" he asked, rather confused.

"I received a call from Jeannette thirty minutes ago. She just learned from Pierre Mauroy that the Soviet Embassy in Paris had released a statement saying you and your family had just been granted visas."

"Nothing of the kind."

"Oh, no!"

"Nancy, this is what I have warned you about; *words are one thing and actions quite another.* Nevertheless, it increases our hope. *There is never smoke without fire.*"

"I understand. I would never have called you at home, but we needed to verify this information immediately."

"I know. Nancy, let's be patient and wait a little. We'll see what happens. By the way, I received the official invitation for our call tomorrow."

"Good. How are you feeling?"

"Nancy, I am absolutely quiet now, like before my release from prison."

"I'm glad. Perhaps Pierre Mauroy heard the news before you, and you'll have something to tell me tomorrow."

"I think Pierre Mauroy was promised this, but we'll have to wait and see."

"Let's not tie up your home phone, because I know it's unwise, and we'll be speaking again tomorrow. My heart is pounding very loud and fast. Can you hear it?"

"Yes," he responded with a laugh.

"OK. Shalom until tomorrow."

"I'm very grateful for this call. Shalom, Nancy, until tomorrow."

I was wide awake and unable to return to sleep; thoughts were racing through my head. Between now and our next scheduled call to Kharkov, less than twenty-four hours away, people needed to be apprised of the latest developments from France.

I phoned Jeannette. "Yuri has not been informed about the visas, but the news has increased his hope. ' *There is never smoke without fire,*' he said." She understood.

Next I reached Yasha Gorodetsky in New York. He was not surprised by the news but was certainly happy to hear it. The Soviets were ready to get rid of Tarnopolsky, he surmised, after the strong action taken on his behalf during the last two months. He cautioned us to proceed normally, however, until visas were actually in hand. "Yuri may not hear for one to two more weeks, but he should arrive in Vienna before the middle of January. Convey to the French that they should double their efforts by contacting the Soviet Embassy twice a day until we see results," said Yasha.

DECEMBER 5:

"Yuri's on the line, dear, go ahead," announced Moscow.

"Yuri, have you heard anything since yesterday?"

"No, Nancy. No news."

I knew he was depressed. Trying to mask my disappointment and frustration, I responded, "Don't worry. Everything will be OK."

"What do you mean?"

"It could take from a few days to a couple weeks, but we're remaining on top of the situation. As you have said, *let's be patient for a little while.*"

"Can you tell me any details?"

"No. Will you trust me?"

"Yes. Absolutely, Nancy."

"We're working around the clock for your liberation, and we won't quit until you have visas in hand and tickets to Vienna. We're planning to meet you very soon in the Austrian capital."

"I hope so. There was a radio broadcast on Kol Israel that said I had received permission."

"OK. It's premature, but it obviously came from France. Did you hear anything over Voice of America?"

"No, Nancy. It was jammed. Remember, I was promised permission shortly before my arrest. Besides, Andropov promised to free Sharansky in 1982, and nothing happened for four years."

"Don't worry. We won't wait that long," I laughed. "We are strong, and we will take forceful action if nothing happens within a reasonable amount of time. We won't let you down. Keep up your spirits and know that our spirits are high."

"We'll try."

"We're in daily contact with Paris, and you must call us immediately as soon as you have definite news."

"Of course. You have my word. . . ."

Professors Cotler and Dershowitz were apprised of developments, and news of the "unofficial" permission began to circulate. A press release was again dispatched by CASJ:

For Immediate Release
December 9, 1986

SOVIET EMBASSY IN PARIS, FRANCE ANNOUNCES
PERMISSION GRANTED TO TARNOPOLSKY

Chicago Action for Soviet Jewry has been informed that on Thursday, December 4th, permission to emigrate was granted to former prisoner of conscience, Dr. Yuri Tarnopolsky and his wife and daughter, who live in the Ukrainian city of Kharkov.

News of the family's pending release was received by Pierre Mauroy, the mayor of Lille, France, who was phoned by a high-level official at the Soviet Embassy in Paris and informed of this action. Lille is the sister city of Kharkov.

Friday, December 5th, the French newspaper *Le Matin* printed an article on page 4 entitled, "Pierre Mauroy Freed Soviet Dissident." Mauroy talked all about the Tarnopolskys in the article, and it said, "the good news was announced yesterday by the authorities of the Kremlin to Pierre Mauroy through the Soviet Embassy."

Tarnopolsky has not received official notification from OVIR as of this date.

Leading scientists from across the country who were active in the campaign began phoning around the clock to the Soviet Embassy in Washington, expressing concern and pressing for visas.

The scientific community, including many Nobel laureates, sent telegrams to Pierre Mauroy.

> TO: PIERRE MAUROY
> WE AMERICAN NOBEL LAUREATES CONCERNED WITH FATE OF DR. YURI TARNOPOLSKY ADMIRE YOUR ACTIVISM ON HIS BEHALF. URGE YOU TO SEEK IMMEDIATE RESPONSE CONCERNING PROMISED EXIT VISAS FROM SOVIET EMBASSY IN PARIS AND DEPUTY CHAIRMAN ALIYEV IN MOSCOW.

> TO: PIERRE MAUROY
> WE MEMBERS OF NATIONAL ACADEMY OF SCIENCE CONCERNED ABOUT FATE OF COLLEAGUE, DR. YURI TARNOPOLSKY, APPLAUD YOUR TENACITY ON HIS BEHALF, REQUEST ASSISTANCE TO SECURE CLOSURE REGARDING GRANTING EXIT VISAS FROM SOVIET EMBASSY IN PARIS AND ALIYEV IN MOSCOW.

> TO: FIRST DEPUTY CHAIRMAN, GEYDAR ALIYEVICH ALIYEV
> WE, MEMBERS OF NATIONAL ACADEMY OF SCIENCE, CONCERNED ABOUT FATE OF COLLEAGUE, DR. YURI TARNOPOLSKY, ARE ENCOURAGED BY YOUR PROMISE TO SECURE EXIT VISA FOR YURI AND FAMILY. APPRECIATE ACTION TO OBTAIN VISA FROM OVIR.

> TO: FIRST DEPUTY CHAIRMAN, GEYDAR ALIYEVICH ALIYEV
> WE, AMERICAN NOBEL LAUREATES, CONCERNED WITH FATE OF DR. YURI TARNOPOLSKY, APPLAUD YOUR INTERVENTION ON HIS BEHALF. URGE YOU TO FOLLOW WITH IMMEDIATE ACTION CONCERNING EXIT VISAS.

Pierre Mauroy promised to continue pressing the case.

DECEMBER 12. MAYOR HAROLD WASHINGTON'S OFFICE:
"Yuri, is there any news?" I asked hopefully.
"No. Nothing."
"I'm at the mayor's office in Chicago, and our call is being televised and

aired on the radio. All networks and newspaper reporters are here since this is a big event in Chicago. We are waiting for Mayor Washington to arrive, and when he does you will speak with him."

"Nancy, I am afraid that something is wrong. We have heard nothing about visas. Perhaps it was a trick."

"No, Yuri. You must have faith in the system and in your supporters. It might take a little time, but there's light at the end of the tunnel, and we can see it shining brightly. Trust us."

"I trust you, absolutely. What is the reason for the delay?"

"Things take time. It won't be a long delay. Trust us. I understand that you also had a call from Monsieur Guffroy at the Municipal Building in Lille."

"Yes, Nancy. He told me to wait a little."

"Yuri, scientists, poets, and world leaders are rallying behind you and giving their support. Trust us. Trust the action on both sides of the Atlantic. We are pressing hard. Continue to keep that fire burning and keep digging that tunnel."

"I'll try, Nancy."

"Last night Sharansky was in Chicago, speaking to a crowd of several hundred people. He thanked his supporters for helping win his release, and he said that the little book of psalms from Avital is what kept his spirits alive throughout the long years of imprisonment. He always kept it in his breast pocket, and it was in his breast pocket last night. Can you hear me?"

"Yes, of course. I'm listening intently."

"When I was introduced to Sharansky, he requested that a message be delivered to you: 'Be strong and have faith, and I hope to meet you soon in Jerusalem.'"

"Thank you, Nancy."

"One moment, Yuri. Mayor Washington is coming to the telephone."

"Hello, Yuri. Shalom. This is Harold Washington, the mayor of the city of Chicago. How are you?"

"I am fine, thank you, Mayor Washington."

"I am calling to remind you that both your countrymen and my countrymen are in solidarity with you and your struggle for human rights."

"I hear you. Thank you very much, Mayor Washington."

"We are doing everything we can to take care of our own backyard in Chicago, but that doesn't mean that we are blind to the struggles of other people everywhere in the world. The cause of Soviet Jews is right up there alongside the cause of blacks in South Africa as a priority issue with us here. We know the pressure from mayors and other elected officials in the rest of the world can make a difference, and we're going to try to supply that difference for you."

"Yes. I think it is a good parallel."

"I'm glad you agree. We've been following very closely your situation over there. We are pleased to hear that you seem to have been granted permission to immigrate to Israel. I was there a year ago this past June. It's a marvelous country, and I must get back. I can see why you are so desirous of getting there."

"I'm glad to hear that, Mayor Washington."

"We are concerned that official notification hasn't come through. How is everything now?"

"We were very disappointed, but I believe in the support of my friends."

"So, you think it will work out?"

"I hope so."

"We all hope, too. We are praying for you. Is there anything we can do here to help you? Do you have any specific requests?"

"I don't know the situation. I was told I have already been released, so this is all quite new to me. I'm in suspense."

"We wish you the best, and we will maintain all necessary pressure."

"I think it is very necessary to maintain pressure."

"Yes, and with as many officials as possible. Here in Chicago there is tremendous interest. We have our local officials, among them some of our aldermen, and we will continue to do as much as we possibly can to bring this about."

"I agree it is the right thing."

"If it is successful, and we know it will be, you'll be more than welcome here in Chicago. You have many friends who would like to see you here."

"Thank you very much, Mayor Washington."

"I'm going to say good-bye, but hold on for a moment." The mayor handed me the telephone.

"Yuri, it's Nancy."

"Nancy, I feel great esteem toward Mayor Washington. I'm very impressed."

"I'm so glad. He was pleased to speak with you."

"Nancy, this is the first time that I don't clearly understand my own situation. I am afraid that Soviet officials will procrastinate as long as possible in order to disarm you."

"No. There is no way for Soviet officials to dampen our efforts. Pierre Mauroy will not be deceived, and the State Department has been apprised of the situation. Both Professor Cotler and Professor Dershowitz are working on the case at this time, and everyone has been informed about the delay. We won't let you down, and we feel success is close at hand."

"I'm waiting patiently, but I am an analyst. For Olga it is more difficult. She has been very nervous."

"You know, Yuri, that I am not a patient person by nature, but this is the end of the struggle, and we must wait it out. It won't be long now. Trust us. Please, Yura."

"I trust you, Nancy. By the way, I am worried about the health of Yacov Alpert. He is an unusual man and a highly qualified scientist. Yacov is seriously ill, is facing difficult surgery, and he needs a certain type of medicine that cannot be obtained in the Soviet Union."

"Professor Che knows about the medicine, and he will secure it from Paris as soon as possible."

"Nancy, from now on you may call me at home. Please schedule next week's telephone call at the apartment."

"That's fine. Remember, Yuri, that we are all in this struggle together. It's taking a lot of self-control, on my part as well as other's, to remain patient. We are hoping to spend the upcoming holidays together in Vienna. Olga and I share a mutual birthday; the new year is approaching. . . ."

"I understand."

"How soon can you be packed up to leave the country once your visas are in hand?"

"About a month. We have a lot of official business to take care of, and my mother is very ill. I don't think she will be able to return to Kharkov."

"I understand, Yura. We all wish you the very best, and we send our love. Perhaps there will be better news next week."

"I hope so, Nancy. . . ."

After many long years, freedom seemed imminent. Yet Yuri's frustration was understandable. Eight days had passed since he had received unofficial news of permission to emigrate, and nothing more concrete had occurred. He was justifiably wary of being deceived.

This final leg of the journey appeared to be the most difficult of all.

Dear Nancy   #18   December 13, 1986

Happy Birthday to you, and many returns of the day! We all wish you good health, beauty and happiness. May your inexhaustible energy and noble impatience displace the mountains. . . .

My plans for the future are connected entirely with scientific work. . . . A famous biologist once said that in his youth he went fishing with the biggest hooks because there was "more honor in *failing to fish* a big fish than a small one." My hooks are very big, and, as you know, I am ready to take risks. . . . I anticipate great difficulties, but, dear Nancy, you have a chance to be a spectator (and a participant, if you'd like). . . .

No one participating in Tarnopolsky's case had time to rest that week. The coordinated effort kicked into high gear and involved supporters at all levels. Our representatives on the Soviet desk at the State Department were on alert; the attorneys were looking for every angle; the French were maintaining a constant vigil at the Soviet Embassy; and the scientific community, worldwide, was adding pressure.

On December 19 we spoke with Yuri again, and he was anxious to learn if there was any news. World leaders were closely following the situation, we said; a promise had been made, and everyone was waiting to see when this promise would be honored.

Yuri was still skeptical. "Remember, it is most important *not* to believe in promises," he said. " *Actions speak louder than words. . . .*"

It would be a serious mistake, I countered, for the Soviet government to ignore the promise or to wriggle out through trickery since it was trying to maintain good relations with Paris.

"I propose a headline for *Le Matin*: 'Soviets Deceive Pierre Mauroy,'" Yuri persisted.

I advised him to think positively and to endure for just a little longer. He said that he felt quiet, but Olga was somewhat nervous. That was understandable. Nonetheless, they had to continue as normally as possible throughout these final days. Family and friends should remain supportive.

"The door is opening, Yura. Be patient. . . ."

But my distant friend's patience was nearly exhausted. The rest of our conversation consisted of the same form of argument--I would try to give him hope; he would all but smother it with his increasing pessimism. I told him about the telegrams to Moscow from the scientific community as well as a letter from Senator John Glenn requesting Ambassador's Dubinin's intervention.

Yuri then told me about his concern over new Soviet regulations that were scheduled to become law by January 1. I assured him that the new law was merely a codification of the existing regulations.

"It makes it possible to either release or refuse everybody. That's why I have told you that *words mean nothing* . . . ," he insisted.

The new law was not applicable, I argued, since it would not be enacted for two weeks. Even after the first of January, it could not affect his situation because his case was "special."

"It could signify a quick release, but nobody here believes it."

"Give us a little more time," I pleaded.

Finally Yuri budged--a little. "We heard Irina Ratushinskaya has been released," he said. "This is not just words; this is action."

"Yes," I responded. "She arrived in London."

Yuri agreed that it signified "some movement."

Telegrams and calls to the Soviet embassies in Washington and Paris continued all week. I kept the faith. Then news from Kharkov arrived during our next phone call.

DECEMBER 26:

"Nancy, there is news," remarked Yuri somberly.

". . . Go ahead, Yura. I'm listening," I said apprehensively.

"On December 24th, the chief of Kharkov OVIR informed me that there was no decision about my permission to emigrate. I was told all sorts of usual nonsense. That evening, a man from the militia paid me a visit at our apartment, the same man who had once threatened me. He asked me about my occupation, and I learned that he had questioned our neighbors in the building as if we were criminals. He gave a very vague explanation for his visit, but his tone was menacing. I asked him if I should regard his visit as a resumption of the policy of frightening and intimidating refuseniks. He answered, 'I'm aware of your capability to think logically. You should know that militia in the USSR visits only former or potential criminals.' So, I drew the conclusion that I was again considered by Kharkov officials as a criminal. My response to this action is the following:

> I consider Kharkov to be a prison for myself, and I refuse to contact any Kharkov officials, including militia, as long as I'm refused to emigrate. I reject all this barbaric nonsense like I rejected it in the Kharkov prison in 1983.

"This is my message, and I'm very surprised by the action."

"Yes, I'm surprised, too," I said softly. "What was the official reason for your summons?"

"He demanded that I reapply for permission to emigrate, but I refused by insisting that my old application should be considered. I applied in 1979, and all my documents are in order. *I refuse to be humiliated again.*"

"I understand. Did he respond?"

"No. There was no response."

"Did you inform him of the message which came from the Soviet Embassy in Paris?"

"No. This is quite a separate topic. What refuseniks are told in OVIR is absolute nonsense. It is rubbish. It is useless to speak to them. I suspect that he was lying about there being no decision."

"I agree. I don't buy his story either."

"By calling me into OVIR and sending the militia that night, I understood that it is a new kind of intimidation. If I am regarded as a criminal, I will behave as I did in the Kharkov prison, by refusing all contacts with officials. Nevertheless, *I consider this to be the response to Pierre Mauroy, and I want you to inform Lille.*"

"I shall inform Lille. I think the officials are playing a game with you to determine your reactions."

"It is a very dirty game, and I don't want to be a part of it. I refuse to partake in dirty games played by KGB." He was burning.

"It is outrageous, but it is unfortunately a pattern we have seen played many times before. However, they will fail at their own game, because they cannot break you. You are strong, and so are we. None of us will buy their story, nor will we be intimidated by their allegations."

"You are right, Nancy."

"Strong actions are continuing on both sides of the Atlantic. We are digging very hard to rescue you by continuing to press so that your government *will* honor its commitment to you. We will not stand for any lies from Kharkov OVIR. The word from the Soviet Embassy in Paris came directly from the Kremlin, which was issued by both Aliyev and Zagladine."

"They are very high officials."

"It was relayed to the Soviet Embassy in Paris, who then conveyed the information to Pierre Mauroy. This is official."

"Yes, Nancy, but I must inform you that this is not Soviet style. You know about some important action, not just words, regarding Sakharov. It was an important event, an unprecedented action which has not occurred for seventy years."

"Yes. This week the newspapers are filled with news of Andrei Sakharov returning from exile."

"I characterize the action against myself as being typical Kharkov-style intimidation."

"OK. But, Kharkov cannot act alone."

"I am not sure it was authorized by Moscow. I don't want to blame high Moscow authorities for what took place here on the 24th, because I see some real action."

"I agree. What do you think about Sakharov's remarks concerning the new policy of openness in the country?"

"As many ex-prisoners in the Soviet Union, my position is to wait and see."

"Our newspapers in the United States have been filled with the text of Sakharov's comments to Gorbachev during his phone call from Gorky."

"That is interesting. However, you should know that Soviet newspapers did not print a word of this conversation."

"I'm not surprised. Sakharov is pressing on with human rights violations, and he spoke about the new policy of openness in the country and praised Gorbachev. But, at the same time, he is pressing for the release of all prisoners of conscience, and he refuses to stop his fight against human rights violations. He also spoke about the change in newspaper coverage, which he found to be very interesting."

"Yes, I know. So, I think it is an important step, but I can't say there have been any general changes. Let's wait and see. I do feel it is best to encourage our chief of state to continue this policy."

"Of course. I'm not going to place any emphasis upon words from Kharkov KGB."

"Yes, I reject everything."

"The general consensus of opinion here is that the actual visas sometimes take longer to obtain than we would like to see happen, but the days of waiting are numbered."

"I hope you're right, but I'm very worried and surprised that there is no amnesty for political prisoners."

"I know. We'll have to watch this closely."

"In Soviet newspapers, Sakharov and his wife are regarded as criminals. It was reported they were given clemency."

"Pardoned criminals. That's interesting. But, nevertheless, there is movement."

"There is movement, but the general situation is unstable. I'm eager to get out of this country as soon as possible."

"We know the policy is unstable, and we are very eager for you to leave as soon as possible. We are looking forward to that rendezvous so we can look each other in the eye and be able to speak."

"Oh, Nancy. How I am looking forward to that," said Yuri emotionally. "You cannot imagine."

"I know," I responded smiling. Several beeps followed, and the line went dead. Frantically I dialed the international operator, and she quickly restored the connection.

"Nancy, I'm here," said Yuri reassuringly. "I want to tell you that I am still extremely worried about the absence of a large portion of my poetry. Please contact Kevin Klose at the *Washington Post* because I sent everything to him in 1982. I think it was forwarded to Ardis Publishers."

"We'll try and get to the bottom of it and report back to you next week."

"Thank you, Nancy."

"Remember, Yura, that dragging out your case while the world is watching will do nothing to promote the good image your country is trying to portray. Rest assured that we are maintaining our strength as we press onward."

"Thank you, Nancy, and best wishes for the new year. We love you."

The period of waiting was agonizing. All of us were tiring of words without actions, yet we on the outside had to maintain a positive attitude to help keep up the morale of those on the inside. In our hearts, we felt the end drawing near.

Yuri's message regarding the December 24 incident had immediately been sent out in a press release. Telegrams and letters were dispatched to Ambassador Dubinin, General Secretary Gorbachev, and other public officials. Intervention was requested with Kharkov KGB, which was working against detente as well as the new Soviet human rights position.

Professor Cotler felt that several recent incidents had pointed to a pattern in Soviet policy; namely, that a political decision could take up to four to six weeks to implement. He did advise, though, that waiting it out was not the best course. Rather, we should intensify action.

At the State Department, Ambassador Richard Shifter, whose office was in charge of human rights violations, promised to contact Aliyev and Zagladine in Moscow at once.

Chapter II

"PERMISSION RECEIVED"

DECEMBER 31:
The news that we had long been awaiting arrived in Paris by telegram.

PERMISSION RECEIVED!
Love, Yuri

JANUARY 2:
"Nancy, have you received my telegram?"

"Yes, Yura," I screamed ecstatically before bursting into tears. Fighting to regain composure, I continued unsteadily, "We are so excited, Yurochka. Congratulations! Mazel tov!"

Yuri told me that their permission had come through on December 31.

"Jeannette phoned at 2:30 this morning, Chicago time, after she received your telegram. Because of the holiday, your cable to me just arrived moments ago. Pamela, Marillyn, Sandy, David--everyone sends their love and congratulations!"

"I see," he responded with a new lightness in his voice.

I wanted to know everything: how he had learned of the permission and when they were planning to leave. Yuri described how OVIR had requested his presence and the simple meeting that had taken place there. He hoped to leave the country by the first of February.

The actual process of emigrating was as bound by red tape as the decision-making process had been. Numerous documents had to be filled out, and signatures of release had to be obtained from remaining family members and former employers authorizing their permission and confirming that there were no "holds." Apartments had to be inspected and returned to the state since there was officially no such thing as private property. Airline tickets would have to be purchased in Moscow, and there were meetings to schedule with embassy officials. Possessions were sorted and dispersed among family and friends, since the Tarnopolskys would be permitted to take very little out of the country. When everything was in order, the family would receive visas. After packing, there were painful good-byes. . . .

I commented to Yuri that their "permission" was the most wonderful Chanukah gift and the best way to begin the New Year. I asked him if they had been lighting the Chanukah candles. Yuri told me that they used oil since there were no candles, but they had forgotten to continue lighting them after the fifth day. When they learned about their permission to emigrate, they forgot about everything else. "You know, Nancy, Chanukah is the holiday of victory."

I told Yuri we had received his twenty-five-page scientific paper and that I had made twenty copies. "*Twenty*?" he said with a chuckle. "Oh, Nancy," he laughed, "there is no need to publish it." Disregarding his comment, I happily repeated that a title page had been added with his name and date, and the paper had been forwarded to several prominent scientists. It was going to be submitted to the American Association for Artificial Intelligence. Although he was now concentrating solely on leaving and felt this was something he could soon take care of himself, he was pleased with my effort.

On the subject of his poetry, I told Yuri that Kevin Klose did not have the material. The poetry had not been found in the file at Ardis Publications either. Misha had mentioned that the "problem" with the poems had been in the quality of the microfilm, which had ranged from fair to poor. "Now I understand everything," replied Yuri. I detected a trace of consternation in his voice. He said we would discuss it again in a few weeks.

We had been through so much together in five years, and I was anxious to share these last moments. What had happened in their lives since receiving the news? Yuri had cut himself off from everything during the past three days, he said, because his good friend from the labor camp had arrived to visit them and it would be the last time they would meet. Sadly, they would not be able to see his mother before they left; she remained very ill in Siberia.

Their friends in Kharkov were excited for them and had taken renewed hope from the Tarnopolskys' permission to emigrate.

Irina would not be returning to school following the winter holiday. "She is glad to get rid of this school," said Yuri.

He asked me to update his relatives in New York and Haifa. I planned to spend most of the day on the telephone, I said, informing people of the wonderful news. Certainly I would be happy to speak with his relatives in New York and Israel.

Hanging up, I was filled with immense joy and exhilaration. All those sleepless nights had been worth it. Yuri planned to begin preparing for departure the following day!

What a difference from last week's conversation, when the tone had been somber. The Kharkov KGB had made one last-ditch attempt to harass and intimidate both Yuri and his Western supporters but had failed to break our resolve. The monolithic Soviet Union could not withstand the morally powerful gaze of the West. In the end, a government founded on terror and violence was doomed to crumble before an analytical and democratic Western society.

We had won a battle, but the war went on. Thousands of Soviet Jews remained hostage behind the Iron Curtain, and the fight would not be over until the last refusenik was set free. While my co-workers across the globe and I rejoiced in our victory, and I prepared to meet the Tarnopolskys in Vienna, CASJ and other affiliates of the Union of Councils for Soviet Jews worked incessantly in efforts to release the remaining refuseniks.

For Immediate Release
January 5, 1987

DR. YURI TARNOPOLSKY RECEIVES PERMISSION TO EMIGRATE

On December 31, 1986, former prisoner of conscience, Dr. Yuri Tarnopolsky from Kharkov, USSR, received official permission to emigrate for himself, his wife and daughter.

Dr. Tarnopolsky, a chemist and poet, was released in March of this year from Chita, a prison camp in Eastern Siberia, after serving three years for crimes he did not commit. . . .

Permission to emigrate was granted to the Tarnopolsky family after eight years of a long, arduous struggle. For the past five years, a massive international campaign was mounted to help free them.

JANUARY 9:
"Nancy, we still don't know exactly when we can leave. There are some family problems, but no obstacles remain for our emigration. I will phone you as soon as I have definite information, because I don't want to rely upon a telegram."

"I would appreciate it, because I want to arrive in Vienna before you so I can meet your flight from Moscow."

"Nancy, will our dog, Nika, cause many problems to our friends or to us in America?"

"No. Don't worry." He was very attached to Nika; to leave her behind would have been unthinkable to Yuri.

"Oh, I'm so glad to hear that." I detected a sigh of relief.

"Yuri, Voice of America broadcast news of your permission into the Soviet Union yesterday. Did you hear it?"

"I know, Nancy. People told me about it."

"Also, Sunday's *New York Times* printed an article about you entitled 'Chemistry Professor Granted Permission to Leave Soviet.' Many other newspapers throughout the United States, France, Canada, and Israel carried the news, too. *The Daily News Bulletin*, published by the Jewish Telegraphic Agency in New York, printed a long article on the first page entitled 'Tarnopolsky Family Told They Can Leave the USSR.' It's all so exciting, Yura."

"Our permission is indeed exciting," Yuri responded warmly.

"Yasha phoned from Israel wanting to know your plans, and he will be calling you on Sunday because friends in Israel are searching for a job for you. How should we respond?"

"Nancy, I don't know quite how to respond, but I would prefer another way."

"I understand. Yuri, let's discuss this in Vienna. We don't have to worry about it right now."

"Yes, I agree."

"We sent out hundreds of press releases regarding news of your permission to emigrate, and I am all packed. I just need airline tickets."

Yuri laughed. "We are also packing, although we don't have many belongings and there are limitations as to what we can take with us. Many friends are now coming to visit us to say good-bye, and there are a lot of documents to prepare before we are cleared for emigration."

"I realize the process is long and strenuous. It must be difficult to say good-bye to loved ones."

"Yes, but we hope to see some of them again."

"We all hope for that. . . ."

The long years of waiting for permission to emigrate had been agonizing. The suffering caused by years of imprisonment is unimaginable, the scars permanent. There are fears and uncertainties of beginning a new life in a strange country, but when victory has been attained and freedom is close at hand, they are superseded by a feeling of overwhelming joy. Nevertheless, the initial euphoria is usually dampened by the reality of loss and separation. Knowing you may never see close relatives and friends again is a sorrow unknown to most of us in the free world. It made the departure bittersweet.

In addition, there was the problem of resettlement: Israel or the United States? For former prisoners of conscience this decision was pressing because it was widely assumed that refuseniks would automatically go to Israel, and someone like Tarnopolsky was highly visible. Many considerations had to be evaluated, and the resolution of the problem was usually painful and difficult. Freedom carried a steep price.

JANUARY 16:

"Our documents are in order, and we are going to hand in everything tomorrow," said Yuri. "Then we wait for visas, which will take one to two days."

"Terrific." I was so happy.

"Afterward, we have ten to twelve days to leave the country, but our departure depends upon the availability of tickets. I'll call you as soon as arrangements have been finalized."

"I need to know the exact date of departure, flight number, and time of your arrival in Vienna. What have you decided to do about Nika?"

"We don't know yet. Please, Nancy, be absolutely frank."

"It's up to you. Naturally, it will be more difficult traveling with her, but it would be pathetic to leave her behind."

"OK, we'll decide."

"There's always a way to work it out."

"Is Yury here today?"

"Yes."

"I want to ask him if he could take Nika for a while until we are resettled." Yury reassured him there would be no problem.

"How was your talk with Yasha last Sunday?"

"It was a difficult conversation for me. I think such things can be rather dangerous."

"I understand. I want you to know that my feelings, as well as your friends' here, are not entirely the same as Yasha's. It's something we need to discuss when we meet in Vienna." Yasha's point of view reflected the Israeli position: all Soviet Jews were "obliged" to immigrate to Israel, and Yuri had a responsibility as a former prisoner of conscience.

"Yes, Nancy. We need that. If we are cleared for emigration and can leave on time, we should depart Moscow by the 29th or 30th of January."

"I shall leave for Vienna one day earlier in order to prepare for your arrival."

"I hope to call you next week, Nancy. . . ."

Four days passed without news from Kharkov, and my nerves were becoming frayed. I prayed that nothing had gone wrong. Unable to withstand the suspense, and filled with tension and anxiety over their forthcoming departure, I phoned again four days later.

JANUARY 21, 8:00 A.M. KHARKOV:

"I hope I haven't awakened you, but we were worried because there was no news."

"Don't worry, Nancy. We'll have our visas on Friday, and then we'll go to Moscow on Monday to purchase tickets. Everything is OK." His voice was very reassuring.

"I'm relieved." I began to calm down.

"We're all packed. Now it is just a matter of a few short days before we all meet in Vienna."

"I can hardly wait! I'll speak with you again on Friday, and perhaps there will be more information. . . ."

JANUARY 23:

"We received our visas!"

"Congratulations, Yurochka! I'm tingling with excitement!"

"Me too, Nancy."

"I am so happy for you, Yura. I bet those visas look beautiful!"

"Yes, they do," replied Yuri gaily. "Now, we are leaving Moscow for Vienna February 1st, but we won't have definite confirmation of this until tomorrow."

"I'm going to make my reservations today, Yura, because the travel agency in Chicago is closed tomorrow."

"I see. Tomorrow I will be in Moscow to pick up our tickets, and I'll phone you from there."

"Excellent."

"We will be taking the train from Kharkov to Moscow on January 30th, and we'll spend one day in Moscow before flying to Vienna on the morning of February 1st."

"That's beautiful! We'll be waiting! I'm going to try and leave Chicago on January 29th, which will allow a couple days to prepare for your arrival."

"So, Nancy, I will make two calls tomorrow. I will first call you, and then I will call France."

"Wonderful. Who from France is coming to Vienna, Yura?"

"I know of two people for certain: Jacques Malamet[1] and Jean-Pierre Guffroy[2]."

"What about Jeannette?" I inquired with surprise.

"No. As far as I know, she cannot."

"No?" I responded with astonishment. "There must be some mistake. I'll talk to her. I just assumed she would be there because we've been planning this rendezvous for two years." He laughed. "Yura, I have a message for all our mutual friends in Kharkov: Please send them my love. Tell them I'm thinking about them and my heart is with them. They have not been forgotten, and I will write as soon as I return from Vienna. I did not intend to neglect anyone, but my mind has been preoccupied."

"Nancy, I'll tell them."

"Thank you, Yura."

"By the way, is there any possibility of avoiding Italy?"[3]

"I don't think so, but we'll discuss everything in Vienna. We'll have a few days before I must return to Chicago. Remember, Tanya was a special case

---

[1] Jacques Malamet was president of the Jewish community in Lille, France.

[2] Jean-Pierre Guffroy was a minister in the cabinet of Pierre Mauroy.

[3] Refugees waiting to enter the United States went from Vienna to Rome and then on to New York. Tanya Bogomolny was able to bypass the stop in Italy because of her health.

because of her cancer."

"I know."

"The most important thing is that you have visas . . . we can deal with everything else."

"Yes, Nancy. I know." He teased me about the possibility of being disappointed in him when we met after all these years. I laughed gaily along with him. "I'll call you in the morning."

"That will be our last conversation, Yura, until we meet in Vienna. . . ."

After making travel arrangements, I phoned Jeannette. Yuri had been correct. She was sorry, but a trip to Vienna was unaffordable. Although disappointed, I told her how greatly she would be missed and that we understood. Marty had hoped to accompany me to Europe, but he was unable to travel at this time because it was tax season. Sandy could not go either. Our exchange family from Normandy responded affirmatively to my call. "Why not!" was Maggy's quick response after my proposal of a rendezvous the next week in Vienna. They had followed the events over the years and were pleased to be included in this momentous occasion.

THE NEXT MORNING:

The telephone began ringing at 9:30. I was sick in bed. Apparently the strain of the past several months and the emotional impact of the last few days had taken their toll. Barely able to move, I reached for the phone.

"Moscow calling collect from Yuri Tarnopolsky. Will you accept the charges?"

"Yes!" I replied in a very loud voice.

"Nancy, we have our tickets."

"Wonderful! What is the flight number?"

"We will leave Moscow Sunday morning, February 1st, at 10:35, and we'll arrive in Vienna at 11:45 local time."

"I can scarcely believe my ears, Yura. This is all so incredible."

"Yes," he laughed. "We are flying Aeroflot, flight number SU (Soviet Union) 261."

"I have it. I'll be there two hours ahead of time." He laughed again.

"Now, Nancy, I must return to Kharkov. See you next week. . . ."

It was official. Although there still could be some last-minute problems blocking emigration, my mind refused to consider the possibilities. I was certain that everything would go smoothly. Tarnopolsky was a prominent and highly visible case, and a lot of media attention would be focused on his family's arrival.

My only real disappointment was having to travel alone to Europe. I would miss Marty. I was also slightly apprehensive because I had never before flown unaccompanied on a trans-Atlantic flight and would have to change planes in Frankfurt. Jeannette would be missed too, but I realized it was impossible for her to join me. I knew in her heart she would be with us, and the Tarnopolskys and I would be speaking with her from Vienna.

From my sick bed I began to make arrangements for the trip. My departure for Europe was only five days away, and the schedule for Vienna had to be worked out in advance. CASJ supplied me with all the necessary people to contact. Meetings were set up, press conferences arranged, and everything was coordinated with our Washington office, the UCSJ. Yuri's family in New York was also informed of the plans.

I was very nervous. Would I get well in time to leave on schedule? I was determined to go, regardless of my physical condition. Overnight I had developed a female problem of unknown origin, which the doctor suspected was caused by extreme anxiety. Nevertheless, the symptoms were real. The doctor put me on medication, ordered me to bed, and prescribed pills for Vienna in case of emergency. After all these years of fighting for Tarnopolsky's liberation, now I had to worry about being well enough to travel.

JANUARY 29. DAY OF DEPARTURE:

Nervous excitement had kept me from sleeping during the night, and I arose early, charged with energy. My health had improved, and I was running on adrenaline. After a final check for instructions from CASJ, I was ready.

Early that afternoon, Marty drove me to the airport. It was our twenty-first wedding anniversary, and we would be spending it apart. Even Moscow could not be blamed this time for putting a hex on our day, compelling us to miss our celebration. It was bittersweet, but Marty unselfishly agreed to delay our own plans so that I could fulfill a dream.

Chapter III

VIENNA

Vienna served as a "holding station" for Soviet emigres who were waiting to enter other countries. I stayed at a pension not far from downtown Vienna that had eight guest rooms, a receiving room, and a small dining room for breakfast. It was perfect for a woman alone.

After quickly getting settled, I secured passes from CSCE and arranged a meeting with Ambassador Zimmerman. I was informed that the United States delegation had been briefed on the Tarnopolsky case and was looking forward to the family's arrival. Business accomplished, it was time to return to the airport for Pierre and Maggy, who were flying in from Paris.

The following day, Jacques Malamet and Jean-Pierre Guffroy arrived from France, renting a room at the same pension where I was staying. They wanted to spend time with me before the flight arrived from Moscow. Both men were eager to learn about Yuri's future plans. It was their hope he would go to Israel, and I feared their disappointment if they knew he was leaning toward coming to the United States. Since a decision had not been finalized, this information remained undisclosed.

FEBRUARY 1:
After another sleepless night I arose early to get ready for the airport. Jacques and Jean-Pierre met me for breakfast, and shortly thereafter we were joined by Maggy and Pierre. Next to arrive was Dov Sperling, the Israeli agent from Sochnut, which was the Jewish agency in Israel. Since Dov represented the Israeli government, he attempted to ascertain Tarnopolsky's intentions and would try to persuade him against immigrating to the United States. It was he who would escort us to the airport, in a van provided by Sochnut.

The French press was already waiting at the airport, and Dov obtained VIP passes for all of us to go directly to the gate. Pierre was official cameraman, knowing I'd be too nervous and too busy to bother taking pictures. In my arms I carried one dozen long-stemmed red silk roses, which had been brought from home.

We didn't have long to wait; the flight arrived early. I waited anxiously to catch the first glimpse of our friends, then they suddenly appeared. Yuri was leading the procession, holding on to Nika's leash. They all appeared tired and pale. I hadn't seen Yuri in over five years, had never met Olga, and Irina had been just a child when last seen in Kharkov. She was now sixteen. After I embraced Olga and Irina, I handed the flowers to Olga and threw my arms around Yuri and wept.

Immediately, the Israeli representative asked Yuri to state his intended destination. Yuri declared plans to immigrate to the USA, and Dov quickly departed. Hebrew Immigration Aid Society (HIAS) was summoned to bring a minibus to the airport and pick us up.

A French reporter questioned Yuri as we walked to the baggage claim area, where the Tarnopolskys' luggage surfaced quickly. There were only a few small pieces--a meager memento of a lifetime spent in their native land.

Before long we arrived at the Tarnopolskys' hotel, a run-down rooming house. Following a short delay, the Tarnopolskys were given a key to their quarters: one small room with two beds. It was a dark and dreary temporary "home" for three people and a dog and seemed a somewhat dissatisfying introduction to the free world. Still, everything was going smoothly, and despite the ambience, this *was* a gateway to freedom.

The dining room of their hotel was the setting for our welcome lunch. With a bottle of champagne supplied by the French, we toasted to freedom and a successful new life. The Tarnopolsky family presented me with a beautiful amber necklace, which Olga had concealed under her sweater when they left Moscow. Irina sat quietly, appearing rather shy, and Olga was composed and smiling. Yuri, besieged with questions in both French and English, turned to his family from time to time, speaking Russian. On his face he wore a broad grin. I was aglow.

Maggy and Pierre departed for the airport shortly before the rest of us left to walk back to our hotel. The Tarnopolskys came with Jacques, Jean-Pierre, and me so we could show them where we were staying. Our hotel was conveniently located a short distance from their lodging. After a long, emotionally charged day, everyone soon retired to get some rest.

The next morning Tarnopolsky was summoned for a brief interrogation at Sochnut before walking over to pick me up. HIAS dispatched a minibus to fetch us both at my hotel, and we were driven to the agency where his wife and daughter had been waiting.

A delay of over an hour and a half awaited us there, where we stood in a room packed with newly arrived immigrants, all expecting to be interviewed. Finally the four of us were led into an adjacent office to meet with a HIAS representative. Within moments a guard reprimanded me for having taken a photograph and ordered that I surrender the camera. Flatly refusing, I was promptly thrown out of the meeting. When the conference concluded, we waited another ninety minutes before the family received their documents and Austrian money. Each person was allotted fifty shillings per day ($5.00 each), which was to be spent on food.

Exhausted, we left HIAS and walked to a small cafe for dinner. Although the place was gloomy, we were too tired and hungry to go any further. Later Yuri stopped to buy sausages for Nika, and the two of us returned to my hotel to go over his portfolio. It was there that he received his first debriefing, and we had our long-awaited opportunity to finally "look each other in the eye."

Yuri felt happy and relieved to be in the West, but he was sorry about those left behind. He remained determined to help others get out of the USSR once he resettled in America. The Soviet way of life had always felt alien to him, and it was time to go "home." Although he felt great love and admiration for Israel and her people, he preferred to be near close friends in Chicago. He was anxious to get on with life and pursue the scientific work that was his dream.

Yuri knew he was a part of history, part of the Soviet Jewry movement. He would be the first prisoner of conscience to immigrate to America rather than Israel, a decision that would be loudly condemned by the Israelis. If he were to go to Israel, he would be regarded as a hero. In the United States he would soon be treated as just an ordinary emigre. After living in America for a few months, he would no longer be a spokesperson for Soviet Jews.

Yuri looked imploringly at me for my reaction, and I empathized with him over his dilemma. "I cannot decide your future," I told him. "It is your decision to make. Personally, I would like to see you in America, but it is not for me to render an opinion because you are not an ordinary person. Nevertheless, whatever you decide, I will help you." He nodded gratefully as I continued. "I'm in a precarious position because of my devotion to you. I know it would be better for your career if you were to reside in the United States, but there's a bigger issue to consider." My eyes began to water as I spoke. "Although you may not like living in Israel, you were unhappier in the USSR. It is possible to have both Israel and the United States by first moving there and then making an extensive tour of the USA with a long stopover in Chicago. Later, you could move to America if you are still unhappy with Israel."

He regarded me sadly. "I'm already fifty years old, and I'm exhausted after the long refusal. Just now I feel as if life is returning. Besides my career, what would I do with a Russian wife [who was not Jewish] in Israel? I know it would be better for Olga in America, although I don't want to alienate my supporters. If it is obligatory to go to Israel, I will go."

I felt an enormously heavy responsibility resting on my shoulders. I was accountable to the Union of Councils, but my heart went out to Yuri, who had struggled for years to be free. Having been liberated for barely twenty-four hours, he was now being forced to make a painful choice that threatened his newly earned freedom. Whatever his decision, there were those who would remain unhappy. Softly, I responded. "Yura, you have paid your dues to society. It is time to live. If you choose America, you can work for the Soviet Jewry movement, although you will forfeit your position as spokesperson. You have many friends, myself included, who would warmly welcome you to America and to Chicago." Yuri's eyes never left my face as he responded: "I choose Chicago."

After he had left for his hotel, I phoned CASJ to inform Marillyn and Pamela of Yuri's final determination to come "home" to Chicago. Marillyn quickly replied, "Telephone him at once and get him back, because Pam has an important message." It was midnight. Embarrassed but following orders, I woke Yuri up to request he hurry back. Fifteen minutes later he was at the door.

"Shalom, Chicago Action."

"Marillyn, it's Nancy," I responded excitedly. "Yuri's here, and I'm putting him on right away."

"Yuri," said Marillyn, "we're crying and laughing, and our hearts are there with Nancy since we've been waiting a long time for you. I'm sorry it was necessary to get you out of bed since you must be exhausted, but with the seven-hour time difference. . . ."

"No, it's all right. I'm happy to hear your voice, too."

"Pam is waiting to speak with you at her house, and I don't want to take much of your time. Welcome, and we need your help in Chicago."

"Thank you, Marillyn. . . ."

Smiling after the warm reception, Yuri waited for me to place the call to Pamela.

"Welcome to freedom," said Pam affectionately. "I apologize for awakening you. How are you?"

"It's OK, Pamela. We are all very well, including the dog."

"I want you to know that the world is welcoming you. We have been watching and waiting, and none of us were completely sure that you were going to be able to make this. We are delighted. I wish you every success and every good wish."

"Now I have just one wish: to see my friends get out of Kharkov and Moscow."

"We'll do our best to help them."

"Pamela, when Americans help Soviet refuseniks, they help themselves. What is happening now in the Soviet Union can occur anywhere else in the world. It is important to defeat the very idea of limitations on human rights."

"You're right. Yuri, we received a call today from Yuri Shtern at the Information Center in Jerusalem. He wants to phone you. How do you feel about it?"

"Of course I'll speak with him, but my decision is to come to the United States."

"We know, and we're happily waiting for you. Yuri, I needed to speak with you before your meeting with Ambassador Zimmerman tomorrow. *It is important to stress there is NO emigration from the Soviet Union. Talk with him about prisoners. . . ."*

"Yes, of course, Pamela. It is a very good point."

"How is Nancy? She must be so happy and relieved that you're safely here. It's like giving birth to a baby. . . ." Yuri burst into laughter, nodding with understanding as he glanced over at me.

Already on our "second wind," we placed several other calls to the States that evening. We contacted Yuri's relatives in New York, Tanya Bogomolny in San Francisco, and in Chicago we reached the Verlinskys and Bermans. Finally, we phoned Mayor Harold Washington's office in Chicago and spoke with my sister, Jane, who at that time was working very closely with him. We arranged for a press conference with Mayor Washington from Vienna.

It was not until 2:00 a.m., after we had completed our last call, that Yuri left to get some sleep. Still running on adrenaline, I continued to work on our schedule, trying to get things in order for the next few days.

FEBRUARY 3:
At 8:00 in the morning I was awakened by a telephone call from someone at Radio Free Europe, who had been trying to reach Yuri. He agreed to attend our press conference the next day, when we were to speak with Mayor Washington.

As I lay in bed thinking about our schedule today, Marty called to tell me how much he missed me. It was so good to hear his voice.

Later in the day, when we were received by Ambassador Warren Zimmerman, Yuri expressed his deep concern for friends left behind. He spoke about Professor Yacov Alpert in Moscow, whom he felt was most deserving of an early release. Yacov had remained active during the Andropov terror, conducting scientific seminars in his apartment with refuseniks as well as with visiting foreign dignitaries. His inactivity now was due only to poor health and advanced age. Other cases were highlighted, including those of Eugene Chudnovsky, Sasha Paritsky, David Soloveichik, and Liliya Zatuchnaya.

Yuri informed the ambassador that the first area of concentration should be the release of all prisoners of conscience. Next to be freed should be former prisoners of conscience and their families. The third group would be activists, and finally would come all remaining Jews. Yuri felt a deep responsibility to save Soviet Jewish children so they would not perish.

We left the ambassador's office to rush back to my hotel for our first press conference on Austrian soil, direct to Cincinnati, Ohio. By the time we had arrived, reporters had been gathering in the room, and moments later the telephone rang.

"This is the United States operator with a call for Nancy Rosenfeld." It was from Sandy Spinner in Cincinnati.

"I'm on the line. . . . Sandy? It's amazing being here at the other end of a press call. The Tarnopolskys are with me, and I'm putting Yuri on the phone."

"Sandy, I am happy to hear your voice," replied Yuri. "This is the third day of our freedom, and my family and I are free due to the great efforts of many people at different levels throughout the world. You and your congregation were most helpful. Nevertheless, I am not quite happy, because my refusenik friends are still in the USSR. I think new efforts are needed before they will be released."

"You can say everything you want now, Yuri, because you are free of the ears of the KGB," said Sandy. He laughed. "How did it feel to land in Vienna?"

"To tell you the truth, I felt nothing, because it is natural to be free and quite unnatural to be a prisoner. But I was very glad to see Nancy. . . ."

This time, unlike all those other times in the U.S., I was on the receiving end of a press call and could watch Yuri's face as he responded to questions from American reporters. He looked relaxed and was smiling. Afterward we telephoned Jeannette.

That evening we had a prearranged phone call with North Shore Congregation Israel. The room at the congregation was packed with people waiting to hear Yuri's voice. What a wonderful and odd feeling to be with Yuri when the call came through from my own synagogue.

"Shalom, Yuri," announced Rabbi Bronstein. "We are here with the entire temple staff, a representative from Chicago Action, Rabbi Hart, students from the Hebrew School, and the press. We are thrilled to talk with you. Do you have a message for us here in Chicago?"

"Shalom, dear Rabbi. We are happy. Really happy. We are free. We have been walking along the streets of Vienna with Nancy. But first I would like to thank your congregation for the wonderful gifts. We appreciate the coats for Irina and me."

"You are certainly welcome," responded Rabbi Bronstein. "We hope to be able to show our appreciation in many, many ways. Rabbi Hart would also like to say a few words. . . ."

"Yuri, this is Rabbi Hart. I spoke with you on the eve of Rosh Hashanah, and you told me you would be eating apples and honey with your family. I remember saying that I hoped we would be eating apples and honey together next year, but I never expected it would happen so soon."

Yuri laughed. "Yes, I hope so. . . . I would like to say something to the children." Yuri greeted them in Hebrew, and the children responded in unison with "shalom."

Immediately after the phone call with North Shore Congregation Israel, Yuri and I were able to get through to Moscow. We spoke briefly with Yacov Alpert, who had escorted the Tarnopolskys to the airport the day of their departure. He related an episode that had occurred shortly before they parted. As they were about to board the plane, airport officials had tried to stop them from their taking Nika. Instantly, Olga and Irina had burst into tears over the last-minute display of harassment, until finally they were released to board with the dog.

The following morning the Tarnopolskys and I were received by the French delegation to the Helsinki Commission. Yuri repeated what he had told Ambassador Zimmerman.

By late afternoon the press began arriving for the call to Mayor Washington. Among those represented were the Associated Press, United Press International, Reuters, the French press, the Israeli press, and Radio Free Europe. Joining us also were Ambassador Zimmerman and his associate, Lynn Davidson.

". . . The United States is calling, and Mayor Washington's office is on the line. Are you ready?"

"We're ready, operator," I responded.

"Nancy, it's Jane. There are twenty members of the press here, and television cameras are setting up equipment. Your people from Chicago Action are present, and so is the mayor. He's ready now. One moment."

"This is Mayor Harold Washington. I am surrounded here by twenty members of the local press, and we've all been anxiously waiting for this call to speak with Dr. Tarnopolsky."

"Thank you, Mayor Washington. I would like to express my pleasure for the opportunity of speaking with you again. When I joined you in Chicago in December for the call to Kharkov, the situation with Yuri was very grave. This is an incredible moment for me to be here in Vienna with Yuri and his family and speaking with you in Chicago. Tarnopolsky's freedom is a tremendous victory, and I would like to put him on the phone."

"This is Yuri. It was a great pleasure, Mayor Washington, to speak with you last December, and it is an immense pleasure to speak with you today as a free man. My family has been delivered from slavery after eight years of the refusal. I would like to express my appreciation since your great personal effort contributed very much to our freedom. You also encouraged another mayor, the mayor of Lille, Pierre Mauroy. The joint efforts of both mayors was a great success. . . . You cannot see us now, but I hope to soon be able to express my gratitude in person since I have decided to move to Chicago."

"I'm pleased to hear that. I am surrounded by a lot of people now, your friends and supporters and members of the press. All of them worked avidly for your release. I wish you could see the joy and happiness on their faces."

"I know," said Yuri warmly.

"We look forward to meeting you here. I can display you to our powerful City Council. May I speak with the ambassador? . . ."

"Mayor Washington, this is Ambassador Zimmerman. I am very grateful for the chance to participate in this wonderful moment. We were delighted to hear about Yuri Tarnopolsky's release from the Soviet Union. He's a brave man. He spent time in a Soviet prison, and even more time was spent being refused his right to emigrate. It's wonderful to see him in Vienna knowing he'll be going to Chicago."

"Thank you. I'm very glad to hear you, Ambassador Zimmerman. Could

I have another word with Yuri?"

"Mayor Washington," replied Yuri, "*you were my supporter, now I am going to be your supporter,*" as a burst of approving laughter resounded from Chicago.

"Hurry up," the mayor answered gleefully. Another thunderous burst of applause and laughter was heard. "We have an election in about three weeks." More laughter. "I understand one of your primary objectives is to support refuseniks still there. Would you like to comment on it?"

"I believe you should use the same tactical pressure, and the efforts of many different forces at different levels should be united. Only pressure will make the Soviet government fulfill its promise of liberating refuseniks. But we don't believe in promises or words. We should judge Soviet policy only by actions."

"Thank you, Yuri. May we speak again with Nancy?"

"Nancy, we are very appreciative of your help in arranging this," said the mayor.

"It's a tremendous pleasure for all of us in Vienna. I'm so pleased to know that all my friends from CASJ are with you today, and I want to thank the press for coming.

"Here in Vienna, the East-West Conference on Security and Cooperation in Europe, which is reviewing the Helsinki Accords, is currently meeting, with Ambassador Zimmerman representing the American delegation. . . . I would like Yuri to speak with Pamela. . . ."

"Yuri, on behalf of the Union of Councils for Soviet Jews, we welcome you to freedom. . . . We hope your arrival in the free world will be the beginning of many more releases to come. We've scored a victory, but only a small one because of the countless numbers remaining behind in the USSR. . . ."

The impact of this call was still resounding as pride and satisfaction filled the air. This represented the culmination of several full and emotionally charged days in the Austrian capital. In the morning, I would be returning to Chicago.

When Yuri saw me off at the airport the next day, it was not to be a painful good-bye. Although the week had flown too quickly, we were able to smile and say with reassurance, "See you soon." Happily, we knew it would be only a short separation before all of us were reunited in Chicago. In the meantime, work remained to be done.

Six days in Vienna had left me with a lifetime of memories. Victory had been achieved one month earlier. Freedom had been our goal. The reunion in Vienna was the frosting on the cake.

Was there a price for victory? Of course. Every operation has a price, all goods have to be paid for, and human life is our most highly valued commodity. Yuri paid with eight years as a refusenik and three years in prison. Payment for me came later.

As I closed the Tarnopolsky case, I ended my "official" role as a member of Chicago Action. Rescue had been achieved, and a new chapter was about to begin.

I boarded my flight in a state of suspended animation, experiencing the first stirrings of postpartum blues. After sleeping all the way to Frankfurt, I had to be awakened by the stewardess and was the last person aboard to deplane. Little time had been reserved for sleep in Vienna, and I had been on a constant high.

Chapter IV

PREPARING A WELCOME

When the taxi pulled up to our Deerfield home the next afternoon, my eyes focused on a balloon telegram tied to the front door. The inscription on the card read, "WELCOME HOME, NANCY. LOVE, FROM YOUR FRIENDS AT CASJ."

I was very anxious to see all my dear friends at Chicago Action as soon as possible, but I was exhausted from the trip, both physically and mentally, suffering from jet lag. However, instead of giving my body a few days to rest and heal itself, I plunged right into my new assignment.

After being processed in Vienna, the normal procedure for Soviet refugees trying to enter the United States was to wait in the Austrian capital for two weeks while they were cleared for the second leg of their journey. Next they would fly to Rome for a few days, then on to Ladispoli to wait two to three months before finally being permitted entrance into the USA. Ladispoli is a seacoast resort one hour from Rome by train.

For the average American a two- to three-month tour of Europe would seem like a dream come true. For a Soviet refugee seeking asylum, the "waiting game" was mental torture. They were tired and homeless and could not afford much sightseeing. Even the cost of admission to a museum is out of range when you are forced to keep a tight budget. The limited allowance from the Jewish Agency provided only simple housing and basic food.

After several long and agonizing years trying to exist during the refusal, the Tarnopolskys' only desire was to be allowed to come "home" and begin new lives. To a fifty-year-old former prisoner, the yearning to be home and to get on with life was even more compelling. Yuri felt his most highly productive years were rapidly waning. As a friend I was determined to help shorten the waiting process.

It was not long before I realized the intricacies of the bureaucratic red tape I was trying to disentangle. I was fighting a delicate political battle. If I pushed too hard, I would show favoritism, and it was unfair to request special dispensations from government officials that might cause them to divert attention away from more pressing matters.

The primary concern was for the welfare of thousands of Soviet Jews who were still caught behind the Iron Curtain. The circumstances surrounding our case were now out of my hands and beyond my control, and I found myself in a new position with a diminished sense of power since the rescue operation was over.

The business of resettlement was a new ball game. In this area I was caught in the middle and, at times, felt helpless and alone. My first responsibility was to my organization, CASJ, and then to my friends, the Tarnopolskys. At the same time, I realized that Yuri would not favor my pulling strings to help him, especially if it were to weaken the support for someone else.

Through New York HIAS we attempted to expedite the process of immigration, and all undertakings were coordinated with HIAS in Rome.

While efforts were being made to hasten the Tarnopolskys' immigration, Chicago was preparing for their arrival. The Social Action Committee at North Shore Congregation Israel gave tremendous help and support.

Rabbi Hart; Pat Nisenholz from the Social Action Committee, who had been most supportive and helpful throughout the entire resettlement effort; and I visited the Jewish Agency in Chicago. There we met with the caseworker and she discussed her role and the responsibility of the Jewish Agency to newly arriving Soviet immigrants. The agency would provide monthly rent checks and an allowance for food and miscellaneous expenses.

Financial support would continue for several months, until a member of the family had secured employment. Once the Jewish Agency ceased to provide support payments, the immigrant family was responsible for reimbursing the agency for the cost of their flights. The family would not be held responsible for any additional refund payments.

Medical care was also provided by the Jewish Agency. Because of Yuri's imprisonment and resulting health problems, he had been assigned to a top Chicago hospital for examination and possible treatment.

Many Soviet Jews had resettled in Chicago's West Rogers Park neighborhood, not far from where I had spent my early childhood. This is where the agency found a modest apartment for Yuri and his family, and representatives of the congregation enthusiastically joined the efforts of Soviet emigres in helping to make the new apartment a home. Paving the way for the Tarnopolskys to settle in Chicago became a true community project and a labor of love. Those participating checked out schools for Irina and possible job opportunities for Yuri, though the decisions would of course be made by the Tarnopolskys when they arrived.

On March 6 Yuri told us over the phone that his HIAS caseworker had informed him the March quota for immigration had already been filled. This, obviously, could cause a delay in the immigration process, so we had a few days of anxiety.

That's when Congressman John Porter stepped in and cabled the director of Immigration and Naturalization Services in Rome to request that immediate attention be given this matter.

Just three days after the news from Rome had reached us, Yuri learned by telephone that the U.S. State Department had just intervened on his behalf, sending a wire to the Department of Immigration and Naturalization. A copy of the telegram, which requested that Yuri's case be accelerated and his family be granted entry into the United States before the end of the month, was delivered to the United States Embassy in Rome.

Intervention by the State Department resulted in immediate action. Yuri and his family could leave on the next available flight to New York, which was only four days away. However, that would have meant that the family would be traveling on a Friday and landing in Chicago on Shabbat. Because of Shabbat, their departure was put off for another five days until the next flight that had space.

On March 18, 1987, Yuri Tarnopolsky, his wife, daughter, and their dog boarded an Alitalia Air Lines flight for New York en route to Chicago.

Chapter V

CHICAGO

"I was born in the USSR, but my freedom was born in Chicago."

A large crowd of well-wishers and reporters had been gathering at Chicago's O'Hare Airport for over an hour. The flight from New York was expected to arrive at 7:30 p.m. Everyone was happy and filled with anticipation, and several friends had brought bouquets of flowers. Finally came an announcement over the loudspeaker that the plane was descending into Chicago. Television equipment was moved into position as the crowd moved forward toward the gate. My heart was pounding.

There was a second announcement. "TWA flight number 137 has just landed in Chicago." I felt someone grab my arm. It was Marillyn. "Nancy, we've just received permission for you to board the plane." I rushed forward, carrying my bouquet of one dozen long-stemmed red roses (this time they were fresh, not silk). The passengers were already crowded in the aisles when I stepped aboard. There were nodding glances from the stewardesses. A request was made over the loudspeaker system for the Tarnopolskys to come forward. At last I saw three smiling figures moving slowly forward and waving. Barely was there time to greet each other before we were whisked off the plane.

As we stepped off the runway and into the waiting area, which by now was packed with supporters, the crowd burst into thunderous applause as lights from television cameras were directed at the new Chicagoans. A special room had been prepared for an airport press conference, and officials were on hand to escort us down the hall. When Yuri began to speak, the crowd instantly quieted. Looking tired and speaking softly, he thanked his friends and supporters from Chicago Action, many of whom were there to greet him. Members of North Shore Congregation Israel were present, as were Rabbi Hart and his family. Friends from the Russian community had arrived, including the Verlinskys and Bermans. My parents had accompanied Marty and me, and Rob would be meeting us later at the apartment. Steve was away in college, but Sherri (our future daughter-in-law) was there with her parents.

Soon it was time to drive the Tarnopolskys "home." Baggage collected, we left the airport and headed for the apartment. The only casualty was Nika. On the flight to New York from Italy, her carrier had been damaged and they were unable to bring her to Chicago. Nika was left in New York with Yuri's relatives, and he hoped to return to New York soon to pick up the dog.

The new apartment was on the third floor of a six-flat building in West Rogers Park. On its door were balloons and streamers, and voices greeted us in unison with a loud "Welcome home!" as we entered the living room. Several friends had arrived ahead to set things up for the arrival. As we opened the door, Pat Nisenholz came rushing up to kiss us hello. Behind her were the Verlinskys, the Bermans, Pat's husband and children, and Mom and Dad. Rob walked in a few minutes later. A big sign on the living room wall read "Welcome Home," and flowers were placed throughout the apartment. Corks from champagne bottles were popping, hors d'oeuvres and freshly baked pastries were abundant, and the Tarnopolskys were aglow with happiness. Their sparkling faces matched the glow of their friends, who had enthusiastically and lovingly prepared for this moment.

On the coffee table in the living room was a photograph album filled with pictures of the long journey to freedom, ending in Vienna. The refrigerator and pantry were stocked with food, and a fruit basket from Sandy Spinner was sitting on the kitchen table. Pictures were hanging on the walls, books stood neatly on shelves, and magazines were stacked in a rack. The "welcome team" had made the place a home.

Everyone gathered around the television to watch the evening news, and we saw the replay at the airport. There was the family coming down from the plane, and Yuri's face soon filled the screen. I looked from one to the other and found it hard to believe that we were watching this from *their* Chicago apartment. We were together. They were home. It was like a dream.

The following morning Christine Negroni from WGN News arrived at the Tarnopolskys' apartment with her television crew. She had last interviewed Yuri by telephone in September, shortly after he was told by authorities that he would never be allowed to emigrate.

Now that they were face to face and Yuri had indeed emigrated, Negroni wanted Yuri to tell viewers what the current situation was. "I think that only pressure, hard pressure, can have some effect on Soviet policy," Yuri replied. "If this pressure will continue, I'm sure that all the dissidents will be free."

Our group--the Tarnopolskys, Pat Nisenholz and Cecile Levy from the Social Action Committee at North Shore Congregation Israel, and I--left the apartment and drove to City Hall, where Mayor Harold Washington was waiting to welcome the Tarnopolskys to Chicago personally. When we arrived, reporters from all the television networks, radio stations, and newspapers were busily setting up their equipment. My sister Jane was the first to greet us, and even some Chicago aldermen were present. Coffee was served, and a smiling Mayor Washington entered the room. "We welcome you and your family to Chicago," said the mayor, "and you will find that Chicagoans have a big heart. They welcome strangers, and it doesn't take long before you're no longer a stranger and are a Chicagoan." Grinning broadly, Yuri responded, "*I was born in the USSR, but my freedom was born in Chicago.*" With a twinkle in his eye and a grin on his face, the mayor formally presented Yuri with an autographed photo of himself, a book of Chicago, the Chicago flag, and the key to the city. Yuri was made an honorary citizen of Chicago.

Before leaving City Hall, Yuri was asked to make a public statement for Voice of America.

Our roller coaster campaign had begun in 1982, and now it seemed to be finally over. Yuri was the first refusenik granted permission to emigrate from Kharkov in several years, and his triumph paved the way for others. The door to the Ukraine was beginning to open.

Chapter VI

RESETTLEMENT

The new Chicagoans plunged right into their task of resettling. As Yuri had predicted, I became both spectator and participant in this new phenomenon. It was like watching a newborn baby begin to develop. Everything was a new discovery, and those first few steps were frequently shaky. Sometimes the Tarnopolskys conquered and succeeded; other times they teetered and fell.

Shopping for groceries presented a challenge because of the seemingly infinite variety of goods from which to choose.

Medical and dental appointments for the entire family necessitated learning how to commute from one part of the city to another on public transportation.

The selection of a school for Irina became urgent so she could continue her education and not fall further behind. Although the groundwork had been laid in advance, the final choice was the family's, and they selected Ida Crown Academy, a Jewish day school within walking distance of their apartment. Before being permitted to enroll, Irina had to meet with the rabbi and go through a mikvah (a ritual bath) since the academy was orthodox and Olga was not Jewish. When Irina began school, she was expected to master Hebrew at the same time she was trying to cope with English.

Irina was confronted with many challenges at a very vulnerable age, and my heart went out to her as she tried to adjust to her new setting while also making new friends. Being a stranger in a strange land can be overwhelming, and Irina often felt bewildered. Because she wasn't fluent in English, she was temporarily placed in a lower grade. This just exacerbated her difficulty in fitting in. At an age when girls are particularly sensitive to the reactions of the opposite sex, she was taller than most boys in class, and her refusenik background had matured her beyond her years. I recalled my own feelings of insecurity as a teenager and empathized with her discomfort.

She accompanied Rob to the evening sessions of the confirmation class at North Shore Congregation Israel, and there she found students her own age. Yet she was the only foreigner among students who had been raised in suburbs along the North Shore.

Olga Tarnopolsky enrolled in a special training program for immigrants located in the neighborhood, which taught basic office skills. Her proficiency in English helped eased her transition to the American working world, and her pleasant manner made it easy for her to form new friendships.

Immediately after landing in Vienna, Yuri had begun to work on facilitating the liberation of his good friends Eugene Chudnovsky from Kharkov and Yacov Alpert from Moscow. He had told Ambassador Zimmerman that they were two of the most deserving scientists to be considered for an early release and had spoken with Pamela about intensifying existing efforts on their behalf. Here in Chicago, Yuri and I coordinated our efforts with CASJ to smooth Chudnovsky's emigration and to secure Alpert's freedom.

At the same time, Yuri embarked on a long and frustrating search for employment. Despite his impressive curriculum vitae, a suitable position for a fifty-year-old Soviet chemist was not readily available. His initial hope of finding the right place to pursue his scientific work was rapidly waning; he was plagued with self-doubt. Yuri fought disillusionment, refusing to abandon his dreams of research and development.

Meanwhile, one month after arriving in Chicago, Yuri began a series of lectures about the plight of Soviet Jewry and his personal struggle for freedom. North Shore Congregation Israel formally welcomed the Tarnopolsky family on April 17, and an adoring crowd of over three hundred people came to meet them and hear him speak.

Before Yuri's address the chairman of Social Action, Ed Kooperman, presented me with a plaque for my role in the rescue effort. The gesture took me by surprise, and I was deeply moved by the outpouring of affection expressed by the committee. As I walked to the podium to accept the award, my knees were shaking. I heard my voice tremble slightly as I thanked the president of the congregation and my committee for their support. I was glowing with pride as I turned to introduce Yuri.

The congregation burst into applause as Yuri rose and walked toward the podium. He spoke softly into the microphone, and the audience seemed to move forward in their seats, not wanting to miss a word he was saying. He thanked his supporters and lauded the efforts of Chicago Action:

"A lot of people in different countries contributed to our freedom. There were senators, Nobel laureates, mayors, rabbis, poets, scientists, and ordinary people. Among them were the so-called 'housewives.' In my opinion, they could be called housewives only in the sense that they considered the whole world their house and all Jews their family. They wanted justice, peace, and happiness in this big house. They took close to their heart the suffering of Soviet Jews, and they have been the driving force of a wide campaign on behalf of Soviet Jewry.

"I feel myself extremely lucky that Chicago Action for Soviet Jewry was at the very heart of my campaign. Since the heart is the place for *soul*, I am happy to say that Nancy was the soul. For five years, since 1982, she had been fighting for my freedom and spared no efforts for victory. When we met in

Vienna on February 1st, she told me there were many more brilliant and wonderful women at Chicago Action. . . .

"Tonight you can see, by myself and my family, one of the victorious achievements of this organization of volunteers. You can ask yourself if it was worthwhile to spend such enormous efforts in order to get three people and a dog out of the Soviet Union. You can ask yourself if it is still worthwhile to support a dozen militant women from Chicago Action who do not leave you in peace. You can ask me what is the general sense of what has happened with Soviet Jews. What is going on in the Soviet Union under the great champion for peace and democracy, Mr. Gorbachev?

"I'm not sure that I was worth all the efforts and money spent on me. However, my freedom is by no means the sole result of the campaign. Kharkov, one of the most closed cities in the USSR for Jewish emigration, has been opened slightly.

"Ten days after my departure from the USSR, which was the first victory in eight years, three other friends of mine, Jewish activists and participants of the unofficial Jewish University, received permission.[1] Two of them, Eugene Chudnovsky and David Soloveichik, had been adopted by North Shore Congregation Israel. Some other refuseniks, Jewish activists, also received permission. Kharkov is now more open than some other Soviet cities, which is why I feel great satisfaction and believe our sacrifices and your efforts were worthwhile. It is a real victory. It happened because of constant pressure on both sides. *Nancy Rosenfeld and I were like two miners digging a tunnel from both sides. The difference was that I could use only my nails.*

"We can understand what has been going on in the USSR since 1970 only in terms of victory and defeat; in terms of war. The Soviet system has been waging war against human rights, freedom of religion, freedom of speech, private property, freedom of movement. . . .

"Jews were only one sector of the front in the war against dissidents, nationalists, Christians, and all Western-thinking people. Every Jewish activist represented a small battlefield in this war. For a prisoner, it meant not only his soul, but his very body became a battlefield in this war. . . .

"Since Soviet Jews did not want to live in the USSR, they were declared traitors and enemies of the Soviet people. They were treated like enemies. When I describe the plight of Soviet Jewry, I use the term *Moral Holocaust,* the mass destruction of souls. We can see physical consequences of this destruction. The numbers of Jews in the USSR has been moving towards zero, and not because of emigration. . . .

"Many eminent people, not only Jews, were released from prisons, labor

---

[1]Tarnopolsky's permission was the catalyst that opened the door in Kharkov for other refuseniks waiting to emigrate.

camps, exile, and some emigrated. More freedom, or less slavery, was promised to Soviet people. Something began to thaw in that deeply frozen country, although spring is still not in sight.

"To explain what is going on in the Soviet Union, there is an old Jewish parable. An old Jew lived in a small room with his big family. He came to the rabbi and complained about it. 'Bring the goat into the room,' advised the rabbi. After some time the Jew returned, lamenting, 'Vayez mir, now it is a real death for us with this goat.' 'Then take the goat away,' responded the rabbi. The next day the smiling Jew came to the rabbi again. 'Thank you for your advice. Now we feel like we are living in a big palace.'

"Gorbachev has been gradually taking away Andropov's goat of extreme political repression, which is unprecedented since 1937. However, a small, closed, and stuffy room of Soviet life has not increased in size. There is no free emigration, no freedom of religion, no free elections, no real openness of society. There is no reason for jubilation in the West. . . .

"Released political prisoners are presented to Soviet people as pardoned criminals. . . . True criminals, like Soviet KGB chiefs, remain in power. . . . Soviet government is disturbed by the weakening of the Soviet Union as a world power. . . .

"The main principle for dealing with the Soviet Union should be as follows: No credits. Pay cash and pay in advance. Give us refuseniks, and we shall offer something in exchange. . . .

"For myself and my family, the refusal was a real war, longer than World War II. In my soul, I never felt enslaved. I felt like a soldier. . . .

"I was assimilated by Russian culture, but I never forgot I was a Jew. When I was eight years old, I read a small book about a Nazi concentration camp in Treblinka. Afterwards, such books disappeared in the USSR. . . .

"In 1972, a small group of Jewish activists visited the Siberian city where I lived. I was listening to Yiddish sounds for the first time in my life, and I felt something echoing in my soul. It was the very beginning of a long journey, and this path leads always out of the USSR. . . .

"In 1977, I moved to my native city of Kharkov, and I began to prepare for emigration. . . . For the first time, I faced open and flagrant anti-Semitism in the Ukraine. . . .

"In 1979, I applied for emigration and was refused like thousands of other Jews. . . . I felt myself part of my people, I found my big family although I wasn't a perfect son. *I felt myself a link in the whole chain of generations.* To some extent, *I felt that the chain depended upon me.* . . .

"Soviet Jews have had to make a difficult and fundamental decision. We had to either give up our future freedom or fight for it. There was another choice--to wait. The majority of refuseniks chose to wait. Most are still waiting. Without those who sacrificed their relative comfort and personal freedom, such as Anatoly Sharansky, Ida Nudel, Joseph Begun, and all prisoners of Zion, there would be no hope for Jewish emigration. . . .

"The plight of Soviet Jewry and the struggle for freedom is one of the most recent and still uncompleted pages of Jewish history. American Jews can be proud of their contribution to this struggle, and I hope that we shall gain the final victory."

Yuri had been perspiring profusely throughout his lecture and from time to time stopped to wipe his brow and drink some water. His talk continued for over an hour as he recalled the agony of the refusal and the nightmare of the labor camp where he had been held prisoner for three years. It was evident that he was putting himself through torture as he relived his experiences. He looked pale and somewhat unsteady.

In early May, Yuri departed for San Francisco, where he had been invited to address an open forum of chemists at Berkeley. This had all been arranged by a Berkeley nuclear chemist, Dr. Michael Lederer, a longtime friend. Mike energetically organized the symposium at which over fifty chemists participated.

Yuri's lecture, which was entitled "Civilization and 'Evilization'--Branches of Social Evolution," expounded on current Soviet policy and the comparison of American and Soviet systems of government. He warned that Gorbachev was giving up political prisoners to the West "one by one, procrastinating as much as possible . . . and presenting them as pardoned criminals, not as innocent victims of repression." Following his speech, Yuri was invited to lunch by members of Scientists for Sakharov, Orlov and Shcharansky (now spelled Sharansky).

A warm reception awaited Yuri at the Bay Area Council on Soviet Jewry, which was hosted by its chairman, David Waksberg. Yuri had met David in Kharkov five years earlier, when he arrived on the heels of our trip. It was through the efforts of the Bay Area Council that Yuri's California trip had been made possible.

Like many newly arriving Soviet Jews, Yuri purchased a used car over the summer even before learning how to drive. Driving lessons became our next joint project. Two to three times each week I drove from the suburbs to the city for his lesson. My "student," very nervous and stiff behind the wheel, complained, "It is hard to teach an old dog new tricks." Mastering the art of driving did not come quickly, and his chagrin was apparent when he failed to pass the driving test. It was not until the third try that he was victorious, and a beaming Tarnopolsky rushed into the waiting room to proudly announce his success. Someone might have thought he had just finished swimming the English Channel.

With a new feeling of independence after acquiring mobility, Yuri finally accepted a "first" job in Chicago. After five unsuccessful months in search of a post commensurate with his ability and stature as a scientist, he was compelled to accept a less satisfactory position at a small Chicago chemical company. Now he had successfully completed his next few steps in the process of adapting to a new way of life.

Although happy for Yuri, I experienced a feeling of personal loss. My role as rescuer had ended several months ago, and my duties at CASJ were greatly diminished. I had assumed an active role in the resettlement process, which had helped to fill a void.

After Eugene Chudnovsky and his family were granted permission to emigrate in May of 1987, he was able to secure a tenured position at Tufts University before they even arrived in Boston on June 9.

Our one remaining joint task was to help liberate Professor Yacov Alpert, and Yuri and I joined forces to intensify efforts in the deliverance of his friend.

Preparations were under way for the annual meeting of the Union of Councils for Soviet Jews, which would be held during September in Washington, D.C. For five years I had been making this pilgrimage with co-workers from Chicago Action. While attending seminars at the conference and exploring new methods of rescue, my primary goal had been to help build support and lobby for Yuri and his family. This year Yuri would be joining us at the conference--for me, it was the ultimate achievement. He had become a *cause celebre* despite his natural inclination to maintain privacy.

PART SIX: INNER CONFLICT

"The course of life is unpredictable . . . no one can write his autobiography in advance."

Abraham Joshua Heschel

Chapter I

OVER THE PRECIPICE

As our plane approached the runway of Dulles Airport in Washington, D.C., the stately dome of the U.S. Capitol shimmered in the distance. Rising proudly toward the sky amid the serene waters of the Potomac, it is the symbol of freedom for oppressed people throughout the world.

I glanced up at Yuri as his eyes gazed with wonder upon the majestic view below. We spotted the Washington Monument, the Jefferson Memorial, and the White House. It was a beautiful, sunny morning in the nation's capital when we arrived.

During the next few days I delighted in playing the role of official tour guide for Yuri. At the Vietnam Memorial he stood solemnly as he reflected on that most tragic time in American history.

Over two hundred representatives gathered together for the annual conference from all chapters of the Union of Councils, including delegates from Soviet Jewish action groups in England, France, and Israel. Newly liberated refuseniks and former prisoners like Yuri Tarnopolsky were flown in from all over the country and abroad for this meeting. Among the most illustrious were Avital and Anatoly Sharansky as well as Tanya and Zachar Zunshine. We had a large delegation from Chicago Action present, and among us sat Yuri.

For three days there were lectures, seminars, and think tank sessions for all representatives to the conference. Among the speakers were former refuseniks, including Yuri, government officials, and appointed members of the Union of Councils. Ambassador Warren Zimmerman, on leave from Vienna, addressed the opening session. He felt hopeful as more cases were being resolved, but the message from a representative of the White House was "We don't need gestures, only justice."

A demonstration was staged in front of the Soviet Embassy by activists carrying signs that read, "LET OUR PEOPLE GO."

From New York and Boston, several buses carrying former Soviet Jews arrived in the nation's capital on the second day of the conference to join members of the Union of Councils at the steps of the Capitol. Not even wet weather could dampen the spirits of an enthusiastic crowd numbering several hundred people, all of whom had gathered to listen to the stories of prominent activists and reports from political figures. Tanya and Zachar Zunshine joined Yuri Tarnopolsky at the podium that had been set up right on the steps of the Capitol. Signs saying "RAISE THE IRON CURTAIN," "LET US REALIZE GLASNOST," and many others with names of refuseniks held hostage were displayed in front of the podium in both English and Russian.

Our stay in Washington was coming to a close. It had been a heady time-- one of the highs on the five-year roller coaster ride. As it turned out, it was in fact an unnatural high.

Over those five years I had worked feverishly without letup in an increasingly demanding position. At stake in my work was someone's life, and that stress left me vulnerable to the increasingly severe ups and downs during our long campaign. Ultimately, I felt as if I were inside a pressure cooker.

Toward the end of our struggle for Yuri's liberation, the intensity and anxiety rose sharply. When victory was finally attained, I was floating in a state of unnatural elation. Waves of euphoria swept over me as I reveled in our sweet victory; the whole world seemed to be smiling down on us. Friends and family were deluged with details as I bubbled on about our achievement. Every minute revolved around preparations for the trip to Austria to welcome Yuri and his family to freedom, and I fantasized for weeks about the moment of their arrival.

Our reunion in Vienna was the realization of a dream and added to my euphoria. Nevertheless, all highs are followed by lows, and the first foreshadowing of an impending breakdown was on the trip back to Chicago, when I was unable to shake the "lows."

The next time for jubilation was the arrival of the Tarnopolsky family in Chicago. This was followed by another, still more difficult period of adjustment. As Yuri began to acquire new tools in the process of Americanization, he grew less dependent on me. He was creating a new life and no longer needed my support; he began to turn to his family and new job for sustenance and strength. In time, my high periods shortened and the lows increased in frequency and intensity. This emotional upheaval reached its peak in Washington.

The incident occurred the day before our scheduled departure. After a long and tiring day of meetings, Yuri and I went for a walk. Near Georgetown, we found a park bench where we could sit and relax. He mentioned his discomfort in not spending enough time with his roommate, a rabbi from the East Coast. The rabbi had been looking forward to meeting Yuri after hearing so much about his case. However, the annual meeting had packed the days with scheduled events and the evenings with dinners. Whenever there was a lull in activity, he and I had hurried off to go sightseeing. One day remained. Yuri thought he should allocate time for the rabbi.

My head began to spin as I felt the hours ticking away, and finally something inside me seemed to snap. No longer did I feel like Cinderella dressed for the ball. The bubble had burst, and I was turning into a pumpkin, dressed in emotional rags and surrounded by mice. After five years I had developed a possessory interest in Yuri's case. I had arrived in Washington with "my" victory trophy, but suddenly I was being tossed out to pasture. When my drowning victim safely reached the shore, I ceased to be his lifeline. I was not indispensable; I had served a purpose, and I felt as if I were now being abandoned.

In a rage, I flew out of control--the lid from the pressure cooker blew off, the pot exploded, hot sparks began flying. I found myself lashing out at the very person whom I had fought to save. Selfishly and irrationally, I began screaming with uncontrollable vengeance, "Damn it, you don't appreciate me. . . . You ungrateful rat. . . . I laid down my life for you. . . ." Immediately, I lost my balance and felt as if I were plummeting to the bottom of the earth from the peak of Mount Everest. Everything around me appeared to be going up in smoke; life was being snuffed out.

This sudden manifestation of instability caught Yuri by surprise, and he was unable to cope. Regrettably, I inflicted great pain on him with my irrational outburst. I was out of control. When I lashed out with unmerciful anger, unable to control my tongue, his face drained of color and turned to stone. He was *not* "my" possession, and he was ready to cut the umbilical cord. His warmth froze instantly like the icy waters of the Arctic. His masked face glared back at me in cold silence.

"Say something," I cried. "Don't just stare at me. . . . You're so damn Russian. . . ." Wracked by sobs, I shivered from the cold, frightened by the transformation--both his and my own. All at once I was that insecure child from my former life.

I feared our friendship was doomed on that chilly autumn day in Washington. I did not recognize the irate figure facing me. I did not understand my own wrath. As the storm moved in, I was being torn to pieces, limb by limb. Thoughts were splintering apart inside my head with hurricane force, and my eyes became sightless as volcanic dust spewed from the air. It is still difficult for me to explain exactly what happened at that time; the ramifications I carry with me to this day.

As the minutes turned into hours, and the time of our departure drew near, the gulf between us widened. Yuri's stony silence incited me further, and my unleashed hostility grew more intense as I sank deeper and deeper into depression and out of control. I felt deeply humiliated and wanted to talk; he was mute ... my vicious tirade continued. From time to time he shot a contemptuous look at me while muttering under his breath, "Stop it, Nancy!" I could feel the venom.

Our confrontation was a catalyst, a microcosm of misunderstandings and cultural differences erupting between East and West on a global scale. If we could not understand one another, how could we expect world leaders to settle their disputes?

Despite my heightened emotional condition, I fought unsuccessfully to get through to Yuri. Although I had been taught to deal with controversy through open communication, Yuri's experience was different. Openness was not known to him; he clammed up.

My co-workers were puzzled by our sudden lack of communication as they somberly observed my irrational behavior and Yuri's iciness. Nevertheless, they could do nothing to help defuse the situation.

We spent the final day of the conference on Capitol Hill, meeting with senators and congressman. Yuri and I had arranged in advance to meet with Congressman John Porter. As we walked to the Hill, we were not communicating. Off in the distance, we heard the screeching sound of sirens, and a caravan of black limousines sped toward us. As they passed in front of us, flying American and Soviet flags, we recognized Soviet Foreign Minister Eduard Shevardnadze and Secretary of State George Shultz, who were en route to their appointed meeting.

Congressman Porter would be joining us for a telephone call to Moscow to speak with Professor Yacov Alpert. This call, like all others to the Soviet Union, had been placed several days ahead. We were joined in the congressman's office by Avital Sharansky and Tanya Zunshine. The call to Moscow did not go through.

Yuri's mind and body had not yet healed from the long years of oppression and slavery. He was shocked and dismayed by my sudden mood swing and transformation from strength to fragility. He looked upon me as a stranger and did not like what he saw.

I had never given myself time to heal following the long, intense years of our freedom struggle. Throughout my commitment to Tarnopolsky's freedom, I never allowed myself time to confront what would happen after our achievement. I did not know that I had been walking a tightrope, very close to the edge. I thought I was invincible. I had begun as a dilettante in search of a cause. I had been converted to an activist. While in the USSR, I met my "intellectual soulmate," a trapped prisoner from whom I was separated by ten thousand miles. When victory was attained and the camera lights died down, I felt as if I were hanging from a precipice. I was blinded by the abyss and fearful of being thrust into oblivion. All at once, I realized that Yuri would be on his way *somewhere*, here today but gone tomorrow, and I would be stranded without an emotional outlet. I was not invincible, but was fighting to keep my head above water. I lost all sense of who I was and where I was. My complete disorientation caused me to feel as if I had arrived at the gates of hell. After the crash, it would take me years to recover from injuries sustained by the severe impact. The scars would always remain.

For several weeks after returning to Chicago, I slept away the days. I could not raise my head from the pillow or move my lethargic body. Feelings of rejection engulfed me like the torrents of a flash flood, and I felt myself drowning in sorrow. Obsessed by the confrontation between Yuri and me, I was filled with reproach and my self-image was shattered. Over and over, the incident was replayed like a recurring nightmare. The visions seemed real: doors slammed in my face, and I fled in a panicky rage as I searched for a return to the womb. All interest in everything around me was lost, and the worried efforts of my frantic family remained unnoticed. Most of all, I turned against myself.

Filled with uncontrollable remorse and self-pity, I felt I had no place to go and nothing worthwhile to do. I was no longer needed, and life lost all meaning. I turned into a zombie.

A constant rush of adrenaline created migraine headaches, and a throbbing pain began between my eyes and extended to the base of my neck. I developed stomach disorders, losing all taste for food. Frequent trips to the bathroom were precipitated by continuous waves of nausea. I began drinking too much, although never admitting to being on the verge of alcoholism. I began popping pills--both painkillers and sleeping pills. Pain, anxiety, and rage filled my days; then emptiness, denial, and memory loss.

One afternoon I found myself standing on the doorstep of a very close friend. When she opened the door, I stood there speechless, dissolved in tears. I shall never forget the fear in her eyes and how she gently led me into the kitchen. Lois prepared lunch but refused my request for a drink. She canceled her plans for the rest of the day. She listened as I opened up, and my feelings of remorse came tumbling out. I shall always be grateful for her lifeline of friendship, extended when I needed it the most.

Several days later I phoned Marillyn at Chicago Action. Immediately recognizing that I was in trouble and in desperate need of help, she gave me the name of a counselor and urged me to contact the woman at once. Never having received professional guidance, I was hesitant to call. "You can't handle this alone, Nancy. You need the sympathetic ear of an impartial person who is trained to treat disorders." It did not take me long to realize that my call to Marillyn was a cry for help. She was right. I was ill and urgently needed help. I made the call.

Chapter II

LONG ROAD BACK

Three days later I nervously entered the counselor's office. As I closed the door behind me, I was relieved to find nobody else in the waiting room. I dreaded being recognized since I was very self-conscious and ill at ease about being in the office of a therapist. Hesitantly I sat down and quickly surveyed the room. It was stark, dimly lit, and instead of a receptionist there was a buzzer for patients to announce their arrival.

As I squirmed in my chair, the door to the inner office opened and I was greeted by a smiling middle-aged woman who ushered me into her study. "You may speak freely here without feeling threatened or being judged," she said gently. Awkwardly, I slowly began talking. Quickly I was put at ease by her warm, understanding tone. In a firm yet sympathetic manner, she kindly beckoned me to relate my story and vent my feelings. As the words came tumbling out, I felt relieved by being able to confide in another person. She responded with compassion and support; I could trust her. Gratefully, I bared my soul and exposed my problems while she offered me a safe haven.

I had traveled from suburban housewife to Soviet Jewish activist. Although I knew many women activists, the difference was that I was driven by compulsion. I had reached the breaking point. I had ceased to function. She listened patiently as I spoke. By nature I am an analytical thinker, and this tool helped me re-create the situation as I focused on my dilemma. I was looking for answers, a quick cure for my problems. That did not exist. She made me probe more deeply. I would have to resolve my own problems through her guidance. It would take years of very hard and intense work as I struggled to regain my health. The balance of the scale did not tip overnight, nor could it be rebalanced without effort.

My relationship with Yuri remained strained. We spoke when necessary. Yacov Alpert's case continued unresolved, and we were obliged to continue our joint effort in bringing the case to completion. It was a difficult task because of my weakened condition and loss of self-esteem. I could barely help myself, and yet I was attempting to help deliver another human being. Somehow I had to force myself to look beyond my own problems so as to behave professionally.

Unlike the all-consuming campaign for Tarnopolsky's freedom, my role in the effort to help liberate Professor Alpert involved others in leadership positions. I had entered the case with Yuri at the tail end, and my official title in this effort was associate coordinator. My commitment was vastly weaker.

Two weeks after meeting with the counselor, I confided in Yuri that I had begun therapy. He regarded me intently, for the first time seeming to comprehend the gravity of the problem. When I divulged my feelings of abandonment, which had arisen following the success of our mission, he softened. It was not his fault that the cage door had opened and he was free. Yet he recognized the pain that no longer feeling needed had caused me and that he was the object of this suffering. Since he had been concerned with only his own plight, he had been unaware of the depth of others' emotional commitment. Despite his joy of freedom, my loss had not been taken into consideration. Nevertheless, our friendship continued to be strained.

Our relationship had changed in other ways as well. Cracks had begun forming on the surface and were threatening to penetrate still deeper. We now saw in each other imperfections that had earlier been hidden from view. I was no longer the invincible one to whom he looked for strength and leadership. He no longer was the oppressed hero.

I registered for a "life-planning seminar" directed by a woman whose background was in career counseling and adult development. The group was made up of twelve women, each of whom had arrived at a "fork in the road" and did not know which path to take. Some had gone through a personal crisis, and the others had arrived at this juncture naturally. All of us were looking for something substantive through which to redirect our energy. We were asked to focus on three specific areas: "Who am I? What is my purpose or mission in life? What will I do in the future?" The program involved weekly sessions over two months. It was comforting knowing that others were experiencing similar problems of adjustment.

Between my weekly counseling sessions and seminar meetings, I found myself beginning to take two steps forward and one step backward. It would be a long and very painful process. I was completely self-focused, trying desperately to regain my strength and purpose in life. Yet I remained in a state of deep depression. It was a most difficult period of time for Marty and Rob since my attention and energy were directed away and I was concentrating solely on my own well-being. They were forced to fend for themselves. Steve was not affected since he was away at college.

I began to purchase self-help books and eventually read every one that I could find on the market. In addition, I read novels and autobiographies about women who had gone through trauma and were seeking new avenues. Reading became an escape mechanism, a trip to a distant world. While focusing on the lives of others, I could avoid my own pain. I found comfort in learning about other people who had suffered severe shocks and were trying to cope with their problems. Although the nature of every situation was uniquely different, the common thread was the need to find a solution.

I joined a Great Books discussion group, hoping to elevate my reading to a higher plateau and take my mind off myself, at least temporarily. Nevertheless, I found it difficult to concentrate on the reading assignments because of my depression.

The struggle continued for Yacov Alpert and his wife, Svetlana. On December 24, 1987, the newly liberated physicist and his wife departed from Moscow on a flight to Vienna. We then intensified our efforts to bring them swiftly into the United States without having to go first to Italy. Because of the professor's age and prominence, this was accomplished. Professor Alpert secured a position with the National Aeronautic and Space Administration (NASA), and Svetlana obtained a research position at Harvard University.

I continued my association with CASJ, although my work was strictly peripheral. I seldom went into the office because it held too many memories of former times when I was successfully engaged in a leadership role and passionately involved in work. Cyrillic classes, for tourists going to the USSR, proceeded as usual at my home. In addition, I remained in my role as Speaker's Bureau chairperson.

As depression continued to weigh me down, I felt a need to do something dramatically different with my life. Becoming a docent for the Chicago Lyric Opera enabled me to escape into another world--for a while. During one school year I worked with elementary school children in helping them stage a production of Rossini's *La Cenerentola*. The music was uplifting, and the children's responsiveness helped take my mind off my own problems. But this work really was just a distraction and brought only temporary relief. As the curtain came down on the final act of *La Cenerentola* after each performance, I retreated back into my shell.

Luba and Yury Verlinsky offered me a voluntary position to head an outreach program for newly arriving Soviet Jewish immigrants. The purpose of the program was to acquaint newcomers with American volunteers who would help to introduce them to the American way of life. It would be run under the auspices of the Jewish Community Centers of Chicago. Grateful for their support and confidence in me, I accepted the Verlinskys' offer.

Donning my new hat in the community, I began to design the program. Lists of new families were submitted by the community center, which were matched as closely as possible with compatible American Jewish families, all of whom were volunteers. Accompanying the volunteers on the initial visit to meet their Russian family, I maintained my presence within the Russian community. We felt satisfied and encouraged by our warm reception from the immigrant families. In time new immigrants came to expect the visit that their friends had told them of, and they looked forward to meeting the "welcome team." Nevertheless, as I plunged into this new venture, I was operating with the same obsessive compulsion that had taken over my life during the years of the Tarnopolsky campaign.

Each visit at an apartment of new immigrants was reminiscent of meetings held with refuseniks in the Soviet Union. We received the same gracious hospitality, and food was prepared Russian-style. The apartments were usually small and sparsely furnished, mostly with used pieces handed down from family, friends, and help from the Jewish Family Service. Mementos from the "old country" were found in every room, from photos to trinkets. Missing were the dread of oppression and the paranoia about speaking in possibly bugged rooms. As with the Tarnopolskys, though, all was not hearts and flowers. For the newly arrived immigrants terror was replaced by anxiety over beginning new lives in a foreign land with a different tongue, new customs, and the pressure of finding employment.

After the introductory visit the volunteer families were on their own to arrange further meetings according to their own needs and schedules. Each volunteer was given a list of guidelines to follow, and they were to report back on their progress. We also dealt with any problems encountered between the families.

Yuri soon began helping me with my new venture, and I relied on him for help with problems or questions that arose regarding the immigrant families. At times he acted as translator if communication difficulties arose. On other occasions he offered advice based on his own recent experiences in dealing with specific situations. As a new Chicagoan, he was sensitive to the needs of other immigrants.

After several months over fifty new Chicagoan families had been matched with American Jewish families. Many successful matches were made, and they became extended families. Others were less successful and the new relationships were short-lived.

On June 10, 1988, over two hundred people gathered to attend a welcome dinner at North Shore Congregation Israel for the new Russian families participating in the program and their matched American families. Upon greeting all the new families as they entered, I felt a renewed sense of accomplishment and pride.

The evening was a beautiful melding of cultures. Each family, Russian and American, had brought a favorite dish, and Hebrew and Russian folk music filled the room. A recent emigre from Kharkov sang and played traditional Russian folk songs on the guitar; a fourteen-year-old who had emigrated with his family from Kiev four months earlier played the clarinet. Finally, Rabbi Hart led the group in song as he sang and played Israeli folk music on the guitar.

When I addressed the group, I spoke about the great strength and courage required to leave one's country and immigrate to a foreign land. "I think of a tree being uprooted and transplanted in a different place. It goes into shock and needs time to begin to grow again. Our Russian friends have been uprooted, they have left many loved ones behind, and they have journeyed halfway around the world to begin a new life, a task which is both exciting and frightening." I concluded with a short address to our Russian guests, which Yuri had carefully helped me prepare so that my Russian would be clearly understandable. As I glanced over at Yuri when I finished speaking, he was smiling and nodding in approval.

Yuri followed me to the podium. He began by making a joke about having to compete with my Russian. Everyone laughed. "We, as Soviet Jews, had a great desire to find a land flowing with milk and honey. We also have a great distaste for every form of slavery, which has been left behind. . . . There is a small number of former Russian immigrants present here today who were more fortunate than we because they arrived in the United States between eight and ten years ago. Like American Jews, they have spent a lot of time and energy to help those of us who have recently immigrated to this country. . . . We hope to join the great American Jewish family and to be together with you as one family."

A new spark of happiness and pride seemed to flow through my veins throughout this enchanted evening, but when it was over I felt like the mother of the bride. Though I was pleased and relieved that everything had gone smoothly, a new wave of depression slowly began to descend on me.

Several months later I finally recognized the need to distance myself from the Russian community. A break had to be made if I were to get well, and what I needed was a complete redirection of my energy.

I decided to return to the work force. Twenty years had passed since I had held a salaried position. I applied for jobs, none very interesting. Everything appeared dull after the absorbing work I had done without pay. Finally I accepted a position as a receptionist at a real estate office. From suburban housewife to Soviet Jewish activist to receptionist? Bored and unhappy, I left after six months.

I had to keep busy. I was reading constantly, but that was only a temporary retreat into another world. I needed to work; there had to be a reason to get up each morning; I needed a place to go. I did not wish to continue with volunteer work as a career because I was ready to be compensated with a salaried position. Nevertheless, my first job had been unsatisfactory.

Soon I concluded that no full-time position for which I was qualified would be satisfying, so I took a new approach.

I registered with a temporary employment agency and began to accept positions that lasted anywhere from one day to a few months. I never stayed anyplace long enough to become bored. My enjoyment came from the independence I felt in being able to control my schedule and assignments. The ever-changing environment and new faces offered greater stimulus. I found myself learning fresh skills and adapting to different situations. I relished the challenge of having to be instantly professional at any given task. The more demanding the position, the greater my enthusiasm. The harder I worked, the less time I had to dwell on myself. Becoming computer literate opened up a whole new range of possibilities.

Nevertheless, my heart was not in my work, and the quest for a solution continued. I was tormented by the notion that I could attain neither peace nor contentment despite my determination to change my life. As my mood swings continued, there were good days and bad days even though my initial emotional upheaval had subsided. The desire to work creatively in an unstructured setting continued to plague me, and I yearned to feel needed. As I searched for stability and purpose, I tried to appear strong. "I'm laughing on the outside but crying on the inside," I wrote in my diary.

By this time Yuri and his family had left Chicago. On December 7, 1988, he left alone for Providence, Rhode Island, to accept a new position. The day he departed from Chicago, Marty and I were in Hong Kong--too far away to be reminded of his "moving day." I could not deal with it. Yuri's family joined him six months later, following Irina's graduation from high school. After twenty-one months in Chicago, he was granted a unique position in his field of chemistry, of the caliber he had long been seeking. At this New England company he was given full range to pursue and develop his own projects. He was accepted as a distinguished scientist and treated with proper respect. Two years later he would receive his first American patent.

I missed Yuri, but I knew that accepting this offer had been the right decision for him. I was proud of him. Although his absence had left an immense void, we would not drift apart. The door remained open for him to return, and I knew I would always be welcome to visit New England.

Gradually I began to accept a broader range of assignments, which kept me busy and stimulated. More energy was directed toward my family, and they welcomed my return. Home took on new interest for me.

Recovery was still incomplete. I was happy with my new life, but something important was missing. The gaping void had never been filled after I removed myself entirely from the Russian scene.

I realized it was impossible to turn my back and completely forget about something that had held great meaning in my life. I had been totally dedicated to the cause of Soviet Jewry, focusing 100 percent of my energy in that direction. By comparison, my present work as an office employee paled.

I could not continue with life, nor could I find peace, until I dealt with my unfinished mission. It was while sitting on a bench in New York's Central Park that I realized I had not fulfilled the obligation of a witness to give testimony. And so I began this book. It was November 1990.

Chapter III

JOURNEY CONTINUES . . .

It is now 1993. Eleven years have passed since my life took an abrupt turn into a world filled with immense opportunities and enormous risks. It was a rocky new path that I followed, scattered with both shattered images and precious stones.

Throughout those years I did not have the luxury of sitting back and reflecting on what was happening--how my metamorphosis from suburban housewife to activist was affecting those close to me as well as myself. Chronicling this tale has allowed me to look at each moment of the last decade and fit it into the total picture. With twenty-twenty hindsight, I now wish I had seen certain incidents more clearly as they were unfolding.

My husband, Marty, had suffered greatly throughout my deepening involvement with Soviet Jewry, but I was unaware of his pain while I was pursuing the rescue effort. When we spent time together, he knew that my head was frequently elsewhere. But despite his anguish and loneliness, he remained my most ardent supporter. No one expressed greater pride in my accomplishments while dismissing my failures. He could not, of course, sit passively by while I retreated further and further into another world, and friction between us inevitably strained our marriage. Nevertheless, Marty remained steadfast while waiting for me to return home. He then immediately supported my plan to write this book, appreciating its potential historical value and contribution to the movement as well as my need to purge my demons.

Both of our sons, Steve and Rob, had felt my absence. I had attended school functions, observed their progress, monitored "minor child crises," and officially assumed the responsibility of motherhood, yet my mind was elsewhere. I had been unable to properly fulfill the role of caretaker and homemaker and was often not in tune with my children's needs. Although my love for them never wavered, it was not until later that I realized my negligence.

To this day I am awed by the fact that the boys--now young men--never failed me even though at times I had failed them. Once they realized the struggle that had taken place during the years of dedication, old feelings of resentment withered away. They both rallied in support of my new endeavor and were excited about the prospects of this book.

Happily, many friends remained faithful and were pleased to welcome me back when I felt ready to return socially. Many of these people had also been actively involved in other worthwhile endeavors, although most found it difficult to comprehend my total absorption with work. Although I had been negligent in my role as "friend," those who stood close by during the years of involvement, and observed in anguish my tumble into depression, remain my dearest companions today.

My life for eleven years was the life of Soviet Jews, and my closely knit group of colleagues at CASJ became my extended family. We shared not only common interests and goals but also mutual respect and admiration. We had worked side by side with a driving, unparalleled intensity to our cause and the mounting danger confronting our refusenik friends. They became our dearest comrades, part of our *mishpocheh,* and we felt a real kinship since most of our families had originated in Eastern Europe.

Most affected, as a friend and "working partner," was Yuri Tarnopolsky. Throughout the years of our struggle, as we fought for freedom from both sides of the Iron Curtain, we formed a formidable partnership. At the same time, we developed a bond that would carry us through life. Following his emancipation from the USSR, our friendship has been like a roller-coaster ride along a bumpy track, with sparks of joy and bursts of sorrow. We've encountered harmony through mutual inspiration, and we've experienced discord as a result of unresolved conflicts. Bound by a common struggle, we are obsessed with achieving our goals while sharing the love of creative expression. Nevertheless, our philosophy of life is different since we emerged from opposite sides of the globe.

I tend to think positively and approach my tasks with optimism. Perhaps I am too idealistic, but I remain convinced that anything within reason is attainable if a person adheres to a strong work ethic. In reaching for the top, I run into danger when I become too intense and my goal becomes an obsession. By that time I'm unable to apply the brakes. Years ago I promised Yuri that I would *never* run short of "impatience" and "persistence"--I couldn't if we were to win our struggle for freedom. Although moderation is safer, only risk takers can attain the heights, and nothing compares with the exhilaration of reaching the top.

Yuri repeatedly risked his life in the battle for liberation not only for himself but also for others. These unselfish acts of bravery cost him years of hardship and humiliation before he was finally granted permission to emigrate. As a result, he feels defensive when threatened by problems that seem to jeopardize his security or block his freedom. Long periods of solitude often follow, and my frequent attempts to alleviate his stress usually fall on deaf ears. Freedom, his most precious possession, remains his ultimate obsession.

As a scientist, he tends to think negatively until theories are proven, although finding solutions to previously insolvable problems is his forte. "I want to prove that the impossible is possible," he said to me one day. As an author and poet, he believes that creativity is born only through pain; the more excruciating the creative process, the finer the work. Anything generated without pain is automatically held suspect. In addition, there can be *no* enjoyment until *after* the work is completed. Friction arises between us when he becomes morose and uncommunicative; I find his addiction to suffering very irritating.

Unfortunately, Yuri's approach to life has been influenced by years of oppression and incarceration. With this I can empathize. I experienced an emotional struggle following Yuri's rescue, but he underwent a violent transplantation. For him life will never be easy. A victim of tyranny, he cannot escape his past.

Two people, two worlds--from tyranny to freedom . . .
Though we cannot change our basic personalities or behavioral patterns, we are learning to be tolerant of one another's shortcomings and to accept our differences since we want to coexist. Neither Yuri nor I can forget the magnetism responsible for drawing us together in the first place; from the very beginning we felt we were destined to meet. We continue to be a source of inspiration for one another and take comfort in the closeness of our friendship. There is an old Russian proverb: "A sorrow shared is half a sorrow, but a joy shared is twice a joy."

It has been difficult for others to appreciate our bond. As kindred spirits, we feel mutual respect and admiration. The strength of our alliance has been tested repeatedly throughout many difficult times, but our friendship has remained steadfast. "Only survivors of thunderstorms and hurricanes can appreciate the sharp delight from the penetrating rays of the sun," I wrote to Yuri after we had resolved one of our most tempestuous conflicts.

After catapulting over the precipice in 1987, I went through a long period of catharsis. Years passed before I began to heal. I realized I could no longer feel the pure joy of an ingenue, nor could I ever again sink to the depths of despair. In coming to terms with myself, I was able to reflect on my years as an activist with pride and gratitude.

I had been given the advantage of bearing witness to one of the most important and colorful periods of Jewish history. My role represented one small part in the total framework of a massive operation. The entire network of activity had been a real *tour de force* . . . it was a privilege to have been asked to participate.

To this day, I believe that my life as an activist was my natural destiny, and I have accepted my fate as well as my responsibilities. There was a price to pay for my decision, and I paid it. I am still paying. Yet I have no regrets for my actions. I feel that I received even more than I gave, and if history were to repeat itself, I am certain that I would follow the same path. The future is filled with uncertainties, and the journey of Soviet Jews from tyranny to freedom remains unfinished . . .

Birth is a beginning
And death a destination.
And life is a journey:
From childhood to maturity
And youth to age;
From innocence to awareness
And ignorance to knowing;
From foolishness to discretion
And then, perhaps, to wisdom;
From weakness to strength
Or strength to weakness-
And, often, back again;
From health to sickness
And back, we pray, to health again;
From offense to forgiveness,
From loneliness to love,
From joy to gratitude,
From pain to compassion,
And grief to understanding-
From fear to faith;
From defeat to defeat to defeat-
Until, looking backward or ahead,
We see that victory lies
Not at some high place along the way,
But in having made the journey, stage by stage,
A sacred pilgrimage.
Birth is a beginning,
And death a destination
And life is a journey,
A sacred pilgrimage-
To life everlasting.[1]

Alvin Fine

[1]Reprinted by permission of the Central Conference of American Rabbis, New York.

EPILOGUE

"There are signs that the pendulum is swinging back."

Drastic changes in Soviet policy have occurred since my days as an activist. Throughout the 1980s only a trickle of Soviet Jews was permitted to emigrate, and a large percentage were entering the United States. Jacov Mesh, whose family hosted the Rozentals during our visit to Odessa, emigrated to New York in January 1986. The following January, Lev Blitshtein, our chief Moscow contact, received permission to emigrate. He rejoined his family, who were also living in New York.

Some chose Israel. Mark Nashpitz, former prisoner of conscience and dentist from Moscow, emigrated in October 1985. From Kharkov were Liliya Zatuchnaya and her son, Valdimir, who emigrated in March 1987; former prisoner of conscience Alexander Paritsky arrived with his family in April; and the Soloveichiks went to Israel in May.

On October 15, 1987, newly freed Ida Nudel arrived in Israel with her pet collie aboard the private jet of Armand Hammer, who accompanied her from Moscow. The headlines read, "REFUSENIKS *GUARDIAN ANGEL* NUDEL WELCOMED IN ISRAEL BY THOUSANDS." Everyone from Jane Fonda to the Israeli cabinet, including Prime Minister Yitzhak Shamir and Foreign Minister Shimon Peres, was waiting at the airport to greet her.

Alexander Yoffe, the Moscow physicist whose film Marty and I had taken with us to Paris, was permitted to leave Moscow with his family in January 1988. They immigrated to Israel. Judith and Leonid Byaly arrived in Israel one month later, followed by Natasha Khassina in April.

In June 1988 the Pekar family emigrated from Moscow . . . destination unknown.

The ratio of Jews immigrating to America over Israel changed in October 1989 with the enforcement of a United States law stating that only those Jews with first-degree relatives would be eligible to enter the USA.

In July 1989 Chicago newspapers reported: "CHICAGO'S ABE STOLAR COMES HOME AFTER 58 YEARS." Abe and his wife, Gita, who had immigrated to Israel earlier in March, returned to his native city for a visit. Hundreds of fans, including Senator Paul Simon, were waiting to greet him.

By June 1990 the door to the Soviet Union began to open, and thousands of Jews started fleeing the country, mostly to Israel. A fear of unrest leading to possible revolution and growing terror over what might happen "tomorrow" were reflected by the soaring emigration figures.

Boris Kelman was permitted to emigrate with his family from Leningrad in July 1990. They chose the United States and settled in San Francisco. Boris immediately began working for the Bay Area Council of Soviet Jews. Mike Lumar, who received his visa in February 1992 also came to the United States. He settled in Brooklyn, New York.

In spite of glasnost and perestroika, there was little indication that living conditions had improved inside the former USSR in the 1990s. Glasnost, a kind of "rationed freedom," gave rise to staunchly anti-Semitic organizations such as Pamyat. Restructuring attempts under perestroika have failed to ease the shortage of food, and bread lines are longer than ever.

As the Soviet republics began to crumble and break away, the feeling of civil unrest grew. Mikhail Gorbachev suffered a major defeat in 1990, when Boris Yeltsin was elected chairman of the Russian Republic, which encompassed over 50 percent of the population of the USSR and 76 percent of its territory. By 1991 Lithuania, Latvia, Estonia, Moldavia, and Georgia had all declared their independence. A proclamation of sovereignty led to bloodshed as the Soviet military attempted to quell the rebellion.

Gorbachev's weakness was Yeltsin's strength. Yeltsin's platform called for greater independence, while Gorbachev remained staunchly against any form of emancipation.

By the time Gorbachev's unpopularity hit its peak in 1991, the Union of Councils for Soviet Jews had been operating a joint bureau in Moscow for nearly one year. The bureau was established to assist Soviet Jews in the monitoring of anti-Semitism, emigration, human rights, and the rule of law. It was staffed by Soviet Jews and rotating American representatives from the UCSJ. Jewish refuseniks were lining up daily at the bureau, located at 14 ulitsa Novoslobodskaya, for help and information.

In January 1991, 13,600 Soviet Jews immigrated to Israel, but the number dropped sharply in February as a result of the Persian Gulf War. Yet even as missiles were falling on Tel Aviv, immigrants continued to arrive. During February 7,000 Soviet Jews landed in Israel and were handed gas masks as they deplaned. War posed less of a threat than remaining captive behind the Iron Curtain. After military operations were suspended in Iraq, immigration rose to 14,000 in March.[1]

Despite continuing flights between Moscow and Tel Aviv, by spring of 1991 renewed fear surfaced that emigration could be halted at any moment. At that time, between one and two million Soviet Jews were still seeking to emigrate. This concern was echoed not only by Jews in the Soviet Union but also by Western Sovietologists. Increasing instability within Soviet republics, uncertainty

---

[1]Statistical figures obtained through the Israeli consulate.

over the future of Mikhail Gorbachev, and the return of power to military control validated public concern.

Increased emigration did not prevent obstacles from surfacing. While a "window of emigration" was still open, there were signs that it would eventually shut. Jewish visa applicants continued to experience long delays after initiating the emigration process. Some had been waiting for permission for over a year. Other Soviet Jews chose not to apply for fear of being refused, knowing an application for emigration would threaten their livelihoods and the future of their children.

The Soviet Jewry movement documented thousands of cases who were denied visas in 1991. There were indications that thousands of others were refused, but their names are unknown. Suddenly a few OVIR offices began to close, effectively shutting the window in those areas.

A petition to President Bush titled "Emergency Reunification of Divided Soviet Jewish Families" was drawn up and signed by a group of Soviet Jews and Soviet Jewish emigres. This action triggered a proposal by the U.S. Emergency Committee for the Rescue of Soviet Jews to evacuate a limited group of Jews to America. It was endorsed by the Union of Councils. The targeted group consisted of separated families whose spouses, parents, or children were already living in the United States. The committee aimed to reunite these families by exceeding the quota of Soviet immigrants to the United States. The plan was severely condemned by both Israeli officials and leaders of the Jewish Agency, who mistakenly felt it was a conscious effort to divert Soviet Jews away from Israel.

Kharkov, former home of Yuri Tarnopolsky, embodies the problems of the late Soviet Union in microcosm. "Kharkov has changed," explained Sandy Spinner of the Cincinnati Council, which had made Kharkov its sister city, "and yet it's unchanged. Many of the same people are in power but are wearing different hats. The new president of Ukraine was formerly the first secretary of the party. An old Communist, he's now a democratic leader.

"But from the fall of the USSR to just recently, anti-Semitism was far less of a threat to Jews in Ukraine than in the Russian republic as well as the Moslem republics and the Baltics. The reason is the emergence of the Rukh movement, a democratic movement in Ukraine. The first generation of Rukh leaders included former prisoners of conscience and human rights activists. Over the last few months, however, the Rukh leadership changed, and what had been feared became a reality. Rukh was taken over by the nationalistic/Fascist element. A new publication came out, *New Ukraine*, which is nationalistic and anti-Semitic. Writers for the newspaper infiltrated the Rukh movement, some of whom hold positions of leadership in the Kharkov government. Telephone communication continues to be interrupted as calls are disconnected. *There are signs that the pendulum is swinging back.* More people are becoming disenchanted with the democratic movement because nothing in their lives has been improved. The

Communists have won. The Jewish community continues to be fragmented, and people remain suspicious of one another. They have good reason."

Pamela Cohen, returning in December 1992 from the first International Human Rights Conference in Central Asia, told an equally frightening story. "We had just concluded a press conference on the final day of the meeting," reported Pam. "Abdumanob Pulatov, a human rights activist and citizen of Uzbekistan, was kidnapped and arrested in the presence of two journalists, one from *Moscow News* and the other from *Izvestia*. Reportedly, he was indicted for organizing student 'disturbances' early this year in Tashkent. Two others were arrested at the same time, but they were later released."

Shaking her head sadly, Marillyn Tallman said, "It's still happening. This is the case of a nondemocratic country committing an illegal act. Witnesses saw Pulatov pushed into a car, and he was driven over the border back into Uzbekistan by KGB agents. He did *not* instigate student riots, but he did organize an intellectual human rights round table for student discussion."

"This is why we're still here," said Pamela. "We feel compelled to stay active and help those left behind. The big difference in the 1990s is that now we're speaking to all remaining Jews in the former Soviet Union. In the past we concentrated our efforts on activists. Even if we had recognized a long-lost relative on the street in Moscow, we could not acknowledge him. As we all know, only those on our list were approached; anyone else could have been suspect."

Significant changes have taken place since Marty's and my trip to the USSR eleven years ago. Nevertheless, it was clear that our task was far from over.

"Nancy," said Pamela, "we're leaving for Washington in two weeks for a debriefing with Micah [Naftalin, national director of UCSJ] on the Human Rights Conference. Why don't you join us?"

Not hesitating for a moment, I agreed.

In Washington I learned, in briefings with UCSJ staff as well as through constant phone updates from councils across the nation, that conditions were much worse than I had imagined. I heard the harrowing details of the civil war in Tajikistan, where murder, rape, and robbery had forced the evacuation of the U.S. Embassy. I heard that Pulatov was still in prison in Uzbekistan; now the trumped-up charges had been changed to the ludicrous accusation of "insulting the dignity of the president." It was all just an excuse to arrest the man who was slated to become the director of the new Human Rights Bureau opening in Bishkek, Kyrgyzstan.

"Give me your tired, your poor, your huddled masses yearning to breathe free." So says the inscription on the Statue of Liberty, and in Washington in 1993 I found that the cry for the sanctuary promised by the United States of America has grown louder than ever. As a result of pressure from UCSJ, our government agreed to put endangered refugees at the head of the long line of five hundred thousand "homeless, tempest-tossed" waiting to "breathe free," but the process still was expected to take a year. In the meantime, a lot will depend on the recently installed Clinton administration.

Also in the meantime, CASJ and the other councils, here and abroad, go on with their battle to disarm one of the greatest threats facing the Soviet Jewry movement in the 1990s: public ignorance. Many people erroneously assume that the problem concerning Russian Jews in the former Soviet Union has been solved now that a large exodus has taken place. Thus the movement has to deal with not only a revival of serious crackdowns in emigration policies and restrictive U.S. immigration policies, but also the reeducation of the public.

It is my hope that this book, which represents my personal contribution to the continuing struggle for Russian Jews, will help to achieve that last goal. As the pages unfolded before my eyes, they reflected my soul and my search for inner peace.

AFTERWORD

By Yuri Tarnopolsky

I always wanted somebody to tell the story of the rescue of Soviet Jews by American housewives. First of all, I wanted to know what was going on in America while I was in Russia. Second, why American Jews wanted to spend money and time on people they did not know was always a mystery for refuseniks in Russia. Finally, I abided by the conviction, which no American took seriously, that the fall of the Soviet empire and the advent of glasnost were, in practical terms, pushed by American and Israeli Jews. I do not expect this idea to be popular. On the contrary, I expect violent opposition from almost everybody in the world, except for Russian and Ukrainian anti-Semites.

Of course Soviet political dissidents started it all. Sakharov and others formulated the idea that communism failed to achieve its own goals, to withstand the competition with the West, and to create a humane society.

Thousands of Russian, Ukrainian, Lithuanian, and other dissidents paid a high price for expressing their views. The Soviet government responded with psychiatric prisons, labor camps, and exile.

The decision to leave Russia did not demand as much courage as open political dissent. Compared with political and religious dissidents, Soviet Jews who wanted to emigrate appeared to be servile solicitors. Whatever they thought about communism, they did not show any political disloyalty. Nevertheless, they voted against communism with their feet, and on a mass scale.

I wonder if somebody noted that the Jewish exodus from Russia was actually the earliest practical attempt of a nation to split from the Soviet empire.

The state of Israel supported the Soviet Jewish movement, but it had no diplomatic relations with the USSR and no direct leverage. It was the organized campaign of American Jews that hit the foundation of the Soviet empire not just with words, protests, and humble requests but with dynamite. It was, in my opinion, the explosive Jackson-Vanik Amendment that made the first material crack in the foundation of the empire. It tied trade to emigration from the USSR.

For a while Soviet Jews who wanted to emigrate were spared the repressions inflicted on dissidents. They were simply labeled by Soviet propaganda as greedy people who were willing to trade their Motherland for American blue jeans. However, people in the Kremlin finally understood all the implications of the "reunification of families." After a new turn of the cold war in 1983, Jewish refusenik activists were grouped with the rest of the dissenters, and cruel persecution followed.

The grass-roots movement of the Union of Councils for Soviet Jews, which is described in Nancy's book, was the only direct interface between America and the oppressed and disconnected refuseniks in the Soviet Union. The movement accomplished what American Jews had failed to do during the beginning of the Holocaust. It mobilized all political channels of pressure on the Soviet government. It maintained the awareness of the American public. Equally important, it established a lifeline of both moral and material support for refusenik activists and the families of prisoners.

It is the strategy of personal contacts that makes the activity of Chicago Action and the other councils so remarkable. I believe the first Raul Wallenberg Award presented to Pamela Cohen and Marillyn Tallman in April 1987 by Prince Sigvard of Sweden is an excellent tribute in recognition of all those who courageously made their way into a troubled Russia.

Even after I had come to America, I had no complete understanding of the extent of that unprecedented movement until I had read Nancy's book.

Nancy and Martin Rosenfeld and scores of other activists in the Union of Councils went not only to the capital of the Soviet Union, but also to isolated provincial cities. Followed by KGB, they dragged heavy bags with jeans and coats through the streets of the Evil Empire and returned to shabby hotels with names, information, and live impressions. As to the now empty bags, a pair of blue jeans that had managed to find its way to the "traitors of the Motherland" could provide a family of two with food for a month.

For the American Jews who lobbied for the Jackson-Vanik Amendment and supported the refuseniks, it was nothing but a Jewish issue. It was not the same from the Soviet perspective.

For the Soviets, Jewish emigration, as well as political, religious, and national dissent, was just one problem of Western interference in internal Soviet affairs. If they had to deal with one, they had to resolve the others. The result is well known. The resistance of Afghanistan, the courage of the Sakharovs, the perseverance of dissidents, the firm stand of the American government on human rights--all that finally did its job. The failure of communism was officially recognized by the Soviet leaders, and communism lost the cold war.

For Nancy and me, our meetings in Vienna and Chicago turned out to be the beginning of a remarkable friendship. Still, it was not the end of our story.

Ironically, Nancy and I became involved in yet another refusal together. Full of impressions and memories, we were anxious to get our stories out. I was working on my *Memoirs of 1984*, published simultaneously with this book, while Nancy was working on her *Unfinished Journey*. It was extremely difficult to find a publisher for either of them. "It's a nice book, but the Soviet Union does not exist. It is no longer our worst enemy. Nobody is interested in Russian matters anymore." These were standard responses.

This time, being on the same side of the border with her, I could observe

Nancy in action. She became a literary agent for both of us. A quick learner, she grasped a lot of new things. First of all, she learned how to write a book and did it the hard way. She learned how to present manuscripts, promote a concept, contact key people, sell books, communicate by computer, be understanding with partners, accept criticism, and much more.

Again, I was overwhelmed by her incredible energy, patience, optimism, sensitivity, and determination.

And she won the second time.

Our books did not overlap. Nancy and I were on opposite sides of the border during our common struggle, and our experiences were very much different. Nancy's book is a personal story. However, I see it as a part of a larger picture, and I stubbornly insist: "This is how history was made."

American Jews can be proud of their own contribution to the major world event on the break of the millennium--the fall of the Communist Empire. What is not less important, the sad story of the abandonment of European Jews during the Nazi plague, now has a bright counterbalance.

Narragansett, Rhode Island
January 1993

LIST OF COUNCILS

ALASKA: ALASKA COUNCIL FOR SOVIET JEWS
3605 Arctic Boulevard, Suite 1177
Anchorage, Alaska 99503-5789

ARIZONA: ARIZONA ACTION FOR SOVIET JEWRY
7518 North 13th Avenue
Phoenix, Arizona 85021

CALIFORNIA: BAY AREA COUNCIL FOR SOVIET JEWRY
106 Baden Street
San Francisco, California 94131

SOUTHERN CALIFORNIA COUNCIL FOR SOVIET
JEWS
3755 Goodland Avenue
Studio City, California 91604

CANADA: ACTION COMMITTEE FOR SOVIET JEWRY
6767 Cote des Neiges, Suite 321
Montreal, Quebec
H352T6 Canada

VANCOUVER ACTION FOR SOVIET JEWS
CANADIAN JEWISH CONGRESS
950 West 41st Avenue
Vancouver, British Columbia
VZ5 2N7 Canada

COLORADO: COLORADO COMMITTEE OF CONCERN FOR SOVIET
JEWRY
295 South Locust Street
Denver, Colorado 80224

BOULDER ACTION FOR SOVIET JEWRY
934 Pearl Street, Suite F
Boulder, Colorado 80302

CONNECTICUT: CONNECTICUT COMMITTEE FOR SOVIET JEWS
                1045 54th Street
                Brooklyn, New York 11219

DISTRICT OF   WASHINGTON COMMITTEE FOR SOVIET JEWRY
COLUMBIA: 1401 Blair Mill Road, Suite 101
                Silver Spring, Maryland 20910

FLORIDA   SARASOTA CONFERENCE ON SOVIET JEWRY
                P.O. Box 2778
                Sarasota, Florida 33578

                SOUTH FLORIDA CONFERENCE ON SOVIET JEWRY
                10691 N. Kendall Drive, Suite 309
                Miami, Florida 33176

                WEST PALM BEACH JEWISH FEDERATION
                OF PALM BEACH COUNTY
                4601 Community Drive
                West Palm Beach, Florida 33417-2760

GEORGIA: ATLANTA ACTION FOR SOVIET JEWRY
                310 Lighthouse Point NW
                Atlanta, Georgia 30328

ILLINOIS: CHICAGO ACTION FOR SOVIET JEWRY
                555 Vine Avenue, Suite 107
                Highland Park, Illinois 60035

MARYLAND: WASHINGTON COMMITTEE FOR SOVIET JEWRY
                (See District of Columbia)

MASSACHUSETTS: BERKSHIRE COUNCIL FOR SOVIET JEWRY
                22 Marlboro Drive
                Pittsfield, Massachusetts 01201

                BOSTON ACTION FOR SOVIET JEWRY
                24 Crescent Street, Suite 306
                Waltham, Massachusetts 02154

MINNESOTA: MINNESOTA/DAKOTAS ACTION COMMITTEE FOR
                  SOVIET JEWRY
                  111 3rd Avenue South, Suite 112
                  Minneapolis, Minnesota 55402

NEBRASKA: OMAHA COMMITTEE FOR SOVIET JEWRY
                  11217 Woolworth Plaza
                  Omaha, Nebraska 68144

NEW MEXICO: LOS ALAMOS COMMITTEE ON SOVIET ANTI-
                  SEMITISM
                  2377 A 45th Street
                  Los Alamos, new Mexico 87544

                  SANTA FE COUNCIL FOR SOVIET JEWS
                  P.O. Box 9870
                  Santa Fe, New Mexico 87504-9870

NEW YORK: LONG ISLAND COMMITTEE FOR SOVIET JEWRY
                  726 Merrick Avenue
                  East Meadow, New York 11020

                  OCEANFRONT COUNCIL FOR SOVIET JEWRY
                  3300 Coney Island Avenue
                  Brooklyn, New York 11235

OHIO: CINCINNATI COUNCIL FOR SOVIET JEWS
                  1024 Spruceglen Drive
                  Cincinnati, Ohio 45224

                  CLEVELAND COUNCIL ON SOVIET ANTI-SEMITISM
                  6325 Aldenham Drive
                  Cleveland, Ohio 44143

OREGON: OREGON ACTION FOR SOVIET JEWS
                  2323 SW Park Place
                  Portland, Oregon 97205

TEXAS: HOUSTON ACTION FOR SOVIET JEWRY
                  6006 Bellaire Boulevard, #118
                  Houston, Texas 77081

WACO COUNCIL OF CONCERN ON SOVIET JEWRY
5501 Fairview Drive
Waco, Texas 76710

VIRGINIA: COMMISSION ON SOVIET JEWRY OF TIDEWATER
7300 Newport Avenue
Norfolk, Virginia 23505

WASHINGTON: SEATTLE ACTION FOR SOVIET JEWRY
2031 Third Avenue
Seattle, Washington 98121-2418

WISCONSIN: MILWAUKEE JEWISH COUNCIL
1360 North Prospect Avenue
Milwaukee, Wisconsin 53202

UCSJ COMMITTEES

INTERNATIONAL PHYSICIANS COMMISSION
125 Dyer Court
Norwood, New Jersey 07684

PRISONERS COMMISSION
212 Dunvegan Road
Toronto, Ontario
M5P 2P2 Canada

PSYCHIATRIC ABUSE MONITORING COMMITTEE
5335 Yarwell
Houston, Texas 77096

YAD L' YAD
41 Farm Lane
Great Neck, New York 11020

INTERNATIONAL BUREAUS ON HUMAN RIGHTS AND RULE OF LAW OF THE UNION OF COUNCILS FOR SOVIET JEWS

RUSSIAN-AMERICAN BUREAU ON HUMAN RIGHTS AND RULE OF LAW
(Public Council)
Ulitsa Novoslobodskaya 14
Moscow 103030
Russia

ST. PETERSBURG BUREAU ON HUMAN RIGHTS AND RULE OF LAW
(Harold Light Repatriation and Emigration Center)
Ulitsa Rileeva 29/31
St. Petersburg 191123
Russia

CENTRAL ASIAN-AMERICAN BUREAU ON HUMAN RIGHTS
Ulitsa Talmasova, Proezd 2/12
Samarkand 703011
Uzbekistan

CHELYABINSK BUREAU ON HUMAN RIGHTS AND RULE OF LAW
(Serving the Siberian Region)
Magnetigorsk

UKRANIAN-AMERICAN BUREAU ON HUMAN RIGHTS AND RULE OF LAW
Krasnoarmenskaya St, Dom 134, Apt. 21
Kiev, Ukraine

AFFILIATES AND FRIENDS

INTERNATIONAL

AUSTRALIA: NEW SOUTH WALES JEWISH BOARD OF DEPUTIES
First Floor
146 Darlinghurst Road
Darlinghurst, 2010, N.S.W.
Australia

CANADA: CANADIAN 35'S
118 Aberdeen Avenue
Westmont, Quebec
Canada

ENGLAND: 35'S WOMEN'S CAMPAIGN FOR SOVIET JEWRY
Pannell House
779/781 Finchley Road
London, NW11 8DN
England

NORWAY: SOVIET JEWRY COMMITTEE OF OSLO
Jacob Aallsgt 45A
0364 Oslo 3, Norway

U.S. BASED

NEW YORK: CENTER FOR RUSSIAN AND EAST EUROPEAN
JEWRY
240 Cabrini Boulevard
New York, New York 10033

STUDENT STRUGGLE FOR SOVIET JEWRY
50 West 97th Street, 3F
New York, New York 10025

MARYLAND: AMERICAN ASSOCIATION OF RUSSIAN JEWS
45 East 33rd Street
Suite B2
New York, New York 10016

INDEX

Jackson-Vanik Amendment 144, 259, 260
Jerusalem Post, The 138, 157
Jewish Community Centers 245
Jewish Family Service 246
Jewish Federation 177
Jewish News Weekly 33
Kahn, Betty vii, 86, 106, 113, 115
Kaplan, Sherman 152
Kelman, Alla 59, 60, 63
Kelman, Boris 59, 60, 62, 63, 254
Kennan, George 98
Kennedy, Edward 176, 177
Kessler, Paul 47, 63
Khassina, Natasha 38, 46, 47, 57, 62, 253
King David Hotel 127
Kissinger, Henry 45, 126
Kleiner, Henny 82, 130, 153
Klose, Kevin 201, 204
Kol Israel 30, 193
Kooperman, Edwin 160, 230
Kremlin 41-43, 259
Lambert, Joseph 165, 168
Lantos, Tom 29, 148-150
Last Exodus, The (Leonard Schroeter) 38
Lectures in Pattern Theory, Volumes I-III
    (Grenander) 136
Lederer, Michael 233
Leningrad trials 31
Levin, Joel 58
Levy, Cecile 160, 226
Loiben, Linda (nee Glassenberg)(sister) 12
Los Angeles Times, The 53
Lown, Bernard 161, 168, 169
Lumar, Michael 47, 62, 254
Malamet, Jacques 208, 211
Masada 23
Mauroy, Pierre 155, 156, 166, 191-194, 196,
    198-200, 208, 217
Mauthausen concentration camp 28
May Laws, the 11
McGill University 174, 181
Mednick, Robert 110
Meggido 23
Meir, Golda 30
Memoirs of 1984 (Tarnopolsky) vii, 260
Mesh, Jacov 57, 58, 63, 253
Mesh, Marina 57, 58, 63
Metzenbaum, Howard 154
Michael Reese Hospital 72, 76
Milgrom, Ida 49

Mitterand, Francois 76, 156
Monde, Le 83
Monitor, The 33
Moskovsky Komsomolets 117
Mueller, Erik 166
Naftalin, Micah 32, 114, 256
Nakache, E. 156
Nashpitz, Mark 28, 48, 62, 253
National Academy of Sciences 137, 194
National Aeronautic and Space Administration
    (NASA) 245
National Hotel, Moscow 41, 42
National Jewish Community Relations Advisory
    Council 72
Negroni, Christine 153, 154, 226
New Trier High School 14
New Ukraine 255
New York Times, The 138, 144, 150, 153, 205
Newman, Ruth 139
News Bulletin 79
Nisenholz, Patricia 160, 222, 226
North Shore Congregation Israel vii, 13, 17,
    70, 80, 81, 93, 159, 176, 216, 222, 225,
    226, 229-231, 246
Northwestern University 14, 165, 168, 176
Novoye Russkoye Slovo 153
Nudel, Ida 29, 45-47, 54, 55, 62, 109, 139,
    174, 232, 253
Oberman, Martin 110
Opper, Linda 28, 38, 86
Oppermans, The (Feuchtwanger) 183, 184
Orlov, Yuri 94, 182, 233
ORRT (real estate discrimination) 13
otkaz (see "Description of a Disease") xiii, xiv,
    xv, 6, 7, 53, 67, 70
OVIR (description) 5
Pale of Settlement 13, 126
Pamyat 117, 254
Paritsky, Alexander 3, 54, 55, 82, 83, 92, 94,
    103, 129, 142, 157, 161, 167, 169, 215,
    253
Paritsky, Anna 54, 56
Paritsky, Dorina 54, 56
Paritsky, Polina 38, 45, 54-56, 63, 82, 92
Patkin, Judith 139
Payack, Paul J.J. vii
Pekar, Alexander 47
Pekar, Joseph 47, 62, 253
Pennsylvania State University 168
Percy, Charles 75, 76

BIOGRAPHICAL SKETCH

In 1982 Nancy and Martin Rosenfeld went on a mission to the Soviet Union on behalf of a grass-roots organization called Chicago Action for Soviet Jewry. There they met, among many other "refuseniks," a scientist and poet named Yuri Tarnopolsky. Deeply affected by the plight of Soviet Jews who were desperate to emigrate but denied that right by their government, Nancy was moved to spearhead, upon her return to the United States, an intensive international campaign to rescue Tarnopolsky. His subsequent arrest and internment as a "prisoner of conscience" shortly after the Rosenfelds' return to the Chicago suburbs made Nancy's task more urgent, and her work became an obsession. That the Tarnopolsky family finally was granted permission to leave Russia in 1986 is a tribute to the work of Nancy and an "army of American housewives" and similar groups, whose humanitarian efforts are memorialized in this touching book.

Nancy and Martin, who have two grown sons, still reside in a Chicago suburb and travel widely together. Nancy remains dedicated to helping the Russian Jews whose inspiring story she has witnessed and whose struggle she has joined--a struggle that goes on despite the collapse of the USSR.